REVISIONING INDIA'S NORTH-EAST THROUGH THE LOOK EAST POLICY

Revisioning India's North-East through the Look East Policy

SAYANTANI SEN MAZUMDAR

Maulana Abul Kalam Azad Institute
of Asian Studies, Kolkata

MANOHAR
2018

Disclaimer

The views expressed are of the individual author and do not express the viewpoint of the Institute

First published 2018

ISBN 978-81-935609-2-1

Published by
Ajay Kumar Jain *for*
Manohar Publishers & Distributors
4753/23 Ansari Road, Daryaganj
New Delhi 110 002

Typeset by
Kohli Print
Delhi 110 051

Printed at
Salasar Imaging Systems
New Delhi 110 033

Contents

Preface

The term 'North-East' is a misleading one as it upholds an image of a state or a group of states comprising homogenous attributes and confronting identical problems. But this image is far removed from what may be considered as the reality of the North-East region (NER) of India being a region of intense disparity and distinctness. There is considerable lack of congruity among the states of the North-East and there are persistent intra-state conflicts and insurgencies. The people outside this region often get puzzled due to the existing practice of clubbing the highly distinct states under one caption and thus misunderstand the dynamics of the entire region. India's North-East has attained a critical position in India's foreign policy due to its much coveted Look East Policy (LEP). North-East India, geographically and economically, is in a privileged position to be the economic bridgehead to South-East Asia. It is generally accepted that the North-East region suffers from acute economic backwardness and under development. The LEP endeavours to promote this region as a springboard to India's thriving equations with its South-East Asian neighbours.

North-East India is the epitome of diverse and rich cultural heritage of India and has the credibility of being the harbinger of economic progress through a comprehensive manoeuvring of cultural exchanges with its South-East Asian neighbours. The chain of festivals in the NER, as exemplified in this study by the Hornbill Festival of Kohima, along with their magnificent facets bears the credence of earning international recognition with the firmly embedded prospect of tourism and economic promotion. Economic development of the NER mandates the significance of strengthening India's trade transaction with the Association of South-East Asian Nations (ASEAN) via land route. In this backdrop the geographic proximities of the NER can play a crucial role as it acts as a gateway to Myanmar, the land-bridge to the ASEAN. But the economic development of any region will not be feasible without the adequate development of transport, connectivity and infrastructure facilities. The rationale of the LEP thus pertains to the progress of the NER from the backburner to the limelight of India's foreign policy by addressing to the crucial challenges of development.

Moreover, the NER of India often becomes synonymous with security threat. A deep sense of insecurity generally envelops the atmosphere of the region, which can at times really turn worse. For nearly over two decades since Independence India paid little attention to the ethnic fissures in the North-East which were getting articulated on primordial lines and were acting in a manner inimical to India's long-term progress. It is an undeniable fact that in case of NER a security prism engulfs any intellectual deliberation. The region has always been stigmatized as retaining conflict-ridden political atmosphere, weak connectivity and infrastructure facilities retarding the spree of development. But the Look East Policy of India, conceptualized and initiated since the early 1990s by the former Prime Minister P.V. Narasimha Rao in the context of changing global dynamics after the end of the Cold War and severe domestic economic compulsions challenging the country, is steered to uplift this region from the quagmire of security threat paradigm to the virtues of economic development through such initiatives as border-trade, promoting business enterprise and people to people contacts. The economic potentials of the region, which are often being overshadowed by the magnitude of distressing happenings, have been underscored by this foreign policy strategy. The inherent potentials and the prospects are adequately nurtured and utilized by India's LEP for a better future of the region.

The study proposes to contextualize and inquire into the development of the North-East of India with reference to the LEP. An attempt would be made to decipher the scope of the policy maker's investment into the region as a whole, that is to consider whether the North-East is perceived only as a conduit to rejuvenate cooperation with South-East Asia, more specifically the ASEAN or whether the Indian establishment is conscious of the purposive developmental needs of the region itself. The crux of the study revolves around the debate about whether the LEP signifies the development of only the frontline states of the region by being totally oblivious to the genuine needs and requirements of all the eight North-East states. This study thus is an attempt to unravel the intricacies of the LEP oriented towards the progress and development of the NER through considerable exploitation of the existing and available resources.

This work is the outcome of my experiences of about three and a half years devoted to studying India's North-East region, more specifically, the region's proximities with its South-East Asian neighbours while working as a Fellow in Maulana Abul Kalam Azad Institute of Asian Studies (MAKAIAS). This study would not have been possible without the advice and support of certain immensely important persons around me. First and foremost I am indebted to Omprakash Mishra, Professor of International Relations, Jadavpur University, for introducing me to this dynamic region and for his outstanding pragmatism and encouraging advice. I am indeed grateful to my Ph.D. Supervisor, Samir Kumar Das, Professor of Political Science, University of Calcutta, for his guidance and especially for his trust and the autonomy he has allowed me in my research.

Most importantly my wholehearted gratitude goes to my family members. My daughter, Sampoorna Sen Mazumdar (Pekham), has consistently been an inspiration and encouragement for my research. I am indeed thankful to my husband, Plaban Sen Mazumdar, for having stood by me during the entire tenure and providing me with the much-required strength to fight all the odds. Special thanks to my parents, Smt. Molly Mukherjee and Shri Prasanta Mukherjee as well as to my in-laws Smt. Sharmila Sen Mazumdar and Late Shri

Ashish Ranjan Sen Mazumdar for their continued and intense support. I am also grateful to Shri Aurobindo Dhar for his enriching comments and inputs.

I wish to express my heart-felt thankfulness to all the people I interviewed and interacted with during my field-trips to the five states of the NER, Myanmar and Singapore and whose insightful contribution has helped me articulate my thoughts on the area. The unstinting support and cooperation of all my colleagues and friends have been an encouraging break-through in this entire academic effort. I am grateful to a number of people, many more than I am able to acknowledge, for the production of this outcome. The suggestions and comments of prolific academicians associated have been of immense value. It is important to confess that lapses (if any) in this endeavour are entirely mine.

SAYANTANI SEN MAZUMDAR

Abbreviations

ADB	Asian Development Bank
AEC	Asian Economic Community
AFTA	ASEAN Free Trade Area
APEC	Asia-Pacific Economic Cooperation
APR	Asia Pacific Region
ARF	ASEAN Regional Forum
ASEAN	Association of South East Asian Nations
ASSOCHAM	The Associated Chambers of Commerce and Industry of India
BBIN	Bangladesh, Bhutan, India and Nepal Growth Quadrangle
BDR	Bangladesh Rifles
BIMSTEC	Bay of Bengal Initiative for Multi Sectoral Technical and Economic Cooperation
BISS	Bangladesh Institute of International and Strategic Studies
BOBCOM	Bay of Bengal Community
BSF	Border Security Forces
BTAs	Bilateral Trade Agreements
BWG	BIMSTEC Working Group
CBEC	Central Board of Excise and Customs
CECA	Comprehensive Economic Cooperation Agreement
CLMV	Cambodia, Lao PDR, Myanmar and Vietnam countries
DGFT	Director General of Foreign Trade
EPAs	Economic Partnership Agreements
FDI	Foreign Direct Investment
FRPO	Foreigners Regional Registration Office
FTA	Free Trade Area
GAIL	Gas Authority of India Ltd

GDP	Gross Domestic Product
GMS	Greater Mekong Sub-region
GR	Guaranteed Receipt
HUJI	Harkat-ul Jehad-al Islami
IAI	Initiative for ASEAN Integration
ICP	Integrated Check Post
INR	Indian Rupees
ISI	Inter-Services Intelligence
IT	Information Technology
IWT	Inland Water Transport
KDF	Kuki Defence Force
KIA	Kuki Independent Army
KLO	Kamtapur Liberation Organisation
KNA	Kuki National Army
KNF	Kuki National Front
LEP	Look East Policy
LPG	Liberalization Privatization and Globalization
MFN	Most Favoured Nation
MGC	Mekong Ganga Cooperation
NDFB	National Democratic Front of Bodoland
NER	North-East Region
NH	National Highway
NSCN	National Socialist Council of Nagaland
NSCN (I-M)	National Socialist Council of Nagalim (Isak-Muivah)
NSCN (K)	National Socialist Council of Nagalim (Khaplang)
ONGC	Oil and Natural Gas Corporation
SAARC	South Asia Association for Regional Co-operation
SAGQ	South Asian Growth Quadrangle
SEA	South-East Asia
SEZ	Special Economic Zone
SOM	Senior Officials' Meeting
STEOM	Senior Trade and Economic Officials' Meeting
TEU	Twenty Foot Equivalent Unit
THB	Thai Baht

TMM	Trade Ministers' Meeting
UBI	United Bank of India
ULFA	United Liberation Front of Assam
UNESCAP	United Nations Economic and Social Commission for Asia and the Pacific

CHAPTER 1

Relevance of North-East India in India's Look East Policy

FOCUS OF THE STUDY

The end of the Cold War unleashed a series of developments in international relations and re-invigorated the concerns of geo-economics within the inter-state dynamics. The shift of primacy from the West to the East, the success of the East Asian Tiger economies and the growing convergence of India's economic and strategic interests inspired India to be inclined more towards the thriving economies of East and South-East Asia. Factors like globalization-induced economic reforms, renewed concern about China's increasing assertiveness in South-East Asia as well as India's vulnerability when faced with Beijing's expanding dominance in the Asia-Pacific region propelled the reformulation of the primary orientation of India's foreign policy. Complying with the tenets of globalization and liberalization India was opening up to the world economy and thus the conceptualization of the Look East Policy (LEP) during the nineties. Economic cooperation with the Association of South-East Asian Nations (ASEAN) has been the most significant criterion of the LEP. Trade and investment formed the edifice upon which the policy was structured. The second phase, which began in 2003, is more comprehensive in its coverage, as it brought the greater Asia-Pacific Region–countries like Japan, South Korea–within its ambit with ASEAN as its core. In its second phase, the LEP acquired a distinct dimension wherein the essence of India-ASEAN cooperation was inextricably linked to the economic and security interests of its North-Eastern Region (NER). The deepening of economic linkages with the ASEAN triggered the imperative of development of connectivity and infrastructure facilities in India-ASEAN cooperation. Herein the significance of the NER of India comes to the limelight if the proposition of conducting trade transactions via the landroute between India and South-East Asia is taken into consideration. Development of the NER gained momentum due to its relative proximities with South-East Asian neighbours.

Development, a primary concern of a foreign policy initiative, signifies a structural transformation of a society from its traditional to modern status. Development of a country is generally measured in terms of its economic advancement. Economic development connotes the development of the wealth or prosperity of a country or region ensuing economic well-being or improvement in the life of its people. For accruing economic development a country needs to implement policies that meet broad economic objectives like employment generation, price stability, regulation of financial institutions, trade practices, tax expansion and sustainable growth. Measures to develop infrastructure and connectivity facilities, telecommunication and technological advancement, promotion of educational programmes and projects are also the indicators of economic development of a country. Policies facilitating neighbourhood cooperation yielding job creation, science and technology transfer and resource complementarities are imperatives for economic development. Though the term economic development is used interchangeably with the concept of economic growth, the latter has limited implication and is illustrated by quantifiable parameters like per capita income or gross national product whereas economic development generally encompasses all the facets of economic welfare of a society. The NER despite being abundant with potential suffers from the menace of underdevelopment and economic backwardness. The LEP, as a means to address India's internal development disparity, is envisaged to promote the NER from the 'backward status' to a 'gateway status' to the evolving

India-ASEAN dynamics. The study is an analytical survey to appraise the credibility of the LEP as a foreign policy initiative in situating the relevance of the NER as India's gateway to ASEAN, which in turn, is conceived as a springboard by India to reach out to the wider Pacific Region.

BACKGROUND TO THE LEP

The inception of any substantial course of action or strategy does not take place overnight or in a vacuum. Certain factors stimulate the evolution and it is utterly relevant to foreground the material circumstances influencing the emergence of the policy. The origin of India's Look East Policy can be traced back to the changed geo-political context of the international system in the early 1990s. The policy though first enunciated in 1991, had its genesis in the end of the Cold War, following the collapse of the Soviet Union. The gradual fade of Soviet political, and economic assistance, which India had banked upon for years, had compelled India to endorse a programme of free market restructuring at home and search for new markets and economic partners abroad. The initiation of the policy in India's foreign policy domain successfully brought the prolonged span of mutual estrangement between India and South-East Asia to an end. However, the history of the genesis of the LEP identifies its roots in the early years of Indian independence. India's substantive endeavours of regional cooperation started taking shape in the pre-independence period whereas in the mid-1940s and 1950s there were enterprising initiatives of the country to develop cooperation with Asian and other developing nations of the world. Growing regionalism is visible in domains like territorial aspects, maritime dimension, even space and in a large number of global phenomena where borders are truly irrelevant. Apart from engaging with several other regions in the early 1990s India initiated its Look East Policy primarily to develop greater ties with South-East Asian countries. A region hitherto ignored by India was now viewed as a serious trade partner. The economy of South-

East Asia that was growing exponentially during this time attracted not only China but also Europe, the USA as well as India. The LEP is oriented to rejuvenate cooperative ties with South-East Asian nations because of the deep historical bonding and advanced economic cooperation. India's cooperation with South-East Asia is predominantly fortified through institutional linkages like the ASEAN. It is mentionworthy that the competition factor would always be dominating India's relations with ASEAN as both face the challenges of responding to overwhelming interests of the US and China.

In terms of India's approach towards its neighbourhood, and foreign policy approach as a whole, there are certain levels of consciousness that need to be dealt with. Those are the aspirations, the realities and the possibilities of the changed realities and there is the process too. The foreign policy aspirations are well-articulated, objectives are being well known and the challenge is the transformation of aspirations or objectives into actual achievements based on the existing realities. Certain realities need to be looked at. All countries have their own interests and the challenge of diplomacy is to cultivate convergence to the maximum extent possible. To go forward we need greater clarity, greater certainty and transparency of the equations that we develop with our partners. The engagements with the neighbours mandate essentially three major domains – trade, culture and security. The quest for technological development as well as economic development steer all the financial institutions to follow the logic of trade. With trade comes cultural practice. The security domain indicates maximum exercise of sovereignty and today's world has the ability to affect both trade and cultural changes which involve not just the flow of ideas but also people-to-people contacts. Security domains require decision by design in terms of military strength, relationships, development of partnerships, supplies of export, mutual support and particularly in this age of global terrorism, the exchange of intelligence and active cooperation between the agencies involved is very much required. It is ardent to develop capabilities both in terms of national level and in terms of bilateral equations, which would substantiate the equations among the neighbours. India certainly needs to develop its economic capabilities and also need to develop potentials as well as actualization of potentials, development of standards and the ability to demonstrate itself as a productive manufacturing country that can reach out to wider neighbourhood. Cultural links can revitalize the process. Though there are political diversities in our neighbourhood, economic potentials need to be exploited. India should be enthusiastic in creating stakeholders for encouraging mutually beneficial relationship in our neighbourhood. Free Trade Agreements (FTA) are important and in this context conceptualization, negotiation and implementation of India-ASEAN FTAs, opening of trade and trade negotiations should be taken into account in order to foster mutually supportive partnerships. Positive, proactive approach provides a niche to produce a win-win situation. India needs to recognize and develop the strength of its market. India is truly globalizing its economic engagement and there is need to broaden the domain of trade and economic strength. Integration of the security discourse into the diplomatic discourse, economic diplomacy, military diplomacy, cultural diplomacy are all distinctive parts of India's engagement with its neighbourhood.

The LEP assumes considerable relevance amidst the changing dynamics in international relations, especially since the centre of global economic and increasingly even strategic power has been shifting to the East. The policy is significant in the sense that the Asia-Pacific has always been a part of our civilizational consciousness and our national aspirations are greatly influenced and motivated by centuries of exchange of peoples, ideas, cultures and commerce from and to this region. India's economic, security and geo-strategic interests are intensely related to this region in its extended neighbourhood. Her dynamics with the countries of the Asia-Pacific Region have been escalating in political, security, economic and cultural spheres. Therefore the LEP is being perceived with immense expectations and prospect.[1] In fact, India did not use to share a smooth equation with these countries because of its overt inclination towards Soviet Union. Despite being the repository of abundant resources South-East Asia failed to gain India's attention and India considered ASEAN as the 'Trojan Horse' of the United States. South-East Asia was also apprehensive about India's strategies and was acutely critical of her decision-making process as slow, cumbersome and too bureaucratic ultimately jeopardizing development in the country. The South-East Asian countries were also sceptical about Indians for being too much ideologically-oriented and less pragmatic in their foreign policy, resulting in divergence of approaches between India and the countries of ASEAN. South-East Asian countries refrained from indulging in direct association with India due to the premonition that inclusion of India in any of the institutional arrangements would bring the South Asian conflicts into their own region, which in turn would further complicate their own security issues rather than solving them.

The LEP is largely being shaped by the imperatives of history and geography. The East and South-East Asian countries became for India one of the most priority areas of cooperation under the framework of economic diplomacy. India and South-East Asia share an enduring historical background. K.M. Pannikar, one of India's first strategic analysts and a visionary, coined the phrase 'South-East Asia' for the scattering of British, Dutch, French and Portuguese colonies whose only common link was their Hindu heritage. Pannikar looked to the past, ancient as well as colonial, to argue that India and South-East Asia are connected integrally in their political, social and economic life. It was from India, especially from the south, that the people of South-East Asia learnt the art of writing, wrote an eminent British Indologist, who asserted that the whole of South-East Asia received most of its culture from India.[2] The first Prime Minister of independent India, Jawaharlal Nehru also acknowledged the relevance of South-East Asia in India's foreign policy dynamics, which provided an impetus to redefine India's relations with its regional neighbours. In fact, India's first forays into foreign policy affairs were in South-East Asia in support of anti-colonial movements in that region.[3]

The LEP is the offshoot of the changed global perceptions and compulsions and thus is a projection of India's increased emphasis on regional cooperation with the ASEAN manifesting the avowed economic and strategic relevance of South-East Asia to India's national interests. The LEP validates the thrust of India's economic and financial strategy to restructure the economic framework of the country and rejuvenate trade with the neighbouring countries thereby strengthening its position in the international market.[4] Confronted with the unstable domestic environment characterized by the perils of increasing terrorism and insurgency, political instability, economic downturn and financial crisis the LEP was embarked upon with the presupposition of putting the derailed economy back on track, restoring a semblance of political stability and availing of new opportunities and facing challenges thrown open by globalization and the New World Order.[5] An offshoot of the economic liberalization programme, the aim of this foreign policy initiative was to integrate India economy with the world economy. Sandy Gordon sums up some of the measures taken by the government to reform the economy which were introduced in the budgets since 1991-2 as follows:

- devaluation of the rupee by about 30 per cent against the US dollar, with the motive of achieving full convertibility;
- raising of the ceiling of foreign ownership to 51 per cent and higher in some instances, with partial repatriation of capital at market rates on a 60:40 basis (with 40 per cent being at the government rate);
- smoothening of restrictive controls on the import of most items and lowering of the tariff. The import duty on capital goods was further reduced to 35 per cent from 55 per cent, with a special 25 per cent rate on capital goods destined for priority sectors. The import weighted tariff was to be reduced to 25 per cent in two to three years;

- eradication of the internal licensing system in all but 18 industries;
- arrangements for sale in principle of up to 49 per cent of the government's share in state enterprises;
- reduction of excise duty;
- reform of the financial sector;
- substantial reduction in the rate of company taxation in 1994.[6]

The re-alignment of India with its South East Asian neighbours are backed by certain considerations:

- Myanmar has the world's 10th largest natural gas reserves, estimated at over 90 trillion cubic feet in 19 onshore and three major offshore fields.
- Indonesia is the world's biggest exporter of coal.
- Malaysia and Indonesia are the world's second and third largest exporters of liquefied natural gas.
- Malaysia's East Natuna Gas Field can emerge as one of the world's richest sources of natural gas as further exploration confirms prospective new outlets.
- Vietnam is expected to emerge as a major exporter of oil.[7]

Regional integration arrangements are mainly the outcome of the imperative of the nation-states to integrate their economies for achieving rapid economic development by reducing the intensity of disagreements and conflict and encouraging mutual trust and confidence-building measures among the integrated units. The ASEAN, which is one of the successful examples of regionalism, was formed in 1967 with the signing of the Bangkok Declaration by five original member countries – Malaysia, Indonesia, Thailand, Philippines and Singapore. The remaining South-East Asian countries – Brunei Darussalam, Vietnam, Laos, Myanmar, and Cambodia joined the regional group during the 1980s and the 1990s. The ASEAN declaration of 8 August 1967 highlights the following as its objectives:

- To accelerate economic growth, social progress and cultural development in the region through joint endeavours in the spirit of equality and partnership for strengthening the foundation of a prosperous and peaceful community of SEA nations.
- To promote regional peace and stability through mutual respect for justice and the rule of law in the relationship among countries in the region and adherence to the principles of the UN Charter.

A cursory glance at the aims and objectives of ASEAN portrays that though the socio-economic and cultural facets have been the prime movers of ASEAN activities the political inclination of countering the Communist regime in Indo-China (Vietnam, Laos and Cambodia) is also vividly apparent. It is steered to prevent intra-regional domination by any SEA country. In fact objectives such as regional peace and stability, respect for justice and rule of law and adherence to the principles of the UN Charter are the fundamental political yardsticks of ASEAN. Moreover, the security impression of the region is critically determined by the apprehension of Communism as a political and economic doctrine countering liberal democratic and economic principles.[8]

IMPERATIVES OF INDIA-ASEAN COOPERATION

Though the inception of the LEP had taken place in the 1990s, the policy had its beginnings during Rajiv Gandhi's initiatives towards China and the other countries east of India. P.V. Narasimha Rao, as the then Prime Minister of India facilitated the endeavour, being mindful of the changed post-Cold War global realities in which his government had to frame its foreign policy strategies thereby advancing national interests based on national consensus. The end of the Cold War and the breakdown of ideological barriers led to a more pragmatic approach by India. India's strategic world view clearly shifted from an emphasis on moralspeak to realpolitik based on acquiring and exercising economic and military power.[9] The domestic and external compulsions and concerns of the country at that time motivated Rao to pursue his larger perception of foreign policy abiding to significant shifts in the approaches towards our immediate neighbours, extended neighbourhood, major powers, partners and alliances. New Delhi's economic reform programme changed its equations with many countries. India's strategies signified its intent to be fully integrated into the global market and to do business.[10] India realized the necessity of cooperative ventures and utilize the window of opportunity with South-East Asian countries. Since the enunciation of the Look East Policy India started giving priority to South-East Asia in its foreign and economic policies. The ASEAN states were supportive of the measures adopted by the Narasimha Rao government. After the Bandung Conference in 1955, it took nearly four decades for India and South-East Asia to rediscover each other.

According to Prem Shankar Jha, 'the dark side of the East Asian success story is that there will inevitably be a loser and that India could be one of them'.[11] It was basically these concerns that led the then Finance Minister Manmohan Singh to bring a fresh burst of economic liberalization to the Indian economy during the 1993 budget, one of his stated goals being to catch up with China.[12] The LEP is therefore a substantive manifestation of Rao's nationalist, pragmatist and visionary perspectives. The succeeding Prime Ministers, H.D. Deve Gowda, I.K. Gujral, A.B. Vajpayee and Manmohan Singh carried this process forward adding considerable substance and purpose to this policy, based on national consensus, which has indeed acquired an irreversible and self-sustaining essence and impetus.[13] According to G.V.C. Naidu, India adopted a three-pronged approach in its attempt to forge regional cooperation through the Look East Policy. They are:

- To renew political contacts with the ASEAN member nations;

- To increase economic interaction with South East Asia (trade, investments, science and technology, tourism, etc.,); and
- To forge defence links with several countries of this region as a means to strengthen political understanding.[14]

The government in India while emphasizing its core concerns in foreign policy delineated the imperative of integrating the Indian economy with the global economy. The initiatives and the policy reforms highlighted the importance of ASEAN with which India sought cooperation. The Government of India, for the first time since independence, turned its attention towards the ASEAN region with economics as the most important criterion.[15] The absence of conflict on vital issues and the presence of common challenges expanded the scope of cultivating cooperation between India and its South-East Asian neighbours. To ASEAN, India's enormous size, productive population, educated middle class, convenient geostrategic location, progressive military might, meteoric economic growth posed as favourable factors. Constituents like ASEAN's perception about India's emerging clout and China as a source of security threat, the volatile situation in the South China Sea due to conflicting claims over the Spratly Islands, the terrible atmosphere in the Taiwan Straits and the Korean peninsula and the no-win ties among the US, Japan and China, had motivated ASEAN for a paradigm shift in India-ASEAN linkages. Thus, mutual needs influenced the convergence of their interests. New Delhi's Look East Policy therefore coincided with ASEAN's 'Look West' line and this new-found regionalization impulse ultimately led to an overall smoothening of relations between India and ASEAN.[16]

The flourishing alliance between India and South-East Asia gets clearly visible through the progressive persuasion of India's Look East Policy and from the reciprocity of South-East Asia as well. There was considerable progression in the pace of cooperation between India and South-East Asia. India's ties with ASEAN were upgraded to a Sectoral Dialogue Partnership in March 1993 in three areas, namely, trade, investment and tourism. The Indian and ASEAN officials met in New Delhi on 16-17 March 1993 to identify specific areas of collaboration within the designed sectors. Due to its sustained efforts India-ASEAN relation was advanced to a Full Dialogue Partnership at the fifth ASEAN Summit in Bangkok in December 1995. This rejuvenated the interactions between ASEAN and India from the senior official to the ministerial level and enabled India's participation in the ASEAN Post-Ministerial Conference. At the Post-Ministerial Conference in Jakarta in July 1996, ASEAN and Indian ministers designed a framework of the areas of extensive cooperation. Classifying specific areas for cooperation, like infrastructure, human resource development, science and technology and tourism among others, I.K. Gujral commented that India's Full Dialogue Partnership status was in fact a veritable gateway to India's enterprising participation in other ASEAN-like groupings, like the APEC and the Asia-Europe meetings.

The deepening of cooperation between India and ASEAN has paved the way for the strengthening of not only economic ties but also security linkages, which resulted in India's admission to the ASEAN Regional Forum (ARF) in 1996. The ARF is a dominant forum for security cooperation in the Asia-Pacific Region where global and regional security issues along with disarmament and nonproliferation affairs are being nurtured. The increasing involvement of India in the strategic discourses of the Asia-Pacific Region underscores its deep-rooted commitment and inclination to the objective of sustaining regional peace and stability. India hosted several workshops related to the security paradigms. India became a Summit-level Partner of ASEAN in 2002, becoming the fourth partner after China, Japan and Korea. At the Second India-ASEAN Summit in October 2003, India and ASEAN signed the Framework Agreement on Comprehensive Economic Cooperation leading to the creation of a free trade area by the year 2011 and India's accession to the Treaty of Amity and Cooperation in South-East Asia. The document emphasizes on cooperation to combat international terrorism. India's accession to ASEAN's Treaty of Amity and Cooperation articulates of a growing closeness with South Asia. But of greater significance was the framework agreement aimed at creating a Free Trade Area in ten years as provided in the agreement on Comprehensive Economic Cooperation. The Comprehensive Economic Cooperation Agreement concluded in 2005 arose as a result of the development of close relations with ASEAN in general and Singapore in particular. Today the palpable effects of the process started under the Look East Policy are evidently visible. One concrete example out of this agreement, which suffices today, is that there are 172 flights per week that connect Singapore to various cities in India.[17] India finally signed the most significant India-ASEAN Free Trade Agreement (FTA) with the ten members of ASEAN in August 2009, which bears immense prospect for the booming of India-ASEAN cooperative ties.

India-ASEAN integration has the propensity to enrich mutual competitiveness by adhering to the following mechanisms:

- Encouraging competitive pressures for optimum and efficient production within each economy.
- Shifting output from less to more competent economies.
- Expanding the economies of scale achieved by producers serving the region.
- Accelerating investments in physical, capital and technological spheres.[18]

India's endeavours in South-East Asia were primarily directed towards the containment of Chinese economic and strategic dominance in the region. One of the significant reasons for India's inclination towards South-East Asia was due to China's avowed interest of developing its economically backward Szechwan and Yunnan provinces with Myanmar, which could affect India's North-East Region (NER). The fact that it endeavours to develop infrastructure and communication facilities both within northern Myanmar and in Tibet had a direct impact on India's NER. The initiatives and strategies adopted by China to promote Yunnan and Szechwan by connecting them with Myanmar in certain cases posed developmental impediments to the NER of India. This expansion of Chinese interests motivated India to evolve a definite strategic policy in its immediate neighbourhood and in the strategically important countries of SEA and the Far East particularly Japan and the Taiwanese and South Korean economies, thereby integrating them within its economic and strategic fold.[19]

South-East Asia is the melting pot of the cultural influences of both India and China. I.K. Gujral had stated that 'What look east really means is that an outward looking India, is gathering all forces of dynamism – domestic and regional and is directly focusing on establishing synergies with a fast consolidating and progressive neighbourhood to its East in Mother Continent of Asia.'[20] The pertinent dimension is that the LEP was very much conscious of China's orientations towards South-East Asia and was aware of China's strategies towards the region for establishing its domineering influence and power. Historically China and India had met in SEA and had effectively established the fact that the seas and oceans not only separate but also connect civilizations. Both countries were recognized maritime powers and the two civilizations had met and interacted with each other as land powers with a strong trading relationship. India therefore is inclined towords reviving its East Asian presence which had a positive historical content and which in a sense provides India a role as a balancing power in the region both economically and strategically.[21] With the centre of gravity progressing towards the Asia-Pacific Region, India's LEP is well crafted to play a decisive role in framing the politics of the region in tandem with its own national interest.[22] India's LEP is multi-dimensional in nature. Apart from cultivating economic linkages with South-East Asia and the Asia-Pacific Region it has strategic and political dimension too. In this arena China is being conceived as a major competitor. But there are areas of convergence between India and China too. Both are the emerging and the largest developing economies cultivating common strategic interests.

Both aspire for a stable environment for development and are unanimous in opposing an unipolar world order. India's rise and the US's shift to the Asia-Pacific are quite challenging to China and it thus seeks to overwhelm nations by military might and by developing infrastructure in terms of airbase, port and railway networks. On the other hand, reconciling US military supremacy in South-East Asia and the Asia-Pacific Region and balancing China's influence are the two major yardsticks of the LEP. It also stimulates India's role in regional security. It is an accepted proposition that in addition to ASEAN India has strong reach in the wider Pacific Region but it needs to be more proactive as it lags behind the US, China and Japan in its clout in this region.

NORTH-EAST INDIA: A VARIED CULTURAL MOSAIC

In the beginning the LEP has been a bit myopic about our domestic imperatives. It overlooked the fact that the NER from times immemorial has enjoyed transnational cultural, linguistic, economic, family and ethnic links with Myanmar and northern Thailand (apart from Bangladesh, Bhutan and Nepal). The LEP had to factor in the historical imperative of the close affinity between the NER and its South-East Asian neighbours in order to accord strategic substance to its orientation. Cross border linkages, support and cooperation have often instigated perils like insurgency, transnational crime and the voices in favour of separatism in this part of the country. This can be said to be extra-national dimensions of domestic problems requiring cooperation of our immediate neighbours. There is a case for reviving in a calibrated manner traditional trans-border links which may help the process of restoring normalcy. Cooperation of Myanmar should be seen as the fundamental facet of our LEP. Geographical proximity facilitated cooperation as the Andaman Sea connects India with Myanmar, Thailand, Indonesia, Bangladesh and the Straits of Malacca. India's naval defence strategy is very much aware of the importance of this geographical reality. The defence of India's island territories, exclusive economic zones, sea lanes and resources, energy requirements can best be safeguarded through regional and bilateral cooperation and expanding cooperation with our neighbours.[23]

The underdeveloped condition of the NER is the focal-point of an insightful academic research and assumes special significance for both academic as also policy studies. The term 'North-East' was first used by the British rulers to identify a geographical area. The term 'North-East Frontier' was first coined by Alexander Mackenzie to identify Assam, including the adjoining hill areas and the princely states of Manipur and Mizoram in his book published in 1884.[24] When there was a plan to merge Assam with East Bengal in the late 1890s and the beginning of 1900, there were proposals to name the new province as the 'North-Eastern Province'.[25] Initially the term remained a geographical concept and throughout the colonial period the British rulers referred to Assam as the 'North-Eastern Frontier of Bengal'. Thus in the colonial period the area what now constitutes the North-East was considered to be a frontier of Bengal that needed to be protected and defended militarily. North-East India became a region merely through a geo-political accident. North-East India, which occupies a remote corner of India, is one of the least developed regions of the country. This position of the region is the result of its initial absorption into the world economy as a marginal periphery, a part of the frontier of the British rule and which eventually led to the region's peripheral position within the Indian nation-state after independence.[26]

The separation of Burma from the Indian sub-continent in 1937 and the Partition of 1947 virtually created today's 'North-East Region'. India is a post-colonial state with colonial inheritance and post-colonial aspirations. Both have been reflected into our neighbourhood policy. Colonial inheritance has been reflected in our neighbourhood policy in terms of a number of border disputes which India is still confronting, a number of consequences of a very hastily done Partition. The

Partition redrew the political boundary of Indian territory. The altered political boundary has far-reaching consequences for the economy of North-East India by creating a physical barrier with the mainland and forming what is now called the 'North-Eastern region'. Before Partition there was no notion of a separate North-Eastern region, as every single province or hill region that now constitutes it was closely linked for trade, economy, movement and education to the adjoining areas of the East Bengal, Burma and Tibet.[27] For instance, certain parts of Manipur, Mizoram and Nagaland had direct lineages with Burma, where ethnic affinity existed. The Khasi, Jaintia and Garo Hills maintained close relations with Sylhet, the Mizo Hills with the Chittagong Hills Tracts and Tripura with Comilla, Noakhali and Sylhet. The areas of North-Eastern Frontier Agency (present Arunachal Pradesh) had close contacts with Tibet, Bhutan and also with Burma. All these equations witnessed significant changes all of a sudden in 1947. The partition disrupted the age-old connectivity of pre-independence inland water, road and railway communications through erstwhile East Bengal. There were a number of distortions and disruptions in the connectivity of the NER due to the partitions. The estrangement of the communication lines and well-developed markets with the plains of the neighbouring country, Bangladesh impeded the economic growth of the region. It created mayhem for the North-East making it the most regulated, sensitive border region and the most exposed territory. Using the region's 2 per cent perimeter as a major linkage point with the rest of India and at the same time checking the inflow of goods and people from across the remaining 98 per cent has therefore been a crucial task.[28] B.G Verghese commented that 'if imperial politics distanced the North-East from its trans-border neighbourhood further East, Partition in 1947 all but physically separated the North-East from the Indian heartland'.[29] Due to Partition the region became isolated from the rest of the country. It became virtually landlocked with tenuous connection with mainland India through the 21-landmass, often described as the 'chicken's neck', which is less than 2 per cent of the 5,000 km combined perimeter formed by the seven sister states. This geographic isolation has contributed to the psychological alienation of the states from the mainstream. The loss of connectivity and market access, according to B.G. Verghese, set its economy back by at least a quarter century.[30] The disruption of natural connectivity and the artificial compartmentalization of regions during the colonial era actually built barriers.

There is debate on the rationality of clubbing all the eight states together and defining it as 'North-East'. Udayon Mishra points out that the use of the term 'North-East' is itself problematic as the region represents a varied cultural mosaic and has never considered itself to be one compact unit.[31] At the time of independence 'North-East' basically denoted Assam and the princely states of Manipur and Tripura. In order to deal with various emerging ethnic aspirations new states were formed out of Assam like Nagaland (1963), Meghalaya (1972), Arunachal Pradesh and Mizoram (1987). The concept of North-East was formalized politically and the term became popular with the formation of the North-Eastern Council (NEC) in 1971. Since its inception the NEC functions as a regional planning body for the North-Eastern region. Though Sikkim did not meet the contiguity criterion it was still included in the NEC in 2002. It is argued that by bracketing the eight North-Eastern Indian states, with its diverse tribes, customs and cultures into what is called the 'North-East', we tend to ignore distinct and disparate aspirations of the ethnic groups. More so, the clubbing of the states is an attempt to stereotype and generalize the problems unique to the respective state. This tendency on part of government leaders and policy makers often distorts the nature of problems specific to respective location and geo-political grievances of the states. It is true that the NER suffers from common menace like ethnic unrests, insurgency, immigration, drug trafficking, communication gap, lack of connectivity and infrastructure development. But at the same time there exist severe intra-regional conflicts jeopardizing the pace of development in the region. There exist acute disparities between the hills and valleys as well as between urban and rural contexts in the sphere of socio-economic development.

India as a geographical entity has never achieved political homogeneity due to certain socio-political factors. For the purpose of political development and stability of a nation, the concept of political integration is usually employed. The rationale of political integration is that there is a need to create a 'territorial nationality which overshadows – or eliminates – subordinate parochial loyalties'.[32] These local aspirations or identical primordial attachments pose hindrance to development since the national leaders steer to expand the functions of the political system by complying with undivided loyalty of all the population. The rationale of political integration of the NER with the mainstream upholds the challenge of the political system to bring about 'the process whereby people transfer their commitment and loyalty from smaller tribes, villages, or petty principalities to the larger central political system'.[33] The politicians or the leaders of ethnic communities of the NER get limited representation in national politics. This leads to resentments in various forms from various ethnic communities and the incompetence of the government to address the political aspirations of all the ethnic groups in the region results in secessionist movements. A sense of integration with the national mainstream therefore has faced a serious setback. The North-Eastern Region is marked by acute disparity and diversity in economic pursuits and geopolitical impediments too have restrained the area to develop economically at par with many other parts of the country. The lack of development and industrialization has resulted in the growing economic disparity of the region vis-à-vis the national average and this rising disparity has aggravated the growing sense of alienation among the people.[34] Economic deprivation, disparity, exploitation, lack of development and a growing sense of alienation created a congenial condition for the rise of ethnic conflicts leading to insurgency in the region.[35] The demands for fulfilling the mandates of these movements in certain cases have further deteriorated the situation, as a result of which a sense of integration with the national mainstream has faced a serious setback. For this reason it is felt that 'the region is heading towards a paradoxical state of external integration and internal disintegration thereby frustrating the developmental efforts'.[36] Since the economic backwardness and underdevelopment have intensified the sense of alienation and relative deprivation of the people the Central Government has pumped in crores of rupees as developmental funds with the motto of stimulating economic growth and development in the region.[37] In order to address the problems successive central governments have announced developmental packages for the region. The general notion is that adequate allotment of funds leading to development of the region will capacitate the people of the region to put aside the problems of identity, ethnic assertion and immigration from neighbouring countries thereby succeeding in the abatement of insurgency. In 1996 the then Prime Minister H.D. Deve Gowda announced an economic package ₹6,100 crore, following his visit to the region. His successor I.K. Gujral endorsed this package. To boost economic development of the region the NDA Government led by Prime Minister Atal Behari Vajpayee also announced another package of ₹10,217 crore in 1998. In October 1996, under the 'New Initiatives for North-Eastern Region', it was stipulated that at least 10 per cent of the budget(s) of the Central Ministries/Departments should be earmarked for the development of North-Eastern states. As the expenditure on the North-East by some Union Ministries during 1997-8 fell short of the stipulated 10 per cent target, the NDA government created a non-lapsable central pool of resources to support infrastructure development projects in the region. Between 1990-1 and 2002-3, the region received about ₹1,08,504 crore.[38] So lack of development is not directly related to shortage of funds. It can be stated that there is certain political or psychological neglect but definitely not in terms of allocation and transfer of resources from the Centre.

NORTH-EAST INDIA AND THE LOOK EAST POLICY

The maturing of India's LEP covers within its ambit a wide array of pertinent issues beyond the objective of utilizing the economic opportunities offered by the essence of cooperation. The objective of the policy predominantly focuses on regional economic integration with renewed emphasis on the development of the NER. In spite of being at a congenial geographic location to grasp the benefits from India-ASEAN cooperation the NER has miserably failed to taste the fruits of development. This unevenness has generated a sense of neglect palpable in various forms of unrest in the region. More recently, development of the NER has been the need of the hour and the LEP for the advancement of the region has initiated a number of substantive endeavours. One of the objectives of the LEP has been the economic development of the NER by linking it with the markets of South-East Asia and through strengthening of its connectivity and infrastructure facilities.

Different societies within the NER with certain commonly shared features like history and geography, economic structures and the structural change they have witnessed over time, and their economic and psychological distances from mainland India bind them together.[39] And they have experienced different levels of development within a given time frame.[40] The NER still encounters the basic problem of integration, insurgency and balanced economic development. The creation of several new states instead of solving the existing problems actually induced the smaller ethnic communities of the region to aspire for greater autonomy and hence rising insurgent and autonomy movements in the region. Such carving out of states was a restatement of self-development for the tribes, but the machinery and the governance could not fully attain such goals.[41] Though politico-administrative and cultural integration and rapid economic development were viewed as prerequisites for the security of the North-Eastern borders, most of the resources for the region during this period were directed towards defence purposes and not so much was devoted to and achieved in the field of economic development.

The NER, though a landlocked region, is endowed with abundant resources, which if widely utilized, would boost foreign trade with neighbouring countries. To name a few:

- The region has about 5,000 km of international borders with the countries of Bangladesh, Bhutan, China and Myanmar that has the potential to act as India's gateway to the entire South-East Asian region.
- It has one of the most fertile stretches of land along the Brahmaputra valley, whose potentiality for the cultivation of a wide variety of cash and food crops on a commercial basis is yet to be fully realized. Agro-economic efficiency is considerably high.
- It is the fulcrum of rich mineral resources, many of which have not yet been fully exploited.
- It is the treasure-trove of abundant forest resources with many ethnic products which are unique to the region.
- It is blessed with one of the largest perennial water systems in India (Brahmaputra and its tributaries) with potential attributes in areas of energy, irrigation and transportation and is the possessor of oil, tea and hydrocarbon processing industries.[42]

The region is endowed with rich hydropower potential, coal, forest wealth, fruits and vegetables, flowers, herbs and aromatic plants. Arunachal Pradesh, Assam and Manipur possess considerable potentials to generate hydroelectric power (over 40,000 MW) and proper utilization of the resources would make the region a major power house not only for India but also its neighbouring countries. The adequate exploration of the water resources would not only provide cheap transportation but also promote tourism. The Thai companies which are competent in managing inland waterway networks could avail the opportunity thus offered. There are significant deposits of coal in Meghalaya and Upper Assam which are mainly exported to Bangladesh. Initiatives should be adopted to explore more markets.[43] Moreover the region is well-known for its handloom and handicrafts and produces a large variety of agro-horticultural products thereby yielding employment and income-generating potentials for such industries. The competitive edge of Thailand's processed food industry in the world and the awareness and expertise of South-East Asia's handloom and handicrafts industry in international market offers many opportunities to North-East India for technical and marketing collaborations.[44] Assam, which produces about 50 per cent of the country's tea, has the potentiality to meet the demands of the neighbouring countries. The heavy demand for bicycle in Myanmar can be met by encouraging cycle production in Manipur and by manufacturing cycle parts, tyres and tubes as rubber is produced in the region.[45] In the field of production of natural rubber collaboration of the NER with Thailand (one of the largest producers of natural rubber) will enrich mutual competitiveness. In the field of tourism South-East Asian countries like Singapore, Thailand and Malaysia can pose an example to the NER for revamping its tourism prospect as those are the most enthralling tourist spots with multitudinous potentials. The English language proficiency of the NER and impressive rate of literacy can stimulate the promise of tourism thereby rejuvenating economic development of the NER. The sub-region comprising North-East India, Bangladesh, Myanmar and South-West China is a geographically contiguous area and shares historical and cultural ties. The countries have interacted with each other through the 'Southern Silk Road'. The trade on the Silk Road pertinently contributed to the development of the great civilizations and in several respects helped lay the foundations for the modern world.[46] Several minor-trade routes linking the region with foreign countries also existed through which a significant degree of trade was transacted. Considerable trade was also carried on between villagers on either sides of the international borders.[47] As per reports, the volume of informal border trade between North-East India and the neighbouring countries surpasses the official volume of trade, which exhibits the huge export potentials of the region if informal trade is legalized through governmental policy. The geographical contiguity can expedite the credibility of the resources thereby facilitating restructuring of industries.[48] Moreover the advantageous geographic location of the region inbues it with the credence of fostering economic cooperation under the sub-regional cooperations like BIMSTEC, MCG and BCIM forum. Cooperation with neighbours across the borders can exploit the region's huge untapped potential and transform itself into a commercial hub. The region's geographical proximities and its historical and cultural contiguities with its South-East Asian neighbours therefore can be promoted as a 'soft-power resource' to revitalize tourism and commercial exchange as a means to development of the region.

The mainstream economic thinkers generally blame economic backwardness or neglect as the main source of political turmoil in the NER and that once this problem is taken care of, the main source of political turmoil will go away.[49] The failure in building the local forces of production and human capacity development made the region increasingly dependent on the mainland. Though the region has rich mineral, water and forest resources, the absence of industrialization makes the region a market for manufactured products from industrialized regions of India and spurring the growth of new industries and jobs outside the region. A vast chunk of the money earned is spent on buying consumable items imported from industrial parts of mainland India. The Shukla Commission that submitted a report to the Government of India entitled 'Transforming the North-East' in March 1997 estimated that about ₹2,500 crore worth of consumable items is imported from outside the region every year.[50] The Government of India conceptualized its LEP towards the development of the North-Eastern Region. This policy is reflected in the 'Year End Review 2004' of the Ministry of External Affairs, which stated that: 'India's Look East Policy has now been given a new dimension by the UPA Government. India is now looking towards a partnership with the ASEAN countries, both within BIMSTEC and the India-ASEAN Summit dialogue as integrally linked to economic and security interests, particularly for India's East and North-East Region.'[51]

India has undertaken substantive initiatives at regional and sub-regional cooperation in pursuant with its LEP. Through ASEAN and sub-regional cooperations like the Bay of Bengal Initiative for Multi Sectoral Technical and Economic Cooperation (BIMSTEC), Mekong-Ganga Cooperation (MGC) of India, Myanmar, Thailand, Cambodia, Laos and Vietnam, and the Bangladesh-China-India-Myanmar Regional Economic Forum (BCIM), India strives to forge closer economic relations with East and South-East Asian countries. These regional initiatives are relevant to the prospects of the emergence of a cross-border region of connecting the NER with the adjacent transnational areas on its east.[52] Deeper intra-regional trade is expected to benefit the North-Eastern states.[53] With the intent to reinforce the LEP and link the NER to the dynamic economies of East and South-East Asia India has rejuvenated its cooperation with the sub-regional groupings. Sub-regional cooperation emphasizes the complementarities of resource potentialities of the collaborative partners facilitating economic growth across national borders. Moreover, in sub-regional economic zones, the focus of cooperation expands from trade promotion to rejuvenation of tourism, natural and human resource development and advancement of infrastructure facilities.[54] This renewed perspective of cooperation ordains the countries with the vigour of an immediate neighbourhood from that of the extended neighbourhood.[55] Regional cooperation triggers economic integration, which manifests when goods, services and factors of production flow freely and the financial markets get unified among the countries within a geographic region.

The littoral states of the Bay of Bengal (Bangladesh, India, Myanmar, Srilanka and Thailand) collaborated to form the international organization, BIMSTEC. The organization was formed on 6 June 1997 (issued at the ministerial meeting of the Foreign Ministers of the countries in Bangkok). BIMSTEC is a link between South Asia and South-East Asia. It should not be viewed in opposition to the South Asian Association for Regional Cooperation (SAARC), rather should be considered as a complement to it. It substantiates Thailand's or ASEAN's 'Look West' policies and India's LEP. Due to India-Pakistan differences the SAARC has not made much headway. BIMSTEC, without Pakistan, thus provides an alternative regional mechanism to channelize regional aspirations into workable projects. Bangladesh and Sri Lanka sought the membership of the ASEAN without much success. In this background the BIMSTEC assumes special importance in facilitating access to the SAARC and acting as a bridge to the ASEAN.

BIMSTEC as an international organization conceives of well-formulated plans and objectives. It emphasizes on commonly shared interests and concerns among the member countries by professing the complementarities of their economies. The basic objectives of BIMSTEC can be identified as follows:

- By carefully labeling and implementing specific cooperation projects in the fields of trade, investment, industry, technology, human resource development, tourism, agriculture, energy, infrastructure and transportation, BIMSTEC opts for the creation of a healthy atmosphere for rapid economic development.
- Aims to enhance the pace of economic growth and social progress in the sub-region through collective cooperation and thus rejuvenates the spirit of equality and partnership.
- Encourages dynamic collaboration and mutual assistance in economic, social, technical and scientific areas with special emphasis on matters strategizing common interests.
- It was agreed upon by the member countries to undertake the initiative of offering training and research facilities in educational, professional and technological spheres with a motive of providing assistance to each other.

- Moreover they should participate more effectively in joint ventures leading to national development plans which will enable people to gain a number of benefits for uplifting their living standards including employment generation and improving transportation and communication facilities.
- BIMSTEC should try to maintain close and fruitful congruity with existing international and regional organizations nurturing similar aims and objectives.
- Puts emphasis on projects which can reap benefits on a sub-regional basis among the BIMSTEC member countries, by utilizing the available potentials in the best possible way.[56]
- Agendas like the harmonization of customs procedures, increased mobility of individuals through smooth visa access, upgradation of transportation routes and communication channels, exchange of information at the ministerial level and improvement in economic spheres and particularly banking ties between the countries mandates the functioning of the organization.[57]

BIMSTEC AND INDIA'S NORTH-EAST

It is apparent that the BIMSTEC was formed by countries in the Bay of Bengal basin with the aim to exploit the available synergies and resource endowments towards the cause of their mutual benefits.[58] Economic disparity across the world is a common phenomenon and this incongruity is also apparent within the BIMSTEC with varying magnitude. Some of the land-locked regions like the NER of India, despite being endowed with rich natural resources, have miserably failed to reap the benefits of globalization primarily due to lack of improved technology and efficient infrastructure services. It is therefore necessary to engineer coordinated efforts among the BIMSTEC countries for optimum utilization of the available resources.[59] The cooperation can consolidate the existing strengths of various economies as well as alleviate many of the structural constraints. Economic cooperation if driven by the private sector can facilitate considerable policy initiatives of the governments in the sub-region. A synergy between long-term strategies aimed to strengthen the foundations for greater economic cooperation and the short-term measures necessary for removing the hurdles is ardently required.[60]

Trade and investment in goods and services could accelerate the development of India's NER by greater cooperation with neighbouring Myanmar, China and Bangladesh. Thus, India promotes the BIMSTEC to foster closer economic links with the member countries of the ASEAN to boost the development of its North-Eastern states. It has often been alleged that the intensity of the insurgencies in India's North-East has been fuelled up partly due to India's not-so-friendly relations with neighbours like Myanmar. But the renewed thrust on cooperation with Myanmar, mostly due to security concerns, since 1992 encompassing a wide array of exchange of high-level visits and signing of bilateral agreements yielded some success in tackling insurgencies by both the neighbours. Moreover, the membership of Nepal, Bangladesh and Bhutan makes the BIMSTEC more competent to counter the menace of insurgency and extremism. Secondly, drug smuggling and money laundering from the famous Golden Triangle into India and beyond has been a cause of distress for the country as it sustains many of the secessionist movements in the region. But this problem could not be addressed due to the dearth of an able multilateral mechanism. Third, much of the BIMSTEC region is immensely rich in hydrocarbon and hydroelectric resources. For instance, Bangladesh already has gas deposits and Indian public sector companies, the ONGC and GAIL, have discovered vast reserves of gas in Myanmar. Along with the massive hydroelectric potential of the Himalayan states of Nepal and Bhutan, and a prospective gas pipeline from Myanmar to India, the creation of a sub-regional energy grid becomes a feasible and viable proposition in the BIMSTEC region. Lastly, a number of proposals have also been discussed to bolster infrastructure in this region through the development of highways and rail links.[61]

India has constructed the 160 km Tamu-Kalewa-Kalemyo roads called the India-Myanmar Friendship Road, for smoother trade transaction. According to the 2005-6 report of the Ministry of External Affairs, India seeks greater cooperation and development towards the integration of North-East India with Western Myanmar by building infrastructural facilities like building of roads that would connect North-East with Myanmar. Of particular importance is the Kaladan Multimodal Transport facility that will establish links between Myanmar, the North-East and the Bay of Bengal. In 2002, India, Myanmar and Thailand announced the landmark international highway project, a 1,400 km highway aimed at completion by two years. For the development of the NER, the Trilateral Highway Project between India, Myanmar and Thailand is playing a substantial role. For infrastructure development, major initiatives like the second India–Myanmar border trade point at Rhi-Zowkhathar in the Mizoram sector after the Moreh-Tamu trade sector by upgrading the Rhi-Tidim and Rhi-Falam road segments in Myanmar is being promoted. Besides road links, efforts of developing rail link from Jiribham in Manipur to Hanoi in Vietnam passing through Myanmar is also in the pipeline. Digital connectivity is another area where work is being carried on, particularly through optical fibre cable link between Moreh in Manipur and Mandalay in Myanmar.

As the second phase of India's LEP seeks to channelize the political-economic benefits of the burgeoning India-ASEAN cooperation towards the NER it holds immense potential for trade expansion and regional development for the North-East of India. But sharing common borders with neighouring countries also increases the vulnerability of being perturbed by a horde or issues like illegal migration, and cross-border criminal and terrorist activities.[62] The achievements of the BIMSTEC have a great role to play in transforming the region from a security dilemma to India's 'Gateway to the East'. The current volume of intra-regional trade in the BIMSTEC is not as large as compared to that of ASEAN, EU and NAFTA. The least developed countries (LDCs) and land-locked countries are having higher share in intra-regional trade in BIMSTEC. For example, intra-regional export shares of Myanmar and Nepal have gone up substantially. The joint statement of the 10th BIMSTEC Ministerial Meeting on 29 August 2008 emphasized on poverty alleviation meant to be supported by programmes like the creation of a food bank for the region, flood control, and checking climate change. The regional leaders are endeavouring to implement the initiatives of improved physical connectivity and easier transport and trade flows by 2020 and are also enlisting selected priority projects for fimely completion. The development of transport and logistic facilities is significant for boosting trade within the region and with other regions. A stronger BIMSTEC undoubtedly points to a more stable and prosperous Asia.[63] Certain challenges are being encountered by this BIMSTEC initiative. Many of the ports in BIMSTEC like Kolkata and Haldia in India, Chittagong in Bangladesh, Yangon and Dawaei in Myanmar and Bangkok in Thailand have been restrained from achieving targets due to navigational problems, dearth of multimodal connectivity and deficit of modern port handling equipment. For the BIMSTEC highway and BIMSTEC railway projects it can adopt a BIMSTEC Land Transport Infrastructure Integration Roadmap and Transport Facilitation of Goods Roadmap.

STRUCTURAL AND MEMBER-SPECIFIC CHALLENGES OF THE BIMSTEC

BIMSTEC has been experiencing considerable growth rates since the 1990s. This growth was produced by reforms towards increasing global integration, improving macro-economic management and underscoring the private sector as a key engine of growth. Trade restrictions including import tariffs were reduced. The high growth rate, in turn, created interest across societies and allowed political space for greater regional integration. The resurgence of the BIMSTEC against the background of the global meltdown and a virtually in-effective Doha Round of WTO talks makes closer regional integration not only a pressing necessity but a viable and effective development strategy. Regional economic integration enables countries to share the experiences of their fellow members and thereby equipping themselves with the traits to emerge as a more competitive market for the rest of the world through the process of specialization and exploitation of synergies. Competitive and innovative regional integration holds out prospect for the region in terms of higher income growth, optimal employment of domestic resources, more gainful integration through global and regional trade and investment and greater equity in access, distribution and development. It is essential to ensure easier and economical arrangements for people and goods to move from one place to another. This is the mandate for revitalization of closer integration within the region and for speeding up its economic development. The creation of basic facilities ensue the harmonization in custom codes and tariff alignments at the next stage. Many issues other than transport and logistics are equally important for promoting trade within the region and with other regions. Energy, food security and agricultural development, investment, tourism, technology cooperation and regional security are some of the areas where bloc-level work programmes are needed.

Nepal and partly Thailand are poised for newer twists and turns. Myanmar is facing a growing tussle between the status quo and the demand for change. India is facing outbursts of occasional violence and public restiveness and a slew of policies that often appear to be out of synchronization with people's priorities. Bhutan has opened a new chapter of history in terms of its rising importance in international politics, and Sri Lanka and Bangladesh are still searching for a national identity amidst pulls and pressures. Even as such disturbances continue, big powers – both far and near – eye the region with growing interest as it represents a strategic area on the world map and also a potential mega-market that business and investment today is so eager to tap. And that is perhaps all the more reason why blocs like BIMSTEC have to develop an identity and cohesion among themselves at the earliest.[64]

Bangladesh requires pro-market reforms necessary for economic development. Though its policies are liberal and attract Foreign Direct Investment (FDI) but are precisely low-cost, labour-intensive and recent reports of advancing militancy have adverse effects on investor confidence. In Myanmar agriculture, extraction of natural resources account for 50-60 per cent of GDP and the manufacturing sector accounts for 9 per cent of GDP. Nepal suffers from limited market potential. The severity of decade-long Maoist insurgency also failed to attract FDI, tourism consequently weakening its economy. Landlocked country presents a barrier to industrial development. Thailand, though demonstrates an impressive economic and fiscal scenario, the alarmingly increasing rate of HIV+/AIDS patients, most belonging to the working population. Political climate in Sri Lanka is not yet stable, human rights protection is getting weaker and the country is still coping up with the devastating effects of the tsunami. India requires additional economic reforms. A key area in need of FDI is infrastructure. Entry of FDI and free trade are volatile is in the sensitive political dynamics in India.

Furthermore, the absence of an effective permanent Secretariat (it was established in Bangladesh in 2014) and financing mechanism, need for a proper agenda and its implementation and political commitment are the essentialities for the successful pursuit of BIMSTEC's objectives. BIMSTEC's success could be strengthened by checking bureaucratic delays and red tapism embroiled in traveling and trading between the member countries, standardizing trade rules and products, developing national financial sectors and accelerating means of cross-border communication. BIMSTEC still faces the challenges of the demands of regionalism over nationalism, deepening the process of integration, expanding cooperation areas and arrangements and implementing result-oriented short-gestation joint projects for better understanding among the member-countries.

The development of the NER from the BIMSTEC should take into consideration some aspects which might have some role to play in the integrity of our nation-state. It is required to open the borders in such a way that the resources and the interests of the region are safeguarded rather than being adversely exploited. The geographic location of the member-countries along with the pluralistic nature with shared cultural heritage and the existence of diverse arts, crafts, languages offer good scope for cooperation. Subregional economic co-operations such as BIMSTEC contribute to efforts towards free and fair trade being pursued under the multilateral trading regime.

After the establishment of the BIMSTEC in 1997, followed by the BCIM in 1999, New Delhi conceived of the setting up of a third regional diplomatic structure linking India to South-East Asia – the Mekong-Ganga Cooperation Initiative (MGCI). The project, perceived as a counterweight to China's cultural influence, was announced in July 2000 in the ASEAN summit held in Bangkok by the six concerned Ministers of Foreign Affairs (Cambodia, Vietnam, Laos, Thailand and Myanmar for the riparian countries of the Mekong river and India for the Ganga river). The MGCI was launched with the Vientiane Declaration on 10 November 2000 in the capital city of Laos, with the primary thrust to expand solidarity, harmony and cooperation in the fields of tourism, culture and education for ensuring substantive social and economic development of the Mekong region countries. India and the five South-East Asian nations – Thailand, Vietnam, Laos, Cambodia and Myanmar – were the signatories of that decisive endeavour. The basic thrust of the MGC is to undertake economic development of the Mekong region by developing the infrastructure facilities. For India, MGC offers immense scope for creating linkages with the Mekong countries by connecting them to the sub-continent's economically backward North-Eastern Region. Indian policymakers believe that the development of the North-East is crucial to the promotion of trade and industrial cooperation with the ASEAN countries and the Mekong countries in particular. Road construction linking the North-

East and MGC will facilitate quicker overland transportation of goods between the two regions. The Asian Highway on its completion will link Singapore with the Indian mainland via the Mekong cities and the North-East Region.[65] The declaration expected the MGC to conduct preliminary strategic studies for joint marketing, to launch the Mekong-Ganga Tourism Investment Guide, to facilitate the travel of people in the region, to expand multi-modal communication and transportation links for expanding travel and tourism and to promote cultural-religious package tours. The MGC stimulated the establishment of networking and twinning arrangements among the colleges and universities in the region, endorsed for the translation of the classics of MGC countries into other MGC languages for better understanding and interpretation and assured the participation in book fairs in member-countries on a commercial basis. The MGC can transform the tourism prospects of the NER into economic opportunities as well as strengths of the region.

BCIM FORUM

The Bangladesh-China-India-Myanmar Regional Economic Forum (BCIM Forum) is a Track II initiative which was the outcome of a conference on regional cooperation held at Kunming, the capital of Yunnan province of China. The sub-region under this grouping consists of a number of geographically contiguous units comprising the North-Eastern states of India, southern provinces of China and Bangladesh and Myanmar. This forum focuses on regional cooperation in infrastructure development and thus highlights the importance of improved transport connectivity for efficient movement of goods and people in the interests of both regional and global competitiveness and in order to promote tourism. Although BCIM forum is organized at the Track II level, it provided recommendations to the proper execution of activities and functions of the BCIM initiative at the official level and its evolution into sub-regional programmes at the government level. The trade and economic relations greatly influence the overall India-China relations, which is the result of a conscious effort on both sides to bring bilateral relationship in tune with the present realities by building upon mutual complementarities.[66] There lies ample prospect for following up the Kunming Initiative, especially the proposal to rebuild the Stillwell Road which was constructed during the Second World War. The Stillwell Road connects Ledo in Assam and Kunming in the Yunnan province of China passing through northern Myanmar. The motto for BCIM cooperation is that integration of these strategically located areas, constituting a natural economic zone, possesses the credence to generate enormous economic benefits in the areas of trade, investment, energy, transport and tourism. The economic dynamism of India and China offers wide range of opportunities for growth and development in the region.[67] In its past meetings, the BCIM Forum has come up with ideas for subregional cooperation in some important areas such as trade, transport, tourism, energy security, etc. The BCIM Initiative brings into its fold three of India's most important neighbours closer in a joint pursuit of common prosperity through the increasing use of the mechanisms of regional integration. Taking note of the importance of such initiative, Rajiv Sikri observes that:

> It is not just that we are neighbours sharing common borders; all of us also face similar opportunities and challenges in our respective quests for rapid economic growth, national development and prosperity of our people. In our mutual relationships, there is increasingly greater focus on economic issues, which will enable us to realize the untapped potential of our economic cooperation and make it commensurate with the level of our political relationships.[68]

If India extends support to China's Kunming Initiative, initiated in 1999 to form a regional economic forum among Bangladesh, China, India, Myanmar (BCIM), the NER will be the centre of trade among all these four states because of its geographic locations.[69]

In the 'Dhaka Statement 2007' of the Seventh BCIM Forum on Regional Economic Cooperation held in Dhaka from 31 March to 1 April 2007, the participating countries observed that the successive BCIM forums have identified enormous potential for cooperation in this subregion which is rich in natural and human resources across an area which represents the interface between East Asia, South-East Asia and South Asia. It is now necessary to further cultivate the mutual complementarity that exists among the countries of the BCIM.[70] The Seventh BCIM Forum also agreed that initiatives should be taken to develop concrete proposals for consideration and follow-up action by the national groups, business communities and the civil society. In this context, the areas on improving trade facilitation, strengthening transport connectivity, enhancing tourism cooperation, promoting educational, scientific, cultural and social exchanges. Having about 40 per cent of the world population, a huge reserve of natural and other resources and two of the world's fastest growing giant economies such as India and China in the forum, the BCIM subregional economic cooperation is perceived to have enormous potentials to generate benefits for the region in general and the underdeveloped areas in particular. Bangladesh, Myanmar, the North-Eastern states of India and south-western Chinese provinces could benefit extensively from such regional cooperation. Proper implementation of this sub-regional cooperation could combine the resources of the constituent members in order to gain competitive edge in attracting both domestic and foreign investments and promoting export for the mutual benefit of the members involved. A regional project on developing energy resources could very well be initiated for efficient and more value-added use of these resources. Along with the move in Track II, Yunnan attempts to develop the cooperation framework to the official level (Track I) and an Initiative is under processing to promote the level of cooperation to Track I.

CONCLUSION

The NER is being considered by many experts of India's foreign policy as a veritable gateway to the success of India's LEP and thereby possesses prospects for substantive economic development of the region itself and of the entire country as well. In the backdrop of the changing global dynamics India and ASEAN need be steadily oriented towards their innovative measures with the adequate knowledge of their mutual interests and prospects. The existing opportunities and challenges are to be grappled skilfully. The LEP profoundly endeavours to promote the connectivity and infrastructure facilities of the NER so as to end the landlocked situation and alienation of the region by integrating the region's economy through improved trade and connectivity with the flourishing economies of its South-East Asian neighbours. But the assessment of the ground realities projects that the initiatives and the projects undertaken for boosting connectivity and infrastructure facilities are not being implemented with the required vigour and the prospect of the NER being the gateway to ASEAN remains utterly dim. The thrust of the LEP is to ensure economic development of the NER through regional cooperation but to execute such a challenging mission it needs to address the problems plaguing the region. Whenever we talk about international integration of the NER we need to be convinced about the national integration of the region. The historical inferences of the political integration of the NER significantly uphold that the issue of integration of the region with mainland India has remained a matter of deep concern. The attempts of assimilation and identification with the mainstream have resulted in the outbursts of vehement protests or animosities by various political or ethnic groups of the region. The frustration emanating from the sense of isolation and acute economic underdevelopment might have led to the genesis of the menaces of insurgency, extremism in the region, the occurrences of which have stigmatized the area as a region of security threat. Though the subregional cooperation faces certain challenges and structural and member-specific limitations, it has the prospect for offering ample scope for cooperation among the member-countries steered towards the optimum utilization of the available resources of respective countries thereby reinforcing the essence of cooperation among India and its South Asian and South-East Asian neighbours. The LEP needs to impart its due importance to the NER. The government should not continue with any ad hoc policy and must have specific document wherein every detail must be spelt out. Though much is talked about the intent of the policy to develop the NER, the realistic appraisal of the policy projects little implementation defaming it as a mere political slogan or euphoria for the NER. It is undoubted that India has made considerable headway in its Look East venture but the prospect is visibly less in the NER. The LEP should address its limitations by being well-versed with the ground realities and undertake a whole-hearted approach to utilize and incentivize the resources of the NER, aiming at projecting the region as a significant gateway to its proper accomplishment. From 2015 the LEP has developed also an Act East Policy. The high-level exchange of visits and the contemporary executive itinerary exhibit the changing power dynamics and national priorities with relative importance. And all Act East policies presuppose a stable and developed NER, a prospective commercial hub, which mandates a comprehensive peace plan for the eight North-Eastern states that can integrate with our eastward foreign policies. In this endeavour India should also devote its potentials to utilize the available resources in the NER in their best possible ways. Cooperation based on mutual trust and confidence would bolster the very essence of India-ASEAN cooperation thereby administering India's emerging eminence in South-East Asian and Asia-Pacific Region.

The Introduction to this book aims at evaluating the implications of India's Look East Policy on its North-East Region. The first chapter explores the relevance of North-East border economy in the LEP. North- East India's crucial engagement with Myanmar qualifies as the most pertinent way of translating the substance of the LEP into reality. To realize the essence of bilateral cooperation in its fullest possible context both India and Myanmar need to promote border economy through boosting of border trade between the two countries. Moreover, the development of the border trade would lead to the revamping of North-East India's economy thereby transforming the region from its landlocked position to a 'gateway status'. This is primarily a case study on Moreh based on the field trip conducted in Imphal. The focus in the second chapter is on the tourism prospect of NER through the Mekong-Ganga Cooperation Initiative. It is pertinent to underscore that increased regional cooperation in the field of tourism facilitates the promotion of landlocked regions into land-linked regions. One of the core aspects of the MGCI is to economically develop its landlocked NER for which the opening of the region is ardently required. In this lieu North-East Region's enthralling scenic beauty can play a vital role. A case study on Kohima's Hornbill Festival based on a field trip to Kohima proposes to highlight the strength of the NER as an impetus to the successful pursuit of the LEP. The third chapter studies the newer vistas of cooperation between North-East India and Myanmar as well as the influence of China on Myanmar in its transition to democracy – more specifically from its 'isolationist past' towards a modernized liberal state. Finally, the major findings of the study are analysed in the Conclusion. Certain paradigms need to be emphasized by the LEP in order to meet the objective of developing the NER.

NOTES

1. Salman Khurshid, in A.N. Ram (ed.), *Two Decades of India's Look East Policy: Partnership for Peace, Progress and Prosperity*, New Delhi, Manohar, 2012, pp. 9-10.
2. Ibid., p. 49.
3. G.V.C. Naidu, 'India and Southeast Asia', *World Focus*, vol. 17, nos. 10, 11, 12, October, November and December 1996, p. 82.

4. K. Shankar Bajpai, 'India in 1991: New Beginnings', *Asian Survey*, vol. 32, no. 2, February 1992, pp. 207-16.
5. Prakash Nanda, 'Look-East Policy Takes Shape', in Prakash Nanda (ed.), *Rediscovering Asia: Evolution of India's Look-East Policy*, New Delhi, Lancer, 2003, p. 267.
6. Sandy Gordon, *India's Rise to Power in the Twentieth Century and Beyond*, New York, St. Martin's Press, 1995, p. 121.
7. Jayanta Roy, 'How to Energize India's Look East Policy: Among Neighbours', *The Telegraph*, 17 May 2012.
8. Indrakumar Konthoujam, 'Mapping India's Look East Policy: Shifting Alignments', in Thingnam Kishan Singh (ed.), *Look East Policy and India's North East: Polemics and Perspectives*, New Delhi, Concept Publishing Company, 2009, p. 30.
9. Amitabh Mattoo, 'ASEAN in India's Foreign Policy', in Frederic Grare and Amitabh Mattoo (eds.), *Beyond the Rhetoric: The Economics of India's Look East Policy*, New Delhi, Manohar, 2003, p. 93.
10. Baladas Ghoshal, 'India, ASEAN and APEC', in Nancy Jetly (ed.), *India's Foreign Policy Challenges and Prospects*, New Delhi, Vikas, 1999, p. 151.
11. Prem Shankar Jha, 'Stagnation and Sovereignty', *The Hindu*, 15 July 1992.
12. Hamish Macdonald and Jaya Sarkar, 'India: The Money Jaugernaut', *Far Eastern Economic Review*, 11 March 1993, p. 16.
13. A.N. Ram, 'Introduction', in A.N. Ram (ed.), *Two Decades of India's Look East Policy: Partnership for Peace, Progress and Prosperity*, New Delhi, Manohar, 2012, p. 12.
14. G.V.C. Naidu, 'India and Southeast Asia', *World Focus*, vol. 17, nos. 10, 11, 12, October-November, December, 1996, p. 83.
15. Annual Report: 1992-3, Ministry of External Affairs, Government of India, New Delhi, 1993, pp. 6-27.
16. Tridib Chakraborti, 'Explaining the Penumbra of India's Look East Policy', in K. Raja Reddy (ed.), *India and ASEAN Foreign Policy Dimensions for the 21st Century*, New Delhi, New Century, 2005, pp. 53-4.
17. Sunanda K. Dutta Ray, *Looking East To Look West: Lee Kuan Yew's Mission India*, New Delhi, Penguin, 2009, p. 150.
18. Sunanda K. Dutta Ray 'Competitiveness and Leverage', in Michael G. Plummer and Chia Siow Yue (eds.), *Realising the ASEAN Economic Community: A Comprehensive Assessment*, Singapore, ISEAS, 2009, pp. 139-42.

19. Preet Malik, 'India's Look East Policy: Genesis', in A.N. Ram (ed.), *Two Decades of India's Look East Policy: Partnership for Peace, Progress and Prosperity*, New Delhi, Manohar, 2012, p. 34.
20. Statement by I.K. Gujral, Ministry of External Affairs, New Delhi.
21. Preet Malik, 'India's Look East Policy: Genesis', in A.N. Ram (ed.), *Two Decades of India's Look East Policy: Partnership for Peace, Progress and Prosperity*, New Delhi, Manohar, 2012, p. 38.
22. Thingnam Kishan Singh, *Look East Policy and India's North-East: Polemics and Perspectives*, New Delhi, Concept Publishing Company, 2009.
23. Amar Nath Ram, 'The First Decade of India's Look East Policy: An Insider's Account', in A.N. Ram (ed.), *Two Decades of India's Look East Policy: Partnership for Peace, Progress and Prosperity*, New Delhi, Manohar, 2012, p. 77.
24. Alexander Mackenzie, *History of the Relations of the Government with the Hill Tribes of the North-East Frontier of Bengal*, Calcutta, Cambridge University Press, 1884, p. 6.
25. Amalendu Guha, *Planter-Raj to Swaraj: Freedom Struggle and Electoral Politics in Assam 1826-1947*, New Delhi, People's Publishing House, 1977 (rpt. 1988), p. 73.
26. Rafiul Ahmed and Prasenajit Biswas, *Political Economy of Underdevelopment of North-East India*, New Delhi, Akansha, 2004, p. 50.
27. Subir Bhaumik, 'Insurgency in North East', *Aakrosh*, vol. 1, no. 1, October 1998.
28. Gulshan Sachdeva, 'Demystifying Northeast', *Dialogue*, January-March 2006, vol. 7, no. 3.
29. B.G. Verghese, *India's Northeast Resurgent: Ethnicity, Insurgency, Governance, Development*, New Delhi, Konark, 1996, p. 2.
30. B.G. Verghese, 'Unfinished Business in the Northeast: Priorities Towards Restructuring, Reform, Reconciliation and Resurgence', *Seventh Kamal Kumari Lecture*. Available at https://isdsnet.com/ijds-v6n8-17.pds (accessed on 10 October 2017), 2001.
31. Session report by Udayon Mishra in the first Civil Society Dialogue on Peace (CSDP) in the Northeast held on 12 October 2001 in Kolkata. Available at http://www.mcrg.ac.in/civilsociety dialogue1.htm (accessed on 23 November 2009).
32. Myron Weiner, 'Political Integration and Political Development', *Annals of the American Academy of Political and Social Science*, vol. 358, March 1965, p. 52.
33. Gabriel A. Almond and G. Bingham Powell, Jr., *Comparative Politics:*

A Developmental Approach, Boston, Little, Brown & Co., 1966, p. 36.

34. Alokesh Barua and Arindam Bandyopadhyay, 'Structural Change, Economic Growth and Regional Disparity in the North-East: Regional and National Perspective', in Alokesh Barua (ed.), *India's North-East: Developmental Issues in a Historical Perspective*, New Delhi, CSH and Manohar, 2005, p. 239.
35. P.C. Dutta, 'Problems of Ethnicity and Insurgency in North East India', in S.K. Agnihotri and B.Datta Ray (eds.), *Perspective of Security and Development in North East India*, New Delhi, Concept Publishing Company, 2005, p. 112.
36. Gurudas Das, 'Understanding the Underdevelopment of North-Eastern Region of India', *Journal of Indian Anthropological Society*, vol. 29, nos. 1 and 2.
37. Zarin Ahmad, 'India: Package for the North East', *Institute of Peace and Conflict Studies*, Article no. 338, 8 March 200.
38. Gulshan Sachdeva, 'Demystifying Northeast', *Dialogue*, January-March 2006, vol. 7, no. 3.
39. Alokesh Barua, 'Introduction', in Alokesh Barua (ed.), *India's North-East: Developmental Issues in a Historical Perspective*, New Delhi, CSH and Manohar, 2005, pp. 14-15.
40. Manorama Sharma, 'Socio-Economic History in Pre-Colonial North-East India: Trends, Problems and Possibilities', in Mignonette Momin and Cecile Mawlong (eds.), *Society and Economy in North-East India*, vol. 1, New Delhi, Regency, 2004, p. 16.
41. Rafiul Ahmed and Prasenajit Biswas, *Political Economy of Underdevelopment of North-East India*, New Delhi, Akansha, 2004, p. 4.
42. J.S.R. Khathing, 'Indo-Myanmar Border Trade', in Gurudas Das, N. Bijoy Singh and C.J. Thomas (eds.), *Indo-Myanmar Border Trade*, New Delhi, Akansha, 2005, pp. 42-5.
43. S.P. Shukla Commission Report, 'Transforming the Northeast, Tackling Backlog in Basic Minimum Services and Infrastructural Needs', New Delhi, Planning Commission, 1997, pp. 67-76.
44. Amita Batra, 'India's Northeast and Southeast Asia: Strengthening and Integrated Space', *IPCS Issue Brief*, no. 107, June 2009, p. 3.
45. G.P. Parasin, 'Indo-Myanmar Border Trade: Resource Base and Export Potential of the North Eastern Region', in Gurudas Das, N. Bijoy Singh and C.J. Thomas (eds.), *Indo-Myanmar Border Trade: Status, Problems and Potentials*, New Delhi, Akansha, 2007, p. 197.
46. Francis Wood, *The Silk Road: Two Thousand Years in the Heart of*

Asia, Berkeley, CA, University of California Press, 2002, pp. 9, 13-23.

47. B.B. Kumar, 'The Border Trade in North-East India: The Historical Perspective', in Gurudas Das and R.K. Purkayastha (eds.), *Border Trade: North-East India and Neighbouring Countries*, New Delhi, Akansha, 2000, p. 6.
48. *Future Directions of BIMSTEC: Towards a Bay of Bengal Economic Community*, New Delhi, RIS Publication, 2004, p. 2.
49. Sanjib Baruah, 'Governor as Generals: The Parallel Political Systems of Northeast India', *Himal South Asian*, vol. 14, no. 6, June 2001.
50. S.P. Shukla Commission Report 'Transforming the Northeast, Tackling Backlogs in Bassic Minimum Services and Infrastructural Needs', New Delhi, Planning Commission, 1997, pp. 67-76.
51. 'Year End Review 2004', Ministry of External Affairs, Government of India, New Delhi.
52. Shibashis Chatterjee, 'Conceptions of Space in India's Look East Policy: Order, Cooperation or Community?' *South Asian Survey*, vol. 14, no. 65, 2007, p. 77.
53. Faizal Yahya, 'BIMSTEC and Emerging Patterns of Asian Regional and Inter Regional Cooperation', *Australian Journal of Political Science*, vol. 40, no. 3, September 2005, p. 392.
54. Isabelle Saint-Mezard, 'The Look East Policy: An Economic Perspective', in Frederic Grare and Amitabh Mattoo (eds.), *Beyond the Rhetoric: The Economics of India's Look East Policy*, New Delhi, CHS and Manohar, 2003, p. 40.
55. V. Suryanarayan, 'Prospects for a Bay of Bengal Community', Seminar 487, March 2000.
56. Declaration on the Establishment of BIST-EC, Bangkok, 6 June 1997.
57. '5-Point Agenda for BIMSTEC', *The Hindu*, 1 July 2000.
58. CSIRD, 2006.
59. Wisarn Pupphavesa, *BIMSTEC-Japan Comprehensive Economic Cooperation: A Step in the Future*, New Delhi, Bookwell, 2008, pp. 1-10.
60. UN Economic and Social Commission for Asia and Pacific, *The BIST-EC Development Programme, Overview and Sectoral Cooperation*, New York, United Nations, 1997, p. 1.
61. G.V.C. Naidu, 'BIMSTEC and its Geo-strategic Importance', in *World Focus* 337, January 2008, p. 3.

62. Ishani Naskar, 'Pangs of Proximity: India's North East and her Eastern Neighbours', in Jayanta Ray and Rakhee Bhattacharya (eds.), *Development Dynamics in North East India*, New Delhi, Anshah Publishing House, 2008, pp. 54, 55.
63. Prabir De, 'Connecting Mekong Region with India through Infrastructure Linkages', *Financial Express*, 5 November 2008.
64. *BIMSTEC Cooperation Report 2008*, New Delhi, Bookwell, 2009.
65. P.V. Rao, 'Sub-regional Strategies of Cooperation in ASEAN: The Indian Approach', in K. Raja Reddy (ed.), *India and ASEAN Foreign Policy Dimensions for the Twenty-First Century*, New Delhi, New Century, 2005, p. 155.
66. Address by Rajiv Sikri, Secretary (East), Ministry of External Affairs, at the Sixth Bangladesh-China-India-Myanmar Forum, New Delhi, accessed at http://www.meaindia.nic.in/speech/2006/03/30ss01.htm on 15 October 2014.
67. Mustafizur Rahman et al., 'BCIM Economic Cooperation: Prospects and Challenges', Centre for Policy Dialogue, Dhaka, Paper no. 64, September 2007, p. 1.
68. Address by Rajiv Sikri, Secretary (East), Ministry of External Affairs, at the Sixth Bangladesh-China-India-Myanmar Forum, New Delhi, accessed at *http://www.meaindia.nic.in/speech/2006/03/30ss01.htm* on 25 February 2015.
69. Sanjib Baruah, *Between South and Southeast Asia: Northeast India and the Look East policy, CENISEAS PAPERS 4*, Guwahati, 2004, pp. 24-8.
70. *Dhaka Statement 2007*, Seventh BCIM Forum on Regional Economic Cooperation, Dhaka, 31 March to 1 April 2007.

CHAPTER 2

North-East Border Economy in the Look East Policy

India's LEP is an integral initiative of reformulating its foreign policy pursuits in accordance with the dynamics of global reconfiguration in the post-Cold War international politics with the objective of economic development underlying its principal mandate. India's orientation towards privatized, liberalized and globalized economy was essentially manifested through its enterprising endeavour of opening up the market economy with the onset of its LEP in the early 1990s. The deepening of economic linkages with the ASEAN unleashed the imperative of the development of connectivity and infrastructure facilities in India-ASEAN cooperation. Herein the significance of the North-East Region (NER) of India comes to the limelight if the proposition of trade transaction via landroute between India and South-East Asia is taken into consideration. 'South East Asia begins where North-East India ends' is often used to define the social, cultural and psychological proximities and bonds of North-East India with India's South-East Asian neighbours. The disparate and distinctive attributes of the NER of India places the North-East in a unique geographical and political space that often reflects its ethnic and genealogical connections to the rest of South-East Asian highlands.[1] Geographic realities validate the significance of the NER as a gateway to Myanmar, which in turn, is the springboard to reach out to the South-East Asian region. Even a cursory assessment of India's foreign policy orientation reveals that the inclusion of Myanmar into ASEAN as a full member in 1997 accords an extraordinary impetus to the NER.

North-East India's crucial engagement with Myanmar thus qualifies as the most pertinent way of translating the substance of the LEP into reality. To fructify the essence of bilateral cooperation in its fullest possible context both India and Myanmar need to promote border economy through revitalizing border trade between the two countries. Moreover, the development of the border trade would lead to the revamping of North-East India's economy thereby transforming the region from its landlocked position to a 'gateway status'.

India's NER, a distinctive geopolitical entity, comprises the states of Assam, Meghalaya, Tripura, Mizoram, Manipur, Nagaland and Arunachal Pradesh. It is spread over an area of 2.55 lakh sq km, which accounts for 7.8 per cent of the total landmass of India and 3.73 per cent of India's vast population. Except for the formerly princely states of Manipur and Tripura, all other states were parts of British colonial Assam. An eighth state, Sikkim was included to the key policy-making institution, the North-East Council in 2001. The unique characteristics of the region get manifested through its varied components and its ethnic, linguistic, cultural, religious and physiographical diversities.[2] The region, once a frontier of the British Empire, shares 98 per cent international borders with Bangladesh, Myanmar, China, Bhutan and Nepal but just over 2 per cent with the Indian mainland. The bifurcation of a state resulting in the creation of more and more states proliferating the resurgence of regional, subregional and ethno-nationalistic movements has somewhat destabilized the essence of unity and solidarity that once used to be the spirit of India's nationalistic struggle against British colonialism.[3] The prevalence of multifarious facets and the occurrence of violent activities and insurgencies in the NER delineate the realistic underpinnings of the political history of India. The Partition thwarted the traditional arteries of communication of the NER with the country's heartland, virtually reducing it to a landlocked region. Using the 2 per cent perimeter of the region as a major linkage point with the rest of India and at the same time checking the inflow of goods and people from across the remaining 98 per cent have been both a tedious and a counter-productive activity.[4] The Partition led to the disappearance of a crucial buffer and brought the Chinese army right to the borders of India and the virtual closure of the border with Myanmar added to the isolation of the region. The flourishing trade with the plains of adjacent East Pakistan, Tibet, Bhutan and Myanmar also came to a halt. The separation of communication lines and well developed markets with the neighbouring countries hindered the economic growth of the region. It turned the NER into a most regulated, sensitive border region thus making it the most exposed territory. B.G. Verghese commented that 'if imperial politics distanced the North-East from its trans-border neighbourhood further East, Partition in 1947 all but physically separated the North-East from the Indian heart-land'.[5] The North-Eastern region was converted from a frontier region during the British rule to an internal periphery in the post-independence period. Since independence the region has been looked upon as a place for extracting natural resources, the process which basically had its onset during the British era.[6]

Contemporary NER is impeded by the perils of intra-ethnic conflicts, rebel movements, grievances emanating from the absence of adequate political representation at the national level as well as from the vulnerability of its geographic peculiarities. This sort of instability and political degeneration has retarded economic development by severing infrastructure development and communication progress of the region.[7] The LEP of India as a foreign policy strategy espouses the imperative of thrusting the NER from the backburner to the lime-light by utilizing the resources of and opportunities in the region. The LEP is of immense significance especially in the contemporary geo-political backdrop where the centre of global economic and strategic power is shifting towards the East. India's association with the countries of the dynamic Asia Pacific Region is on a rising trajectory – be it in political, security, economic or cultural field. Today the LEP, as a foreign policy strategy, encourages an impression of promises, potentials and expectations for the people of India.[8]

K.J. Holsti has provided a useful definition of foreign policy strategy. He designates it as 'a state's fundamental strategy for accomplishing its domestic and external objectives. A nation's general strategy is seldom revealed in any one decision but results in a series of cumulative decisions made in an effort to adjust objectives, values and interests to conditions and characteristics of the domestic and external environments'.[9] The interconnection between foreign and domestic politics is getting ever more significant in international politics. The interdependence between the development of nation-states and the globalization of economy predominantly raises this significance. The escalating relevance and the primacy of economic affairs in international relations with the end of the Cold War have made domestic interest groups and coalitions all the more conspicuous. According to C. Raja Mohan, India's vision of grand strategy divides the world into three strategic circles.[10] First, he mentions the immediate neighbourhood where India has sought primacy and a veto over the actions of outside powers. In the second, the extended neighbourhood is talked about, which encompasses an area stretching across Asia and the Indian Ocean region where India has sought to balance the influence of other powers and prevent them from undermining its national interests. This cites India's interests in the Indian Ocean region where India considers itself as a pre-eminent power. In the third, Raja Mohan discusses about an area which includes the entire global stage where India has tried to establish its place as one of the great powers, a key player in promoting international peace, security and development. India's aspiring great power status largely depends upon its regional position, as the then Secretary of East (2004), External Affairs Ministry, Rajiv Sikri believes,[11] which will consequently determine the importance of Asia in tomorrow's world. India's LEP is an offshoot of such new environment, driven by strategic perceptions and economic considerations towards SEA. The LEP can said to have been shaped by the imperatives of history and geography. India's LEP while conforming to the basic tenets of foreign policy postulates, is oriented to cultivate India's external objectives by rejuvenating cooperation with its South-East Asian neighbours keeping tandem with its domestic imperative of developing the NER. Therefore, India's LEP has articulated its foreign policy orientations in alignment with the interests of the NER.[12] One of the objectives of the LEP has been to develop the troubled NER and to find lasting solutions, ensuring advancement of the landlocked NER.

The LEP has accorded an added momentum to the development of the NER, more specifically during its second phase, due to its proximities with South-East Asia. Moreover the onus of cooperation has extended beyond the ten ASEAN member-nations to the wider Asia-Pacific region, which has always been significant to India's civilizational consciousness. The exchange of ideas, communication, cultures, businesses and people-to-people contacts between India and the Asia Pacific region bears certain connotations on our national pursuits. India's greater interests, be they economic, security or geo-strategic, are more or less in accord with this region in our extended neighbourhood. The broad objectives of the LEP during the 1990s were three-fold – to institutionalize linkages with ASEAN and its affiliates; to strengthen bilateral relationships with member-states of the ASEAN; and to carve a suitable place for itself to prevent South-East Asia from falling under the influence of any one major power.[13] A successful and accomplished LEP will not only contribute to India's growth and dynamism but also ensure development and stability of its disturbed and strategically sensitive NER. The LEP 'envisages the North-East region not as the periphery of India, but as the centre of a thriving and integrated economic space linking two dynamic regions with a network of highways, railways, pipelines and transmission lines crisscrossing the region'.[14]

The domestic implications of LEP have given impetus to local economics and bilateral trade, which would in the long run expand the economic profile of the NER. All the eight states of the NER are on international borders and share geographical contiguities with the thriving and dynamic South-East and East Asia economies. By developing border trade and gradually integrating this region through cross-border market access with the markets of the neighbouring countries the NER can become the bridge between the Indian economy and the fastest growing and thriving region in the world. But all these mandate the development of improved infrastructure and connectivity facilities as better connectivity across borders will help India to have access to and penetrate the region thereby strengthening its strategic leverage there. India's NER, with multifaceted talents, has the credence of becoming the hub of the country's growing trade and business with South-East Asia. Till recently there was no integrated roadmap for the development of the region but with the release of the *Vision 2020* document in July 2008 by the then PM Manmohan Singh this lacuna has been addressed. The presence of diplomats from Czech Republic, Brunei, Indonesia, Laos, Malaysia, Myanmar, Singapore, Thailand, Vietnam and Arab League at the fourth North-East Business Summit at Guwahati on 15 September 2008, underscores the growing importance of the NER in the foreign policy agenda.[15] It is expected that the synchronized and calibrated approaches of the Central Government and the state governments can utilize the abundant potentials of the NER for it to emerge as a strategic base for domestic and foreign investors motivating them to tap the prospects of contiguous markets of China, Myanmar, Bangladesh, Laos, Thailand, Vietnam, Cambodia as well as Malaysia, Indonesia and beyond.

It is indeed that the economic advancement of the NER mandates the development of the border trade, which in turn necessitates the improvement of the communication and transportation facilities ardent for the opening of the region. It is often being cited that the insurgencies and the violent outbursts in the region are the outcomes of acute economic underdevelopment of the region. Herein the prospect of developing border trade can be dealt with to accrue economic progress of the region. Though it has been mentioned earlier that the political instabilities or the violent activities in the region are the consequences of economic depression and frustration, it can also be stated that political instabilities in certain instances have caused economic underdevelopment. The study thus will be an attempt to review the pros and cons of economic backwardness with vivid illustrations.

The focus on the relevance of the NER is backed by two primary considerations. First the assets of the NER need to be exploited and utilized and second, the region can be better explored if it is integrated with mainstream India and with the countries to its east. Herein it can be cited that while speaking at the Guwahati Conclave in June 2007, Jairam Ramesh, the then Minister of State for Trade and Commerce, clearly spelt out that the future of India's NER lies in its 'emotional and political integration with the rest of India and economic integration with the rest of Asia'.[16] The economic development of the region can take place with the smooth and necessary ease of movement of goods and commodities adding boost to its border trade. This would also provide a large market for the products in the entire ASEAN region for which the NER needs to develop its production base, preferably using its own resources. It is mention worthy that the close proximity of the NER with the immediate resource-rich neighbour, Myanmar can facilitate the prospect of reaching out to the expanded South-East Asian markets. Economically the NER is blessed with biodiversity, hydro-potential, oil and gas, coal, limestone and forest resources. It is favourable for a whole range of plantation crops, spices, fruits and vegetables, flowers and herbs, much of which could be processed and exported to the neighbouring countries. For example, the tea industry in Assam, started in 1886 by the British, produces approximately 25 per cent of the world tea production and employs approximately 7.4 lakh labourers. Assam accounts for nearly 53 per cent of the all-India tea production. Similarly, Assam's oil refinery sector, one of the oldest in Asia which started in 1897, is performing well. The NER has natural gas reserves of 190 billion cubic meters, coal reserves of 909 million tons, hydroelectric potential estimated at 49,000 MW, oil reserves of 513 million tons, limestone reserves of 4,933 million tons and a forest cover accounting for 25 per cent of the country's forest area which is the highest forest protection record in the country. The NER has 38 per cent of the country's hydropower potential.[17] The focus of the Indian government is to foster cooperation with its neighbouring countries by sharing of respective aptitudes on the basis of knowledge, resources and skills. Herein the NER can play a vital role since it is the repository of myriad assets and talents. Therefore to advance its economic position and to be the economic bridgehead to South-East Asia the NER needs to primarily focus on its border trade development. This chapter, thus, is an attempt to delve into the intricacies of the development of border trade between Moreh of Manipur and Tamu of Myanmar as a measure of LEP to develop India's NER.

INDIA-MYANMAR BORDER TRADE

India's Myanmar policy till date has not taken a concrete shape primarily due to the military junta regime in Myanmar and the security-related concerns emanating from the existing Indian militant groups across the India-Myanmar borders. It has been imperative for both the neighbours to formulate a concrete rational policy addressing the impeding ambiguities. As Myanmar is the gateway to SEA and an essential component for the success of India's LEP, India cannot afford to ignore and thus calls upon its proactive engagement with Myanmar. This could help India facilitate greater national interest thereby promoting the economy of the region extensively.

The resources of the NER can strengthen the process of regional integration in this age of globalization. The NER can correspond to the market of 800 million people, linking the strengths of countries like Bangladesh, Nepal, Bhutan, southwest China and ASEAN. Its intensely important strategic location and natural resources make it credible to be India's next powerhouse. Great strength is being provided by the Brahmaputra valley through its fertile soil for cultivating horticultural products, plantation crops, vegetables, spices, rare herbs and medicinal plants bolstering dynamic agro-export processing zone. It could also be a green tourism destination with the rare flora and fauna, natural scenic beauty, unique performing arts, and varied cuisine and handicrafts, and its market proximity to South-West China and South-East Asia. All these make the NER a strategic base for foreign and domestic investors to tap the world's largest market consisting of SAARC, BIMSTEC and ASEAN. The NER has also an excellent intra-regional distribution capacity with internal waterway linkages connecting Bangladesh and Myanmar, giving access to the ports of Chittagong (Bangladesh), Kolkata and Haldia (West Bengal in India) and Sittwe (Myanmar).[18] The subregion comprising North-East India, Bangladesh, Myanmar and South-West China is a geographically contiguous area sharing enduring historical and cultural bonding. The growth of trade and commerce precipitates the formation of a regional common market with a possibility of establishing free trade area by 2020. In this backdrop it is ardent to conceptualize a common house in the form of a Regional Economic and Trading Cooperation (RETC) on the lines of global trading practices to ensure free and fair competition, remove tariff and non-tariff barriers and standardize the trading system among the participants' countries. This sub-regional cooperation must deal with possible trade disputes and provide a platform for dispute settlement. It should delve into certain essentialities like balance trade practices, encouraging competitiveness, promoting mutual partnership, enriching innovation and ensuring sustainable development in the region. It also needs to nurture the opportunities of possible market expansion in the near future with other regions and global organizations. [19]

Myanmar is the second largest nation amongst the ten member-countries of the ASEAN to which it was admitted in July 1997.[20] Physically, India's NER shares direct border with Myanmar. India, through its NER via Myanmar can directly link to other South-East and East Asian countries. India shares a land boundary of 1,643 km connecting Arunachal Pradesh, Manipur, Nagaland and Mizoram with mainland Southern Asia through the Myanmar states of Kachin, Sajang and Chin. Mainland India's ties with South-East Asia have predominantly been through the sea route, thus being primarily maritime and not continental. The imperative to explore land connectivity to reach out to South-East Asia intertwined with the objective to open and promote the landlocked NER has propelled India to undertake a number of road, rail and connectivity projects in its NER, particularly with the neighbouring Myanmar since improved road and communication network is required for the realization of better future of the region. The then foreign minister Jaswant Singh made two visits to Myanmar in 2001 and 2002: the first visit was to inaugurate the India-Myanmar Friendship Road, and the second to initiate deliberations on building the ambitious Trans-Asia highway project. However, the implementation of the proposals and planning in the field of physical connectivity has not been done yet due to a number of political and administrative hurdles, thus most of them are in the discussion stage. To accelerate the magnitude of trade between the two neighbours, India and Myanmar have sealed a deal to convert the border trade at Moreh-Tamu and Zokhwathar-Rhi border to normal trade, paving the way for trade at Most Favoured Nation (MFN) rates for all goods barring a handful of restricted items. Moreover, the Joint Trade Committee decided to further open trade at a new border point Avankhung-Leshi.[21]

Against this backdrop PM Dr. Manmohan Singh's visit to Myanmar in 2012 is noteworthy in the annals of India-Myanmar bilateral cooperation. During this visit, in only three days India and Myanmar signed a number of pacts encompassing a vast array of topics including providing Myanmar with a US $500 million line of credit, establishing a Border Area Development Programme, and setting up a rice biopark. The neighbours have also consented to building and developing border haats, a joint trade and investment forum. The agreements signed during the visit are listed as follows:

(a) Memorandum of Understanding regarding US $500 million Line of Credit.
(b) Air Services Agreement between India and Myanmar.
(c) Memorandum of Understanding on the India-Myanmar Border Area Development.
(d) Memorandum of Understanding on Establishment of Joint Trade and Investment Forum.
(e) Memorandum of Understanding on the Establishment of the Advance Centre for Agriculture Research and Education (ACARE).
(f) Memorandum of Understanding on Establishment of Rice Bio Park at the Department of Agricultural Research in Napyidaw.
(g) Memorandum of Understanding towards setting up of Myanmar Institute of Information Technology.
(h) Memorandum of Understanding on Cooperation between Dagon University and University of Calcutta.
(i) Memorandum of Understanding on Cooperation between Myanmar Institute of Strategic and International Studies and Indian Council of World Affairs.
(j) Agreement on Cooperation between Myanmar Institute of Strategic and International Studies and Institute for Defence Studies and Analysis.
(k) Cultural Exchange Programme (2012-15).
(l) Memorandum of Understanding on establishing of Border Haats across the border between Myanmar and India.[22]

From the viewpoint of Indian industry and business, Myanmar is a bridge between India and South-East Asian markets, and a gateway to South-East Asia. While Indian economic relations with other ASEAN countries such as Thailand and Singapore are thriving, Indian business questions Myanmar's credibility, not only in the domain of bilateral economic cooperation but also for regional cooperation due to its geo-strategic significance and geographical contiguities with India. As Myanmar is part of both the BIMSTEC and the ASEAN, it is crucial for some regional projects like the Trans-Asian highway and railway projects. (Myanmar is being linked to the rest of South-East Asia under the Trans-Asian highway project from Iran to China.) And India is keen to import gas from Myanmar. India's Oil and Natural Gas Corporation (ONGC) Videsh Limited is reportedly negotiating with South Korea's Daewoo International Corporation to buy a 30 per cent stake in Daewoo's offshore exploration block in the Arakan offshore in north-western Myanmar. Formal trade between India and Myanmar through the Moreh Land Customs Station in Manipur was opened on 12 April 1995 by the then Minister of State for Commerce, Government of India, Shri Chidambaram along with his Myanmar counterpart Lt. Gen. Tun Kyi, the Minister of Trade. Moreh is the only land customs station through which trade across land route from India to Myanmar is being conducted. Interestingly, despite the enormous potentialities of both Myanmar and the NER of India in terms of contiguity of border, proximity of markets and natural resources, the value of export-import trade between India and Myanmar through the NER represents a small fraction of the total export-import trade of the entire NER.[23]

Development of border trade between India and Myanmar thus forms one of the prime attributes of the economic cooperation between the two neighbours. An effective joint border management supported by institutional mechanism is required to encourage cross-border trade and discourage illegal trade in the India-Myanmar border as the latter already has outshined the magnitude of legal trade between the two regions. Along with illegal trade, deadly diseases, drugs and small arms trafficking are also providing the sustaining ground for militant groups. Hence, permanent settlement of the border disputes and development of the border area are necessary for establishing an effective border control mechanism. This will help in legitimizing the institutional relationship between the two and also help to tackle the militancy problem in the NER. Some policy experts in the region are sceptical about the development and construction of roads in the border region, apprehending that free cross-border movements will give easy access to the insurgent groups thereby fuelling problems and instigating them to act against India. However such scepticism should be aware of that underdevelopment of the region breeds insurgency to a massive extent in the region. One security analyst suggests that underdevelopment of the region will alienate the law-abiding lot and in turn will feed insurgency, the effects of which would be much greater than allowing a few insurgents to pass through the highways. However, an effective monitoring set-up must be put in place to prevent the misuse of the highways.[24] Thus developing the border regions and putting effective border management mechanisms into place are necessary to promote border trade. It has to be borne in mind that the sensitization of local communities in the borderlines and ensuring their participation in the economic activities and acting against illegal forces is also equally important to realize India's vision of regional integration.

The India-Myanmar Trade Agreement provides for mainly two types of movement across the border. These are:

(a) Free movement not related to trade regulated under a simple Border Pass or Permit issued by the immigration authorities of either country. This is restricted to 12 hours per day and takes place between Tamu/Namphalong (Myanmar) and Moreh (India). This form of movement is restricted to ethnic locals living on both sides of the border up to a distance of 40 km on either side of the international border and is in keeping with the customary practice existing prior to the introduction of formal trade. Traditional free movement and exchange in the form of visits not related to trade does not entail exchange or barter of local produces for commercial purposes. Consequently, free movement or exchange taking place all along the international border are not regulated by Customs or Director General of Foreign Trade. However, this sort of movement as indicated in Article II of the India-Myanmar Trade Agreement restricts goods to local produce only and its consumption within the 40 km zone.

(b) Movement in connection with 'Regulated Trade' is permitted through a 'Special Identity Document' called Travel Pass, which is equivalent to and similar to a passport. Visits of such pass holders are restricted to a period of 7 days with an option for Indian traders to travel up to Kalemyo-Mandalay in Myanmar and for Myanmar trader to come up to Imphal in India. Free movement related to trade is regulated under a simple Border Pass or Permit issued by the immigration authorities of either country. This is restricted to 12 hours per day between Tamu/Namphalong (Myanmar) and Moreh (India). This sort of movement restricts trade to the exchange of locally produced commodities (as contained in the Annexure I of the India-Myanmar Trade Agreement) in head loads and on payment of customs duty. The value of the goods so traded is not to exceed US $1,000 per transaction and are exempt from declaration on the prescribed Guaranteed Receipt (GR) Form in terms of the Reserve Bank of India notification (No. FEMA.23/2000-RB Dated 3 May 2000).[25]

Types of Trade allowed under the Trade Agreement:

Unlike trade through other land borders, as per the India-Myanmar Trade Agreement a three-tier system of trade was introduced. The tiers are:

(a) Traditional exchange of locally produced items up to US $1,000 between indigenous people residing up to 40 km on either side of the border under simplified documentation without GR formalities, on payment of customs duty.

(b) Barter Trade of 22, which was extended to 44 afterwards, was agreed upon exchangeable items up to US $20,000 with GR formalities as per DGFT PN No. 289(PN) 92-7 and on payment of customs duty.

(c) Under this system, traders should possess IEC allotted by Director General of Foreign Trade (DGFT). The items that can be traded under this system are locally produced commodities, mainly agricultural produce and minor forest products as appended – mustard/rape seed, pulses and beans, fresh vegetables, fruits, garlic, onion, chilies, spice (excluding nutmeg, cloves, mace, cassia and cinnamon), bamboo, minor forest products (excluding teak), betel nuts and leaves, food items for local consumption, tobacco, tomato, reed broom, sesame, resin, coriander seeds, *katha*, ginger, soyabean, roasted sunflower seeds.

(d) Normal or Regular Trade under the Letter of Credit System as per EXIM Policy guidelines.

The Reserve Bank of India also formulated its policy in line with Article II of the India-Myanmar Trade Agreement, which, inter alia, laid a condition that imports from Myanmar to India:

(1) Shall precede exports from India to Myanmar and such exchange should be balanced within six months from the date of import, in case of barter trade upto US $20,000 and
(2) Preferably within a day or two, in case of traditional exchange of locally produced items up to US $1,000.[26]

As the India-Myanmar land border passes through India's NER and Myanmar's north-western region, it has tremendous security implications for India. Since a number of ethnic insurgent groups of the NER have set up their bases across the border, a strategic partnership between India and Myanmar can only address the nation's security concerns arising out of the operations of ethnic militants. As the NER is far away from the national market centres, markets across the borders can act as the vent for the surplus of the NER. Thus NER can reap the benefits of India's LEP if the region could be economically integrated with the economies of South-East Asian countries through Myanmar.

India's engagement with Myanmar has far reaching implications for the development of the NER. First, physical integration of the NER with Myanmar would help to break its landlocked conditions that stand in the way of the region's economic growth. Although the NER is rich in resources like hydrocarbons, forest, hydroelectricity, and minerals, high transportation cost has not allowed it to grow according to its comparative advantages. The connectivity bottlenecks have made the region perpetually underdeveloped and hence politically volatile. A two-pronged strategy of development may help the region to overcome the predicaments of land-lockedness. First, as the NER shares 98 per cent of its borders with the neighbouring countries of Bhutan, Bangladesh, China and Myanmar, it is important to integrate the region with the South-East Asian as well as South Asian markets across the borders. Second, restoration of its traditional routes by way of transit corridors through Bangladesh for movement of goods and passengers between the NER and mainland India and establishment of physical connectivity with Myanmar to reach the ASEAN markets can only address the adverse geographical impact of the Partition and ensure speedy development. Once cross-border connectivity is improved, cross-border trade and development cooperation can be promoted, markets in the neighbouring countries could act as a vent for surplus generated in the region. As the development of the bordering regions can hardly be promoted through the framework of development of nation-states, the strategy of cross-border cooperation for the frontier regions can only provide the necessary stimuli for their growth. The model of market-led growth initiated through economic reforms by most nation-states is generating growth only in those areas having comparative advantages in terms of transport cost, transaction cost and labour cost. Firms tend to locate their operations in areas which help them to remain competitive in the market. As the peripheral areas are located far away from the main centres of national markets and international connectivity, suffer from high transportation and transaction costs and lack skilled labour, market forces are unlikely to boost growth in them. In order to counter the limitations of the market forces, the nation-states are trying to develop these areas through higher resource allocation in terms of plan allocation and centrally sponsored schemes. In India, since 1996, the Central Government has focused on the 'New Initiative for North East'. Under this initiative, 10 per cent of annual budgetary provisions of all central ministries and departments are earmarked for the development of the NER. A 'non-lapsable pool of fund' has also been created to ensure transfer of fund from the Centre to the NER, for the time period of 1998-9 to 2012-13 on amount of INR 23,210.50 crore has been allotted to the non-Lapsable Central Pool of Resources (NLCPR) for the NCR. In order to monitor the development activities in the NER, a separate department called Department of Development of North-Eastern Region was created at the Centre. The Government of India also framed a separate industrial policy for the NER in 1997, which aims at providing infrastructure facilities, creating growth centres and free tax zones as well as supplying various incentives in order to promote industrial development in the region.

Besides these economic measures, political measures have also been taken up to engage various militant secessionist groups in peace talks in order to restore business confidence in the region. Efforts are also being made to improve the quality of governance along with the accountability to resource transfer. Border trade should be viewed as a strategic tool for the long-term development of the frontier areas. The responsibility of developing these areas needs to be borne through cross-border cooperative endeavours rather than through national efforts alone. It is thus beneficial for the nation-states to cooperate with one another and provide scope for the market forces to properly function in the landlocked areas.[27]

As the 1994 agreement aimed at legalizing much of the informal exchanges, its initial implementation gave a fillip to formal border trade which reached INR 466.9 million and INR 623.9 million in 1996 and 1997, respectively.[28] Since then, despite the opening of the Champhai border post, formal border trade has remained much lower and the overall balance shows a deficit-between 1995-2004 – total formal exports through Moreh represented INR 938.5 million while imports amounted to INR 1,108.3 million. The volume of trade of the Mareh-Tamu border point is estimated to be around 300 million. Though numbers fluctuate significantly from year to year the total annual border trade now usually amounts roughly to INR 100 million in Moreh as well as in Champhai. Since informal trade, according to some Burmese refugees in Aizawl, may well represent up to 70 per cent of total exchanges, examining, informal estimates can be more revealing. Informal border trade in Moreh is four to five times higher than that of Champhai – INR 1,816.9 million against INR 460.4 million in 2003-4. Champai, despite being one of the largest trading centres, its market faces are predominantly driven by illegal trade. According to LCS, hardly any trade takes place through rokhawthar nowadays. The 21 January 1994 agreement allows for the following 22 exchangeable which, in due course of time, about 40 treadable commodities to be traded legally items to be traded legally. These are largely locally produced agricultural goods: 'mustard/rape seed, pulses and beans, fresh vegetables, fruits, garlic, onions, chillies, spices (excluding nut meg, mace, cassia and cloves), bamboo, minor forest products excluding teak, betel nuts and leaves, food items for local consumption, tobacco, tomato, reed broom, sesame, resin, coriander seeds, soyabean, roasted sunflower seeds, katha, ginger, any other commodities as may be mutually agreed'. M.P. Bezbaruah points out that products manufactured in a third country dominate informal trade, whereas the 22 items allowed are produced locally and or in the trading countries-India, Myanmar. Formal exchanges mainly include agricultural products, wheat flour, soya nuggets and betel nuts. Indeed betel nut had grown in 2003-4 to almost 100 per cent of the formal imports of Moreh. Informal border trade follows more or less the same overall composition in Moreh and in Champhai. The main items imported are electrical and electronic items and textiles but they are imported in different proportions in Moreh and Champhai. Electrical and electronic goods represent 57.38 per cent of Moreh's imports while textiles, blankets in particular, top Champhai's imports at 36.48 per cent. The import of livestock pigs in particular constitutes a big difference between the two as it takes up to a quarter of informal trade in Moreh and does not happen in

Mizoram. Thus India's LEP in the past two decades has not accorded much space to Mizoram despite the refocusing of the LEP on the NER, and despite Mizoram's two major assets – a peaceful situation and an educated population. At a time when greater connectivity has become the central motto of an euphoria that projects the NER reintegrated with its surrounding region, it is relevant to examine the challenges to the LEP in Mizoram that are implied by the increasing of connectivity.[29]

The comparative study of two significant and operational border points between the NER and Myanmar (Moreh and Tamu and Champhai and Rhi) puts forth a realistic assessment of the intensity of the border trade from these points. Comparisons between Moreh and Champhai-Zokhawthar reveal that from the early days there was inkling in favour of Manipur's border trade post. Although both towns were included in the 21 January 1994 border trade agreement between India and Myanmar, Moreh experienced rapid development since its inauguration in April 1995 while the border trade at the Champhai-Rhi post officially commenced only in 2004, after a bridge was built in 2002. Whereas the Government of India presently develops an Integrated Check Post (ICP) at Moreh, authorities finalized in September 2007 a small composite Land Customs Stations building at Zokhawthar. The disregard in Champhai is perhaps backed by certain considerations. For instance, the distance from Guwahati to Champhai is about 660 km of winding road and a drive of 35 hours whereas Moreh is only around 470 km from Guwahati and a 20-hour drive. Moreh also sits on the most direct Guwahati-Mandalay road, and therefore appears as the most sensible choice for a transportation hub. With the implementation of Kaladan Multimodal Project possibly in 2019 as the route for gas extracted off the Arakan coast, Shwe gas reserves, there a scope for improvement of Champai district. In fact Bangladesh's refusal to host a pipeline has propelled the Indian government to improve Mizoram's riverine connectivity with Myanmar. From southern Mizoram a pipeline will relay the gas through the western side of the state, but as no tap-off point seems incorporated in the project, the possibility of Mizoram reaing benefits out of it seems quite dim. National Highway (NH) 502A is a part of the connectivity drive in NER. There is a proposition for another highway connecting NH 502A to Bangladesh and Tripura. To the north the NH 502A will be linked to NH 54 which will connect Silchar in Assam to Manipur. In the east, the road connecting the town of Champai to Myanmar is being broadened. It is expected that the completion of this project will make the movement of goods through Mizoram to Manipur and beyond possible. The Champai district in eastern Mizoram upholds the importance of this highway 502A as a huge volume of trade is conducted between Myanmar and Mizoram through this district. The opening of a Land Customs Office (LCO) at Zokhwathar, a small village about 30 km to the south-east of Champai, adjoining the Myanmar border, in March 2015 by the then Commerce Minister, Nirmala Sitharaman, underscores the burgeoning efficacy of the border trade.[30]

From Moreh to Tamu

Moreh is a fascinating expression of the North-East's idyllic beauty. It is the most fascinating place in Manipur, which is itself a splendid place to visit. Nestled deep within a lush green corner of North-East India is the little Shangrila called Manipur – 'a jeweled land' – with a total area of 22,327 sq km. of this area, nine-tenth constitutes the hills surrounding the valley. Lying between 23.80 and 25.69 degree North Latitudes and 93.03 degree and 94.78 degree East Longitudes it is bordered by Nagaland on the north, Assam on the west and Mizoram on the south, along the east it shares a 398-km long international boundary with Myanmar astride the proposed South East Asia Super Highway. It is 120 km from Jiribam in Manipur through the adjoining Cachar district of Assam from on the Indo-Bangladesh border. Manipur is inhabited by three major ethnic groups – the Meities including Meiti Muslims in the valley; and the Nagas and the Kuki-Chin-Mizo tribes in the hills. People are predominantly Mongoloid, and speak Tibeto-Burmese languages. Manipur is rich in art, culture and sports and is endowed with a beautiful landscape and is gifted with several unexplored fascinating destinations promising great tourism potential. There are a number of advantages of investing in Manipur – excellent air connectivity including cargo services, trade with Myanmar and other South-East Asian countries. High a value exotic fruits and flowers grow in large quantity, rare medicinal and aromatic plants are available in abundance, tourism opportunities including healthcare, opportunities for contracts in roads and power sectors are also present. Law and order situation is also improving in Manipur.

Manipur has the advantage of acting as India's gateway to the East through Moreh town, which is the only feasible land route for trade between India and Myanmar and other South-East Asian countries. A Land Custom Station already exists at Moreh for the existing volume of trade. The tradable items permissible through Moreh were 22 commodities which increases to 44 commodities in 2012. Major exportable items include cement, engineering goods, transport equipment, motorcycles, iron and steel, medicines, chemicals and allied products, cotton yarn, etc. The items imported from Myanmar through the barter mechanism are betel nuts, turmeric, red kidney beans (*rajma*), kuth roots, gram, resin, dry ginger, etc. The volume of trade at the Moreh-Tamu border point in 2001-2 was INR 95.48 million and 298.19 million in 2009-10 an average increase of 39 per cent p.a.[31]

A BRIEF ASSESSMENT OF INDIA-MYANMAR BORDER TRADE

Major exports into Myanmar are cotton yarn, auto parts, soyabean meal and pharmaceuticals, and major imports from Myanmar are betel nut, dried ginger, green *mung* beans, black matpe, turmeric roots, resin and medicinal herbs. According

TABLE 2.1: VOLUME OF BILATERAL BORDER TRADE

(in million US $)

Year	Myanmar Exports	Myanmar Imports	Total Trade	Balance of Trade
2005-6	11.28	4.13	15.41	7.14
2006-7	11.02	4.75	15.77	6.27
2007-8	10.91	3.92	14.83	6.99
2008-9	5.49	4.43	9.82	1.05
2009-10	7.79	5.95	13.73	1.84
2010-11	8.30	4.50	12.80	3.80
2011-12	8.87	6.54	15.41	2.33
2012-13	25.09	10.57	35.66	14.52

Source: Department of Border Trade, Ministry of Commerce, Myanmar.

to the Myanmar Department of Border Trade, the border trade turnover between India and Myanmar has ranged from US $10 to 22 million, though it is probably higher if the huge unaccounted informal trade is also taken into account.[32]

India's Look East Policy and several new measures taken by both the Central and the state governments to promote and enhance trade link with SEA provide Manipur with a competitive advantage. In recognition of the potentials of Moreh, the Government of India has notified an Integrated Check-Post there. Free Trade Agreement with ASEAN has also opened up fresh opportunities for trade with the ASEAN countries. The ICP at Moreh will expedite speedy movement of export-import consignments and redress the inconveniences suffered by general public in the emerging scenario of India's LEP. It will be a composite check-post facilitating all agencies to operate under one roof with an Pintegrated approach. In order to create an ICP at Moreh in the pattern of Wagah border, the state government has identified 45.50 acres of land near Gate No. 1 within the Customs Notified Area. The Ministry of Home Affairs, Department of Border Management has sanctioned the compensation amount. It is also one

TABLE 2.2: INDIA'S IMPORTS FROM MYANMAR

(in million US $)[33]

Commodity	2008-9	2009-10	2010-11
Pulses and Beans	611.78	851.53	570.82
Wood & Articles of Wood	311.01	404.95	416.16
Products of Animal Origin	2.93	6.22	12.32
Others	2.34	7.19	7.88
Raw Hides & Skin		2.05	4.55
Coffee, Tea, Mate & Spices	0.91	3.07	2.94
Total Imports	928.97	1289.8	1017.67

TABLE 2.3: INDIA'S EXPORTS TO MYANMAR

(in million US $)[34]

Commodity	2008-9	2009-10	2010-11	2011-12
Others	94.17	79.85	111.4	110.12
Meat & Edible Meat Offal	–	1.91	71.59	13.31
Pharmaceuticals	49.92	55.98	61.29	76.09
Iron & Steel	63.93	43.66	40.21	26.29
Sugar & Sugar Confectionery	–	0.07	21.27	–
Electrical Machinery & Equipment	13.62	16.69	16.39	26.81
Chemicals & Allied Products	–	9.81	12.27	5.4
Oil Well & Mining Equipment	–	–	–	75.88
Total Exports	221.64	207.97	334.42	333.9

Source: DGFT, Ministry of commerce, New Delhi.

of the several measures by the government to promote trade link with South-East Asia in the backdrop of the proposed Trans-Asian Highways project. The Saurashtra-Silchar Super Highway project is being extended to Moreh. With the proposed Trans-Asian highways from Moreh of Manipur to Mae Sot of Thailand through Bagan of Myanmar coming up, Manipur will become India's gateway to South-East Asia. The proposed centre shall have an immigration department, local

TABLE 2.4: INDIA MYANMAR BILATERAL TRADE

(in million US $)[35]

Commodity	2009-10	2010-11	2011-12	2012-13
India's Exports to Myanmar	207.97 (6.17%)	320.62 (54.17%)	545.38 (70.1%)	342.94
India's Imports from Myanmar	1,289.80 (38.84%)	1,017.67 (-21.1%)	1,324.82 (30.18%)	570.18
Total Trade	1,497.77 (-10.65%)	(30.17%) 1,870.20	1,338.29 (39.75%)	

Source: DGFT, Ministry of Commerce, New Delhi.

police including women constables for immediate security, land customs department, customs preventive department, forests, narcotics and drug control department, postal department, bank counter, telecom, animal quarantines, plant quarantine, quality certification inspection agencies, export promotion councils, trade facilitation counters and trade related public bodies, food testing laboratory, truck parking facility, staff quarters and basic amenities such as canteen, truck drivers' rest houses, etc.[36]

Manipur is blessed with considerable opportunities and strengths geared towards attracting foreign investments. The India-Myanmar border-trade currently underway in the border towns of Moreh and Tamu has already paved the way for a full-scale trade between India and Myanmar which would further extend to other ASEAN countries like Thailand and Laos through the Trans-Asian Super Highway. There is thus a good scope for investment in creating infrastructure facilities in the areas of road construction, power generation, developed industrial areas, water facilities and information technology services. Moreover the airport of the state capital Imphal is just 7 km away from the city. The percentage of literacy in Manipur is higher than the national average. There is an adequate reservoir of trained and skilled man-power for the IT sector.[37]

In spite of possessing so many qualities Manipur's due recognition continues to be unremitted. The border trade between India and Myanmar has been operational for over a decade now and it is high time that the benefits accruing from that trade be assessed, as also the lacunae plaguing it be identified. The probable causes for the failure of the border trade may be enlisted as follows. India's policy in the 1990s of 'constructive engagement' pursued by the Policy of Eastern Strategy by Jaswant Singh has been followed by an MOU on border trade on 21 July 1994 (Moreh-Tamu). India stands as Myanmar's fourth largest trading partner after Thailand, China and Singapore. The border trade between Moreh and Tamu, which reached its peak in 1998, failed due to the reasons cited below. The problem of insurgency in the state of Manipur 19 insurgent groups in Moreh, poor infrastructure, preference of sea route over land routes and various pressure groups did not allow any trucks to cross the highway to Moreh for nearly four months during 2011. Besides there are also problems of frequent bandhs, a feeling of insecurity among the trading and the non-local communities, no proper electricity supply in the entire Moreh town area, poor telephone, internet and banking system and trade and commerce officials untrained in trade transaction matters. Appallingly there is adequate and competent banking system to deal with the entire trade transactions in Moreh. The dual currency exchange rate system acts as an impediment to smooth trade operations. For example, the official exchange rate of the Indian Rupee against the Burmese Kyat is Re 1 = Kt 0.09 and the unofficial rate of exchange is Re 1 = 19 Kt. Thus the overvalued Myanmar currency in the official market acts as a disincentive to the Indian traders and absence of currency exchange counters adds to the existing problems.[38] The major irritants are the poor conditions of roads, lack of a separate bypass for movement of heavy vehicles, lack of adequate staff, lack of awareness of rules and procedures for conducting border trade, excessive documentation especially for imports, testing, and certification which make the process expensive and time-consuming.

Furthermore, India has been sceptical about the opening up of borders and developing infrastructure linkages with South-East Asian and East Asian neighbours because of the suspicion that the NER could become a dumping ground for cheap goods from China and other economies of South-East Asia. Thus there is a need to explore the export possibilities in NER so that this region could face the competition posed by regional economic integration and could be benefited by the LEP and enhanced connectivity with SEA. At present the NER does not seem ready for competition because industrial production is very limited. However, there is great potential for further industrial development, especially in the hydro-electric, pharmaceutical, tourism and agro-based industries. Therefore, the development of NER as an export base is the need of the hour so that the trade opportunities offered by the enhanced connectivity could be exploited.[39]

ROLE OF POLITICAL INSTABILITY IN ECONOMIC DEVELOPMENT

Of the many causes impeding the magnitude of border trade, the role of political instabilities cannot be ignored. The compound characteristic of distinctive cultural and religious identity enforcements in the NER has characterized the region as one of the most turbulent spots in Asia. The NER, with over 200 ethnic groups, languages and dialects where diverse faiths and practices constantly interact and generate conflicts of interests, is plagued by incessant political rivalries and insurgent activities retarding the pace of development in the region. This somewhat provides explanation for the isolation and seclusion of the region despite being the repository of abundant possibilities and opportunities emerging from its advantageous geographic location. The tide of regionalism in this contemporary globalized world mandates the cohesion and integration of these diverse groups required of an integrative and advanced economy.[40] This argument can be illustrated by the reasoning of a Naga-Kuki clash in Manipur in 2010 jeopardizing the spree of economic activities in the entire Manipur state.

The North-East is marked with diversity in economic pursuits but geopolitical hindrances have prevented the area from developing at par economically with many other parts of the country. It is often alleged that economic backwardness or neglect is the main source of political turmoil in the North-East and that once this problem is addressed the main source of political turmoil will go away.[41] It is true that militant groups, political parties and public opinion in the East Asian region have grievances about the region's economic underdevelopment and this has resulted in the alienation of the people. Once developmental efforts are initiated a host of opportunities will emerge and penetrate into the lower strata of society. Therefore people will cease to resort to insurgency. Some analysts opine that the primary reason for the rise, growth and sustenance of insurgency in the region is the lack of development, and the region as a whole suffers from lack of developmental initiative. It is also true that insurgent groups in the region have been successful in exploiting the prevailing sense of general deprivation among people to further embolden their assertion. However, the belief that the initiation of developmental efforts would automatically end insurgency is wishful thinking. Such a line of thought fails to analyse the problem in its entirety.[42] Though the insurgent groups complain about economic backwardness or neglect, their primary complaint is perceived injustices grounded in the history of how the Indian post-colonial constitutional order came into being.[43] What is striking is that the bureaucrats, politicians and military officers who make North-East policy are either oblivious of the historical issues that insurgencies raise, or consider them too trivial to merit substantive engagement.[44] The lack of development and industrialization has resulted in the growing economic disparity of the region vis-à-vis the national average and this rising disparity has further led to the sense of alienation among the people.[45] Economic deprivation, disparity, exploitation, lack of development and a growing sense of alienation have created congenial conditions for the rise of ethnic conflicts leading to insurgency.[46] But sometimes the realistic appraisal of the economic underdevelopment of the NER recounts the role of political instabilities in the region. Thus economic backwardness and political turmoil are intermittently connected with each other.

An assessment of the causes responsible for the downturn in the intensity of trade promotion signifies the role of political instabilities (among other reasons) in impeding the pace of trade facilitation between the NER and Myanmar. The term 'North-East' is a misleading one as it upholds an image of a state or a group of states comprising homogenous attributes or identical tenets facing similar constraints or limitations. But this image is far from reality as the NER consisting of contiguous seven sister states and the state of Sikkim is a region of intense disparity and distinctness. There prevails limited solidarity among the states of the NER and they are often being threatened by intra-regional conflicts and insurgencies. Very little similarity is visible in the food habits, dresses, customs, and cultures of the people inhabiting the region. So, it is not at all a proper approach to club the highly distinct states under one caption. The people outside this region often get puzzled by this practice of addressing these highly distinct states together and thus end up misunderstanding the existing system of the region. For instance, during the Commonwealth Games of 2010, a leading Indian newspaper mistakenly reported that the North-East participants, wearing Naga attire, successfully earned the appreciation of the audience by performing well in the inaugural programme. But it was actually the Mizo attire, and this misrepresentation by the newspaper created a hue and cry in entire Mizoram followed by bandhs and strikes. From this incident it can be stated that the people of the region are sensitive about their identity and a minor mistake can create an uproar in the region leading to grave consequences. There are several other examples, which can justify this statement. So it is improper to club them under one broad heading.

The border town of Moreh is generally seen as a site from where Kuki-Naga clashes began in 1992 and led to reprisals and counter-reprisals in other parts of Manipur. Lying on the Myanmar border, Moreh is the key route through which a considerable amount of traffic in drugs, small arms, and Chinese goods for sale in Indian markets takes place. In addition, Moreh is strategically important for the many insurgent groups of the NER for many of their headquarters and training camps lie across the border in Myanmar. Although the India-Myanmar border is quite porous, Moreh town is key to the movement of goods and guns as well as drugs. It is often being stated that in the early 1990s as much as INR 60 crores worth of business passed through this route every day. If these figures are correct, today's estimate would be considerably higher.[47] Inhabited on one side (the south) by the Kuki-Chin groups, and on the other by the Naga (the Marin, Anals and Tangkhul tribes), the town has always been something of a disputed territory. The Nagas claim it as their traditional land but the population of the town is not principally Naga, but Kuki. It also comprises Tamils driven out of Myanmar (these groups trade in gems and guns and are said to have strong links with the Liberation Tigers of Tamil Elam in Sri Lanka) and also some Marwaris and Punjabis who moved there principally for commercial purposes. The late 1980s and the early 1990s saw a new development in the activities of the insurgent groups in Manipur. Till then dominated by the Naga, the profile of underground groups now began to change. Being scared of the fact that their identity would be completely submerged the Kukis now began to form their own insurgent groups. These included the Kuki National Front (KNF), the Kuki National Army (KNA), the Kuki Independent Army (KIA) and the Kuki Defence Force (KDF). Soon the Kuki groups began to raise demand for a homeland, Kukil of their own similar to the demand of Bodo groups in Assam for Bodoland. There were now many more contenders for power and the battleground seemed to acquire a heterogeneous character. The NSCN (I-M) and the NSCN (K), for example, were clear in their strategies that they would not spread atrocities and they would not be violent towards women and children. This mental or ethical bent of mind was not necessarily true for the other groups who were brawling for power. Moreh town and the national highway linking Imphal to Myanmar, which passes through Moreh, has been the focal point of this struggle, as it provokes activities like smuggling and drug trafficking thereby fuelling illegal operations. Moreh had been in the control of the National Socialist Council of Nagaland (NSCH), which was in-charge of collecting taxes levied on commercial institutions and residential dwellings. In the Kuki terminology, the Naga exercise of tax collection was stigmatized as extortion. They, therefore, virulently agitated against these Naga activities. The propaganda that the NSCN was determined to drive the Kukis out of Moreh further accentuated the discontent. The ensuing violence assumed a horrific character and spiraled dangerously out of control, conflagrating from Moreh to the heart of Manipur, ultimately degenerating into ethnic cleansing.

Narration of painful stories is the intriguing feature of the contesting claims of both the tribes, the consequences of which acquire precedence over their actual occurrence. One of the stories that became a central issue in these clashes was that the Kukis served a Quit Naga order in Moreh in May 1992, The Kukis' claim although is different. They cite an incident of 12 May of that year in which two Kukis, Holkhojang Haokip and Lhunkhothang Tongkholun, were killed by NSCN (IM) militants near Moreh in Chandel district. Two more deaths (that of a school teacher and a social worker) also took place at that time. The Kukis' grievance was that all these killings took place in the heart of Kuki land where the NSCN-IM had the audacity to demand tax from Kuki villages. Members of the Tangkhul community at Moreh were found to clandestinely engage in providing information to the NSCN-IM. They also supplied ammunitions to the NSCN-IM cadres and served as tax collectors from Kukis. The Kukis did not want to harass the Tangkhul public but such arrogant activities were excruciatingly. A few months later, in Zoupi village the Nagas served a quit order on the Kukis. Though both the sides asserted that they refrained from resorting to violence to alarm the people for leaving but in reality there was violence on both the communities. Due to the general atmosphere of insecurity and animosity among the tribes many villages that were heterogeneous became bereft of one or other community.[48] The sense of identity, which was imbibed from their respective culture, religion, commerce, economy, tradition and customs had played a significant role in the tribal communities existence over a considerable period of time. The two communities became scared of getting marginalized in their own land in terms of skills, livelihood and identity and thus became overtly conscious to proclaim their right to self-determination and their distinctive ethnic identities. The crisis of political subjectivity in Manipur actually accentuates disarticulations in the existing power matrix of the region.

The thrust of my case study in Moreh was to develop an intensive understanding on the afore-mentioned themes. I got mixed response from my interviews, signifying both optimism and pessimism about the relevance of the policy in ensuring development of the North-East Region. As a policy LEP has emphasiges on Mizoram, Manipur, Nagaland, since these states are bordering Myanmar. The policy has somewhat failed to accomplish its target due to the inefficacy of the bureaucratic culture. Political will has always presided over the genuine developmental need of the region. Economic development would pave the way to new services, jobs or engagements for the people, ultimately leading to reduction in the magnitude of the insurgency. Initiatives should be undertaken for identifying opportunities so that people should be trained in vocations, certifying them and providing them with employment. Otherwise the entire region would be torn apart by the social discontent.

The profiles of the insurgents generally tend to evoke the

impression that the people mainly from underprivileged sectors resort to insurgency to get rid of their acute poverty-stricken condition. The economic blockade of 2011 and again in August-September 2014 reiterates the degree of hatred and intolerance of the people towards the armed forces. The blockade of 2014 was the offshoot of the animosity and distrust of the Naga United Council towards the armed forces engendered out of the killing of two youths of Naga United Council by the police. The political antagonism led to acute economic crisis, leading to the insurmountable soaring of prices; for example, petrol cost rose upto INR 500 per litre resulting to extreme distress of the common people. If governance is improved, developmental and recruitment activities are monitored carefully there will be overall development of the region and the problem of alienation will start fading away. It is really disheartening to see that not a single state in the NER experiences development through the LEP. No concrete result of the policy is visible. India can have advantage over China in South-East Asia but things are not happening that way. Involvement of academia, government, bureaucrats and respective governments is sincerely required for the realization of the policy.

Field visit has enriched my understanding about the potentialities of Moreh in expanding border trade. If trade relations are being conducted through the NER then Moreh has immense possibilities, since it is the only commercial centre that is still functioning. The United Bank of India (UBI) in Manipur states that trade value between Manipur and Myanmar till 2011 was above INR 3 crore. Border trade is allowed on 16 km from India till Namphalong in Myanmar, which is in rupees. In Gate No. 2 trade is only allowed upto 16 km. One requires a visitor's I-card to travel. People want the LEP to be pursued but are not that optimistic about it; it is like an appeasement and the promise of the policy is yet to be accomplished. Prices of Indian commodities are exorbitant due to the high transport costs. Chinese goods are relatively cheaper which provoke the people to opt for those.

Qualitatively Indian goods are superior but the cheaper costs of the Chinese products attract the people more. The markets are highly competitive and there is no way to restrict competition, in which Indian goods lose out to the Chinese goods. The Tourism Festival of November was round the corner and preparations were being carried on in large scale. In the festival of 2011, Thailand's enthusiastic participation became considerably palpable, as it opened 30 shops of jewellery and food.

The reason for the failure of Moreh market to come to the limelight might be the incompetence of the products as Moreh people are not at all conversant with modern scientific technologies and thus the state fails to devise its tools to cope up with the ensuing development. Due to lack of good infrastructure, quality education and absence of critical faculty in the specialized field the region may find itself out of place at this juncture and may not grab the opportunity of competitive advantage, opened up by the current wave of regionalism. It is imperative for the policy makers to emphasize on quality education and create socially responsible human resources to ensure effective social and economic participation for overall well-being and development of the region. The geographical and climatic congeniality together with improved infrastructure and communication facilities will invariably stimulate national and foreign participation. This will not only revive the regional economy but also will have a considerable impact on the growth of knowledge economy in the region.[49]

Given the fact that India is a crucial destination for Myanmar's exports and imports after China and Thailand, the record of bilateral reveals that less than 6 per cent is traded through the land routes whereas 82 per cent of China-Myanmar trade and over 70 per cent of Thailand-Myanmar trade are via land routes. Therefore ample scope lies in bettering of trade transactions with the neighbouring countries in local products like tea, spices, handloom, bamboo and cane handicrafts. The significant volume of informal trade that takes place along the India-Myanmar border results in loss of revenue for both the Central and the state governments of the NER. The LEP is motivated to legalizing informal trade leading to the expansion of trade activities as well as generation of considerable revenues for both the Central and the state governments. The economic interdependence along the India-Myanmar border has not developed extensively as that across the Sino-Myanmar border. The prospect of boosting up the border trade commands a thorough review of the differential advantage which the NER can offer to Myanmar and China cannot.

The strife for dominance over trade by multiple communities inhabiting the border area has induced threatening conflicts, ultimately jeopardizing the prospect of economic cooperation. The imbroglio of ethnic insurrections, tribal rebellions and uncontrolled trafficking is a source of major instability in the NER and the internationalization of these secessionist movements has contributed to the worsening of security problems in India and Myanmar. The two countries should cooperate with each other for securing the region. The first joint counter-insurgency, the *Golden Bird Operation*, led by Indian, notably the Assam Rifles and the Burmese armies took place in April 1995. Synergy and focused approach of both the Central and the state governments are the prerequisites for the development of the NER. The allotment of considerable funding by the Central Government for the progress of the region does not guarantee the implementation of the projects undertaken as the dearth of spending efficiency and lack of responsiveness severely impede the harnessing of the abundant economic potential. A combination of these factors endangers the promise of a better future for the region. Moreover, it needs to be gauged sincerely whether the developmental initiatives under the LEP are counter-effective to the progress of the NER.

The adverse impact of the booming trade emanates from the visible crises as large numbers of small-scale traders are increasingly getting replaced by large-scale traders. Moreover, the smugglers, taking advantage of the movement of goods are pursuing their illicit activities rampantly due to the prevailing law and order situation. It is evident that the movement of people acquires more significant dimension than the movement of goods. There is too much expectation from the LEP, but the required awareness level is negligible. State governments are pessimistic, but they must rise to the occasion, as it looks like the last bus assuring development for the region. The government should spell out very clearly the components of the LEP conceptualized by the country. The economic angle requires to be given more relevance than the security one. The state governments of the region, more particularly that of Manipur, must prepare its people to face up the challenge to make the policy a success. It should impart modern science and technology education, particularly to the people living in the border areas. It has to be borne in mind that once opportunity is provided, they are enabled. The 2011-12 competitive examinations reports truly justify the statement. The academic records reveal the outstanding performance of the Manipuri students in public or competitive exams. So the brighter side of the NER also needs to be portrayed. The NER people need more exposure in order to reap benefits out of the policy. The people must be educated to cope with the essence of the policy. The state governments need to bear greater responsibilities towards motivating the people to enjoy the opportunities. Alarmingly there is no document of the Government of India, which specifically spells out the aim of the LEP in developing the NER though it is discreetly mentioned in the speeches of the ministers. There is so much hype about the policy without any substantive content on the region.

For the NER to gain from India's Preferential Trade Agreements and Free Trade Agreements with the economies of the East, the essentialities are improved infrastructure facilities, transit arrangements, creation of new trade routes, custom check posts, advanced banking, telecommunication and electricity facilities and easy visa regime ensuring the smooth functioning of the traders, businessmen and transport operators in the region. The cross-border markets should act as avenues for the surplus produced in NER as well as a source of cheaper imports. Keeping pace with the paramount changes in Myanmar's political and economic landscapes India needs to foster India-Myanmar bilateral dynamics by restoring the traditional links. People-to-people contacts, particularly in health and education need to be emphasized on. Movement of goods and services due to the haloes of globalization and liberalization would definitely boost India-Myanmar bilateral cooperation to a great extent. The mandates for the prospect of economic cooperation and trade facilitation between India and Myanmar include certain crucial aspects like a thorough and extensive understanding of the nature of market consolidating the economic growth and the distributive performances. For realizing the essence of economic cooperation and revitalizing border trade it is required to ensure infrastructure development, develop more custom stations for easy movement of traffic, development of border haat to promote the livelihood pattern of people, to increase integrated check-posts. Most importantly interests ruling needs and demands on both sides of the border need to be identified. Of late, the Central Government has recognized the economic backwardness of the region and that economic backwardness and underdevelopment generate feelings of alienation and relative deprivation among the people. Hence crores of rupees have been spent as developmental funds with the intention of stimulating economic growth and development in the region.[50] The general notion is that by bringing about development the people of the region will put aside problems of identity, ethnic assertion and immigration from neighbouring countries that will finally result in the abatement of insurgency. Therefore, successive central governments announce developmental packages. In 1996 the then Prime Minister of India H.D. Deve Gowda announced an economic package ₹6,100 crore, following his visit to the region. His successor I.K. Gujral endorsed this package. To boost economic development of the region the NDA Government led by Prime Minister Atal Behari

Vajpayee also announced another package of ₹10,217 crore in 1998. In October 1996, under the 'New Initiatives for North-Eastern Region', it was stipulated that at least 10 per cent of the budget(s) of the Central Ministries/Departments should be earmarked for the development of the North-Eastern states. As the expenditure on the North-East by some Union Ministries during 1997-8 fell short of the stipulated 10 per cent target, the NDA government created a Non-lapsable Central Pool of Resources to support infrastructure development projects in the region. Between 1990-1 and 2002-3, the region received about ₹1,08,504 crore.[51] So lack of development could not be due to shortage of funds. It can be stated that the political or psychological neglect was not definitely in respect of devolution and transfers of resources from the Centre. The allocation of developmental funds has not at all diminished the extent of problems faced by the region. The fact is that there is less monitoring and lack of implementation of the developmental packages. As economist and Congress leader Jairam Ramesh has argued, this kind of public expenditure has become very much part of the problem of the North-East.[52] This occurs because of poor monitoring, lack of accountability and non-adherence to the set time-frame for project execution. The need of the hour is the proper utilization of the funds and streamlining of the projects, not just the announcement of periodic developmental packages. Wassabir Hussain listed two main reasons why pumping of funds into the region by the Centre has not had the desired impact. Leakage of funds at various levels of the government machinery and development funds making their way into the coffers of the insurgent groups are common knowledge. There is also lack of capacity by these states to absorb the huge quantity of funds in the absence of training and expertise to successfully come up with implementable location-specific projects and the infrastructure to get some of these projects off the planning stage.[53]

Myanmar needs to figure in India's foreign policy with considerable importance in the backdrop of changing global equations. An intensive understanding of the internal dynamics of the country as well as serious engagements with the government should be the mandates of India's relations with the country. People-to-people contacts should be encouraged for fostering the cooperative ties. In this vein conferences and seminars have a pivotal role to play. The NER bears immense potentials in this aspect. The existing opportunities and the resources of the region can be highlighted or showcased for attracting students from Myanmar to pursue studies, research activities or important projects in the region. For strengthening of academic–exchange programmes the understanding of respective languages should be encouraged. The MOUs signed between the two neighbours should be implemented without further delay. Investments should flow from big conglomerates for which development of infrastructure is needed. India's Myanmar policy should be an inseparable part of India's NE policy. There is also a need for a change from conflict-resolution approach to utilization-of-opportunities approach. It should be ensured that the NER should experience the development. A comprehensive charter of cooperation for economic, technological, educational, anti-terror operations is also needed. India should not try and match the influence of China on Myanmar and instead it should focus on malnourished children, rampant malaria and tuberculosis and the spectre of HIV and AIDS. India should extend its helping hand in these sectors and win the hearts of the people of Myanmar, which will usher a new era of India-Myanmar relations as Myanmar is the transit route of exporting to other neighbouring South-East Asian countries like Thailand, Laos, Korea, Singapore, Malaysia, Indonesia and even China.[54] Smoothening of visa-rules, establishment of knowledge-based industries and setting up of manufacturing units on the basis of products identified by national and regional comparative index must be encouraged. It is pertinent to mention that exchange of high-level visits between the neighbours foster the essence of cooperation thereby strengthening mutual peace and prosperity. A noteworthy development in India's renewed bond with Myanmar has been Prime Minister Manmohan Singh's visit to Myanmar in 2012, the first ever by an Indian Prime Minister in the last quarter of a century. The visit has been courteously perceived as an ideological acknowledgment of the victory and re-birth of democracy in Myanmar and most importantly the revitalization of bilateral ties. Along with other promises between the two neighbours a very significant project for the NER is the announcement of an annual assistance of $ 25 million for next five years for meeting the development and security needs of India-Myanmar border areas. Another discerning aspect of India-Myanmar bilateral cooperation is the democratic icon Aung San Sui Kyi's visit to India in November 2012, which does open up a wide array of opportunities and vistas of bilateral cooperation. Since then there have been reciprocal visits of the minister from both the neighbours.

CONCLUSION

The government should adopt efficient measures for promotion of border trade. There should be a competent law-and-order mechanism to prevent bandhs and blockades; there must be licensed or bonded public or private warehouses. Adequate security is mandatory for the business community. The geographical location and proximity to the neighbouring countries is an added trade advantage for the region. Border trade needs to be highlighted in view of the need to pursue closer commercial and economic links with the larger markets in the fast-developing South-East Asian economies. India should undertake encouraging steps to motivate the Myanmar authorities to initiate a stable policy of trade acceptable to the traders from both sides. There is serious requirement of testing laboratories for the importing of food items. Development of infrastructure is one of the ardent criteria for the smoothening of trade transactions. Improving of banking faci-lities and easing of visa complications for travelling to

Myanmar by land route for business and commercial purposes are needed too. Telecommunication and electricity facilities must be uplifted. Huge revenue to the state government is lost due to corruption and lack of governance. The government of Manipur, particularly its commerce and industries department should take an active interest in developing the Moreh town area, post honest officials there and reward such officials for their honesty. There is increasing competition among different communities inhabiting the border areas for acquiring control over trade, which has ultimately ushered in conflicting or brawling situations on different occasions since 1993. The significant political change in Myanmar might provide the NER with the opportunity to advance the border trade between the two neighbours. The remarkable changes in Myanmar like the triggering of reforms both politically and economically, rising popularity and international recognition of the democratic icon Aung Sun Su Kyi, unprecedented freedom to debate in the Parliament–Pyihaungsu Hlu Haw (Union Assembly) and Pyithu Hlu Haw (People's Assembly) – and the intense urge to instill competitive fervour and transparency to the opaque business sector have in fact reinvigorated India's cooperation with Myanmar. A revision in the foreign policy dynamics of India is the need of this hour. The North-Eastern states have established a large volume of informal trade with Myanmar. The official border trade which had a spurt in the beginning with export of Indian goods worth INR 31 crores and imports from Myanmar worth ₹15 crore in 1996-7 had declined to a level of INR 5 crores in export and import by 2004-5 according to official statistics. The value of export to Myanmar is estimated to about INR 27 crore in 2012-13 while the value of import is estimated as INR 20 crore.

Trans-border trade has failed to provide any benefit to the local people and there are procedural hiccups for obtaining licenses, apart from the failure of law and order and absence of proper infrastructure facilities.[55] With appropriate policies and programmes the region can become an important gateway to affluent Asian markets. We have to identify the potentials, taking into account the historically developed patterns of exchanges across the border and the present volume of informal cross-border trade. Focus should be on the assessment of trade relations, trade flow, and regional development and a framework to strengthen the cross-border economic integration should be suggested between the NER and Myanmar.[56] The cross-border markets in Myanmar are nearer than the far away main markets in the country. The cross-border markets may act as an avenue for the surplus produced in the NER as well as source of cheaper imports. The economy of Myanmar is more integrated with the economies of South-East Asian countries rather than with the developed western economies, thus the NER's prospect of reaching the markets of ASEAN through Myanmar has further brightened with its entry into ASEAN in 1997. The production structure of the border states needs to be reorganized in line with the demand structure of the neighbouring country. As the import basket of Myanmar mainly consists of manufactured goods the NER could benefit from trade with Myanmar only if it could industrialize itself. It is thus important to have a market survey in Myanmar and identify the products which the NER can produce at competitive costs, preferably using its own resources. India needs to envisage border trade as a strategy for the development of the border areas.[57] The NER needs to promote its production base in order to accrue benefits from trade and in this innovative venture the enthusiastic participation and engagement of all the North-Eastern states are desirable.

The LEP is well equipped with the developmental aspects or strategies for the region. The policy framework for the North-Eastern Region is guided by a combination of political, economic and cultural factors, which are predominantly monitored by the Planning Commission and the North-East Economic Council.[58] There is dearth of the much-required zeal to implement the developmental projects and thus the immense financial investments have miserably failed to harvest substantive outcomes.[59] Political prudence combined with the development realities should be the modus operandi for the planning and implementation of any developmental endeavour on part of New Delhi. The uniqueness of each of the eight North-Eastern states is needed to be turned into a common planning and formulation for the region as a whole so that all the states could pursue the issues pertaining to the South-East Asian business corridor and also to facilitate the integration of trade and investment.[60] In this vein the proper synchronization of India's Myanmar policy with the interest of the NER is ardently required. The recent reconciliation between the government and Suu Kyi in Myanmar indicates an upward swing in India-Myanmar bilateral relations. The period since October 2011 has witnessed a chain of high-level exchange of visits which is believed to bear positive fallout. For the momentum to be sustained India needs to adopt a more forward looking mindset. New opportunities stimulate the pace of competition. Herein the challenge is to sustain the creative undertakings. The Indian business community should be respectful of Myanmar's sense of dignity and pursue their policies as responsible investors. They should offer capital, technology, capacity-building and products in accordance with Myanmar's needs rather than as an imposition, and the governments and the strategic communities should contribute utmost to relationship-building and encouraging people-to people contacts.[61] Only then will India-Myanmar cooperation have a positive impact on the NER wherein Manipur would have a decisive role to play thereby situating its relevance in the greater perspective of the LEP.

The ban on barter system in 2015-16 has largely jeopardized the prospect of India-Myanmar border trade. Cross-border trade has suffered an acute jolt due to the suspension of the popular barter system at the India-Myanmar border post of Tamu. Development of border trade is crucial to the facilitation of trade transactions accruing benefits to both the neighbours. Opportunities should be exploited for reaping benefits for both the neighbours in the fullest possible context. The LEP should foster North-East India's multifaceted talents in consonance with the present Indian government's emphasis on 'skill, scale and speed'. The skills of the people in respect of indigenous production, creativity, aptitude and English language proficiency are indeed commendable. But there is need for education and development of human capital in order to tap the full abilities of the demographic dividend for a competent labour force coupled with technological development. Regarding scale, infrastructure development, expansion of the magnitude of exploitation of the available skills and resources through proper training mechanisms and guidance are required and the speed mandates an increase in the pace of the implementation of the projects between the two neighbours.

NOTES

1. Dilip Gogoi, ed., *Beyond Borders: Look East Policy and Northeast India*, Guwahati, DVS Publishers, 2010, p. 1.
2. B.G. Verghese, *India's Northeast Resurgent: Ethnicity, Insurgency, Governance, Development*, New Delhi, Konark, 2004, p. 1.
3. Gogoi, *Beyond Borders*, p. 2.
4. Gulshan Sachdeva, 'Demystifying Northeast', *Dialogue*, vol. 7, no. 3, January-March 2006.
5. Verghese, *India's Northeast Resurgent*, p. 2.
6. Nabendu Pal, 'India's North-Eastern Region: Towards a More Humane Approach', *Bharat Rakshak Monitor*, vol. 3, no. 2, September-October 2000.
7. Gogoi, ed., *Beyond Borders*, p. 2.
8. Salman Khurshid, 'Foreword', in Amar Nath Ram (ed.), *Two Decades of India's Look East Policy: Partnership for Peace, Progress and Prosperity*, New Delhi, Manohar, 2012, pp. 9-10.
9. K.J. Holsti, *International Politics: A Framework for Analysis*, New Jersey, W. Prentice-Hall, Englewood Cliffs, 1967, p. 102.
10. C. Raja Mohan, 'India and the Balance of Power', *Foreign Affairs*, 85(4), 2006, pp. 17-32.
11. Rajiv Sikri, Seminar titled 'Transnationalism and Northeast: Towards A new Asia', *CENISEAS*, Guwahati, 10-11 September 2004.

12. Jayanta Brahma, 'Revisiting Indian Foreign Policy: Mapping the North-East on the Foreign Policy Agenda', in Gogoi, ed., *Beyond Borders*, p. 6.
13. G.V.C. Naidu, 'Wither the Look East Policy: India and South-east Asia', *Strategic Analysis*, vol. 28, no. 2, April-June 2004, p. 332.
14. Rajiv Sikri, Secretary East, Ministry of External Affairs lecture at the *Forum*, 'Northeast India and India's Look East Policy', accessed electronically at http//www.ceniseas.org/sikrilecture.doc on 15 July 2014.
15. *The Assam Tribune*, Guwahati, 15 September 2008.
16. G. Srinivasan, 'India's Look-East Policy Must First Look at North-East', *The Hindu Business Line*, 13 July 2007.
17. B. Bhattacharya and Prabir De, 'Promotion of Trade and Invest-ment between People's Republic of China and India: Toward a Regional Perspective', *Asian Development Review*, 22(1), 2005, pp. 53-4.
18. Dilip Gogoi, 'East through Northeast: India and Southeast Asia in the New Asia', in Gogoi (ed.), *Beyond Borders*, p. 45.
19. Ibid., p. 51.
20. Rahul Mishra, ' Myanmar in India-ASEAN Relations', *World Focus*, Special Issue, Delhi, Meenakshi Press, June 2014, p. 38.
21. *The Assam Tribune*, Guwahati, 17 October 2008.
22. 'Joint Statement on the Occasion of the Visit of Prime Minister of India, Dr. Manmohan Singh to Myanmar', Press Information Bureau, 28 May 2012.
23. J.S.R. Khathing, 'Indo-Myanmar Border Trade', in Gurudas Das, N. Bijoy Singh and C.J. Thomas (eds.), *Indo-Myanmar Border Trade*, New Delhi, Akanshah, 2005, pp. 42-5.
24. Bibhu Routray, 'The Indo-Myanmar-Thai Highway: Impact on Insurgency in India's Northeast', *Bharat Rakshak Monitor*, vol. 5, no. 3, November-December in www.bharat-akshak.com.
25. Khathing, 'Indo-Myanmar Border Trade', in Das, Singh and Thomas (eds.), *Indo-Myanmar Border Trade*, pp. 42-5.
26. Ibid., p. 46.
27. Gurudas Das, 'Implications of Engaging Myanmar for India's North East: Trade, Transit and Security', International Conference, New Delhi, organized by GIF-MAKAIAS collaboration, 15 Feb-ruary 2012.

28. M.P. Bezbaruah, 'Indo-Myanmar Border Trade: The Stakes for North East India', *Dialogue*, vol. 9, no. 1, 2007.
29. Mirza Zulfigur Rahman and Julien Levesque, 'Border State and Look East Policy: Opportunities and Challenges in Mizoram', in Gogoi (ed.), *Beyond Borders*, pp. 194-5.
30. M. Rajshekhar, 'A New Gateway to the North-East Runs into and Jumps over a Corruption Roadblock', accessed electronically at http://scroll.in//article/729210/a-new-gateway-to-the-north-east-runs-into-and-jumps-over-a-corruption-roadblock on 27 May 2015.
31. Accessed electronically at www.investinmanipur.nic.in/border.htm on 2 February 2012.
32. Accessed electronically at www.indiaembassy.net.mm/index.php?option=com_content$view=article$id=165$Itemid=165&lang=en, on 8 May 2013.
33. Accessed at www.enterpriseindiamyanmar.in/india-myanmar.aspx on 22 May 2015.
34. Ibid.
35. Ibid.
36. Interview with the Planning Development Officer, Planning Department, Government of Manipur, Imphal, on 7 September 2011.
37. Interview with an officer, Department of Information Technology, Government of Manipur, Imphal, on 7 September 2011.
38. T. Haokip, *The Shanghai Express*, accessed electronically at www.e-pao.net>features on 13 Mary 2013.
39. Yogendra Singh, 'Integrating India's Northeast with Southeast Asia: Infrastructural Dimensions', in Gogoi (ed.), *Beyond Borders*, p. 83.
40. Mirza Zulfiqur Rahman and Julien Levesque, 'Border State and Look East Policy: Opportunities and Challenges in Mizoram', in in Gogoi (ed.), *Beyond Borders*, p. 196.
41. Sanjib Baruah, 'Governor as Generals: The Parallel Political Systems of Northeast India', *Himal South Asian*, vol. 14, no. 6, June 2001.
42. Bihu Prasad Routray, 'Is Development a Riposte to Insurgency?' Institute of Peace and Conflict Studies, Article no. 770, 25 June 2002.
43. Baruah, 'Governor as Generals: The Parallel Political Systems of Northeast India', op. cit.
44. Sanjib Baruah, *Durable Disorder: Understanding the Politics of North-east India*, New Delhi, Oxford Uniersity Press, 2005, p. 78.

45. Alokesh Barua and Arindam Bandyopadhyay, 'Structural Change, Economic Growth and Regional Disparity in the North-East: Regional and National Perspective', in Alokesh Barua (ed.), *India's North-East: Developmental Issues in a Historical Perspective*, New Delhi, CSH and Manohar, 2005 , p. 239.
46. P.C. Dutta, 'Problems of Ethnicity and Insurgency in North East India', in S.K. Agnihotri and B. Datta Ray (eds.), 'Perspective of Security and Development in North East India', New Delhi, Concept Publishing Company, 2005, p. 112.
47. Interviewing a Manipur government employee in Imphal on 6 September 2011.
48. Urvashi Butalia, 'The Naga-Kuki Conflict in Manipur', Bonn, Evangelischer Entwicklungsdienst.e.V (EED) Ulrich-von-Hassell-Str. 76 D-53123, November 2008.
49. Gogoi, 'East through Northeast: India and Southeast Asia in the New Asia', in Dilip Gogoi (ed.), *Beyond Borders*, Guwahati, DVS Publishers, 2010, p. 51.
50. Zarin Ahmad, 'India: Package for the North East', 'Institute of Peace and Conflict Studies', Article no. 338, 8 March 2000.
51. Gulshan Sachdeva, 'Demystifying Northeast', *Dialogue*, vol. 7, no. 3, January-March 2006.
52. Jairam Ramesh, 'Northeast India in New Asia' *Seminar*, no. 550, June 2005.
53. Wassabir Hussain, 'Interaction on the North East' *Observer Research Foundation*, New Delhi, 18 November 2004.
54. C.J. Thomas, 'Trade and Cooperation Across the Border: Need for a Bold and Balanced policy Towards India-Myanmar Border Trade', International Conference, 'India-Myanmar Relations: Strengthening Ties and Deepening Engagements', organized by GIF-MAKAIAS collaboration, New Delhi, 15 February 2012.
55. T. Haokip, *The Sangai Express*, accessed electronically at www.e-pao.net>features, on 13 Mary 2013.
56. Presidential speech in the inaugural session of a national seminar 'Promotion of Border Trade Between India's North-East and Myanmar: Problems and Prospects', 8-9 November 2011, organized by the Indian Council of Social Science Research, North-Eastern Regional Centre, Shillong, referred in Das, Singh and Thomas (eds.), *Indo-Myanmar Border Trade*, op. cit.
57. Gurudas Das and C.J. Thomas, 'Economy of Myanmar: Trends, Structure and Implications for Border Trade with India's North-

East', in Das, Singh and Thomas (eds.), *Indo-Myanmar Border Trade*, op. cit., p. 32.

58. Gulshan Sachdeva, *Economy of the North-East: Policy, Present Conditions and Future Possibilities*, New Delhi, Konark, 2000, p. 6.
59. Gulshan Sachdeva, 'India's Northeast: Rejuvenating a Conflict-riven Economy', *Faultlines*, vol. 6, 2000.
60. 'Former Indian Ambassador Suggests NE to Form Separate Economic Zone', *South Asia Monitor*, July 2014, accessed at news.webindia 123.com/news/Articles/India/20140709/2421610.html on 5 September 2014.
61. Rajiv Bhatia, 'New Glitter on the Golden Pagodas', *The Hindu*, 15 March 2013.

CHAPTER 3

Tourism Prospect of the North-East Region: Realizing through Mekong-Ganga Cooperation Initiative

The NER of India is a variegated region with unique possession of extreme contrasts. On the one hand it is the epitome of scenic beauty, treasure trove of resources with magnificent tourism prospects and on the other, a hot-bed of turbulence with frequent occurrence of insurgencies and terrorist activities ultimately denouncing the region with a security threat perception. The LEP of India with its objective of developing the region can promote its immense tourism credibility with inherent employment opportunities through the subregional initiative of Mekong-Ganga Cooperation. The MGCI was formulated in 2000 with the intent to bolster solidarity and harmony in the fields of tourism, culture and education thereby ensuring considerable development of the Mekong region countries. India and the five South-East Asian Nations – Thailand, Vietnam, Laos, Cambodia and Myanmar – are the members of the Initiative. In its endeavour to reinvigorate the pace of regional integration the MGCI has accorded intense significance to tourism as it has the viability of stimulating economic development of the member countries. It is pertinent to underscore that increased regional cooperation in the field of tourism facilitates the promotion of landlocked regions into land-linked regions. One of the core aspects of the MGCI is to economically develop the landlocked NER for which the opening of the region is ardently required. In this lieu the NER's enthralling scenic beauty can play a vital role in fostering the prospect of tourism. But the ground realities of the region pose certain crucial challenges to the MGCI for making the tourism potentials extensively effective. The chapter attempts at appraising the credibility of the MGCI as a sub-regional initiative in promoting the tourism potential of the NER as an impetus to economic development thereby rejuvenating India's LEP.

The foreign policy objectives of any country are structured on the basis of domestic and international imperatives. India's LEP is being driven by the thrust of comprehending the dynamics of global reconfiguration in the post-Cold War era in tandem with its own national interests. India's LEP towards South-East Asia is being conceived in the new environment to revive historical connections, facilitate regional economic integration, promote national interest and address security concerns.[1] The advantageous geographic location and the critical proximities with the ASEAN countries endow the NER with a crucial position in India's foreign policy agenda.[2] The essence of regional cooperation motivates the countries with geographical contiguity along with shared culture and traditions to cultivate cooperation through promotion of considerable synergies. The NER despite being a region of immense potentials has been deprived of its due in the annals of international relations. The region did figure in the foreign policy agenda as early as in 1962 during the course of 1962 war when Chinese troops came down to the plains of Assam upto Tezpur. This encroachment by the Chinese troops in fact acquainted the policy makes and political leaders of India with the geo-strategic significance of the region and its relevance in policy-making for the unity and integrity of the nation.[3] The NER deserves to acquire priority in foreign policy matters, especially on neighbourhood policies, and policy frameworks on this front have to be preceded by a series of dialogues, consultations and discussions with the states of the NER. The states also need to play an efficient and proactive role in facilitating the foreign relation initiatives with the neigbours. They should be focussed on reaping long-term benefits for the sake of interests of their states as well as of the whole country even at the expense of their short-term domestic gains. Due to their geographic and cultural contiguities they should foster a neighbourhood policy thereby creating a win-win situation for themselves, the country in general and the neighbouring country as well. Security and defence matters need to be dealt with intense sincerity and caution and the humanitarian issues must be looked upon with intensive care. The ethnic considerations, especially the interests of minorities should be kept in mind while venturing into any bilateral initiative with a neighbouring country. The larger interest of the country should not be undermined in any way.[4]

The realistic pursuit of the Look East Policy mandates the proper utilization of available resources of the NER in order to accrue benefits to the region as the fundamental precept of the policy has been the economic development of the NER. India's NER occupies a vantage position in the geo-political landscape because of its international boundaries. The region is surrounded by five Asian nations – China, Nepal, Bhutan, Myanmar and Bangladesh. Arunachal Pradesh, Manipur, Mizoram and Nagaland share a 1,643 km long border with Myanmar. Assam, Meghalaya, Tripura and Mizoram share an 1,880 km border with Bangladesh. Arunachal Pradesh, Assam and Sikkim share a 468 km border with Bhutan. Arunachal Pradesh and Sikkim share a 1,325 km border with the Tibet Autonomous Region of the People's Republic of China.[5] It is undeniable that the NER suffers from developmental challenges because of its landlocked conditions. The Partition of India in 1947, as B.G. Verghese puts it, 'caused the extreme isolation of the NER'. The Partition and diplomatic and strategic manoeuvres between India and its neighbours turned the NER into a sensitive border region demanding special attention based on national security, which has not been conducive to the region's economic and political well-being. It is thus imperative for the region to get out of the territorial trap and get connected with its transnational neighbourhood.[6] Phase 2 of India's Look East Policy was officially declared at the second India-ASEAN Business Summit, in New Delhi on 4 September 2003, when the then Indian Minister of External Affairs, Shri Yashwant Sinha said, 'India's Look East Policy has now entered its Phase 2. Phase 1 was focused primarily on the ASEAN countries and on trade and investment linkages. Phase 2 is characterized by an expanded definition of "East" extending from Australia to China and East Asia with ASEAN as its core. Phase 2 marks a shift from exclusively economic issues to economic and security issues.'

The MGC was a significant initiative taken during this Phase 2.[7]

The congenial geographic location and abundance of valuable natural resources as well as prevalent contiguities with the South-East Asian neighbours validate the credibility of the region as a land-bridge to India's flourishing engagements with South East Asia. Underlining the linkages, Prime Minister Atal Behari Vajpayee had said:

> When I look at the North-East, I also naturally look at India's extended neighbourhood in South East Asia. This is a region where truly historic socio-economic transformations are taking place. Because of its proximity with South East Asian markets, India's North-Eastern region enjoys a locational advantage of great importance. . . . India is working actively to promote regional and sub-regional trade and economic cooperation. Our North-Eastern States can become our economic bridgehead to South East Asia. Equally, vibrant commercial exchanges with South East Asia can galvanise growth and development in the North-East. I therefore urge all the eight States in the region together to prepare the ground to participate vigorously in the emerging opportunities with our South East Asian neighbourhood. This also includes tourism, where I see a major synergy between the North-East and ASEAN countries.[8]

The NER often becomes synonymous with security threat perception. It is an undeniable fact that in case of North-East India the question of security threat encompasses the essence of any intellectual deliberation. The region has always been denounced as retaining conflict-ridden political atmosphere, weak connectivity, feeble infrastructure facilities retarding pace of development. The lack of proper accessibility and the absence of development of adequate communication and connectivity facilities have physically impeded many of the developmental moves of the government. Nevertheless the attempt could not have been abandoned for a long period because of India's LEP. Under the policy India and the South-East Asian nations felt the necessity to exchange their respective repositories, in respect of trade, commerce, industry, tourism and in a number of other allied and collaborative spheres. The LEP is steered to uplift this region from the quagmire of ambiguities to the virtues of economic advantages through exposure to modernity, better business possibilities, enterprising initiatives of developing border trade and people-to-people contacts. The economic potentials of the region though often overshadowed by the magnitude of distressing happenings must not be discounted at any cost. Rather the prospect should be adequately nurtured and utilized for a better future of the region. In this aspect NER's tourism potential deeply embedded in its enthralling scenic beauty and diversified talents, as exemplified in this chapter by the Hornbill Festival of Kohima, can play a crucial role.

MEKONG-GANGA COOPERATION INITIATIVE

The Mekong-Ganga Cooperation Initiative is one of the momentous outcomes of India-ASEAN cooperation, which aims to promote the prospect of tourism among the neighbouring countries. After the establishment of the Bay of Bengal Initiative for Multisectoral Technical and Economic Cooperation (BIMSTEC) in 1997, followed by the Bangladesh-China-India-Myanmar Forum for Regional Cooperation in 1999, New Delhi conceived of the setting up of a third regional diplomatic structure linking India to South-East Asia – the Mekong-Ganga Cooperation Initiative. In 1996 a draft of the structure, which was presented and was known as the Mekong-6 Axis, delineated its objective of linking the riparian countries situated on the shores of the great Indochi-nese river, Mekong with India (considered as the main cradle of the Indochinese civilization from Laotian kingdoms to the Kingdom of Champa in south Vietnam and the Khmers in today's Cambodia). However, despite the Asian Development Bank's support the proposal failed to take any concrete shape at that time.[9] But four years later Cambodia gave a fresh impetus to the idea of regional cultural cooperation linking Indochina to India. Through the MGC initiative Phnom Penh was endeavouring a rapprochement with New Delhi emphasizing the cultural proximities between India and the countries in the Indochinese peninsula, which was indeed an attempt to move away from Beijing's overriding influence.[10] The project, perceived as a counterweight to China's cultural influence, was announced in July 2000 in the ASEAN summit held in Bangkok by the six concerned Ministers of Foreign Affairs (Cambodia, Vietnam, Laos, Thailand and Myanmar for the riparian countries of the Mekong River and India for the Ganga River). With a breakthrough in cooperative essence between Myanmar and Thailand and greater India-Myanmar cooperation, diplomatic contacts received momentum and the MGC soon saw the light of the day in conjunction with the Mekong Basin Group's activities (without India but with China through the Yunnan province).[11]

The Mekong-Ganga Cooperation Initiative was in fact launched with the Vientiane Declaration on 10 November 2000 in the capital city of Laos, Vientiane with the primary thrust to expand solidarity, harmony and cooperation in the fields of tourism, culture and education for ensuring substantive social and economic development of the Mekong region countries. India and the five South-East Asian Nations – Thailand, Vietnam, Laos, Cambodia and Myanmar – were the signatories of that decisive endeavour. Thailand's Foreign Minister Dr. S. Pitsuwan first proposed the notion of the project. Since Ganga and Mekong are regarded as two of the greatest rivers in Asia, the idea of the project bloomed out of the imperative to create a linkage between the two civilizations. It ought to be feasible because of the prevailing parities between the masses of both the regions in physical appearance, social ideals, religious traditions as well as their food habits. The motive of that initiative was also to render a new definition to the member countries in the new global economy, without actually distorting their native identity. Initially the name of the initiative was Ganga-Mekong Swarnabhoomi Project but it got revised to Mekong-Ganga Cooperation due to some differences among the member countries.

The first conference's agenda consisted of consolidating cultural and tourist exchanges between the six partner countries.[12] The second meeting was hosted by Vietnam in Hanoi in 2001. But in both the cases the achievements were not as expected. As it was contemplated the cultural exchanges got boosted up especially with the development of special tourist tours to the Buddhist destinations, pilgrimages to India, Myanmar, Laos and Thailand under the MGC's aegis. However economic cooperation lagged far behind expectations. The functioning of the MGC highlighted the primary intent of the concerned diplomats of the member countries of developing the cultural and the religious affinities before focussing on the economic and trade flows, which would inevitably flourish with the increasing tourist influx. For all that to materialize the diplomatic rhetoric has been incompetent to facilitate the pace of cooperation and most of the organizations seemed to be incompetent in this aspect. Thus the diplomatic impulse of the developing institutions has largely motivated India to move closer to Myanmar by entering into a regionalist institutional framework.[13] The political progress achieved within the purview of the Indian LEP has demonstrated India's willingness to be at dialogue with Myanmar regime with the motto of reshaping Asia's strategic map by rejuvenating cooperation among the neighbours.

The working mechanism for Mekong Ganga Cooperation consists of the annual ministerial meeting, the senior officials' Meeting and the five working groups namely:

- Working Group on Tourism (Thailand is the lead country)
- Working Group on Education (HRD) (India is the lead country)
- Working Group on Culture (Cambodia is the lead country)
- Working Group on Communication and Transportation (Laos is the lead country)
- Working Group on Plan of Actions (Vietnam is the lead country)

The first Ministerial Meeting of the MGC was held in Vientiane on 10 November 2000 and concluded with the 'Vientiane Declaration'. The declaration underscores the grouping's determination to develop closer relations and better understanding among the six countries so as to strengthen friendship, solidarity and cooperation. The 'Vientiane Declaration' outlines the objectives of the MGC in four specific sectors of tourism, culture, education, and transport and communications.[14] In specific, it mentioned about the launching of the Mekong-Ganga Tourism Investment Guide, establishing networks among tourism training institutions and conducting seminars in tourism promotion, encouraging coordinated efforts to expand the export market for handicrafts and traditional textiles of the Mekong-Ganga Cooperation countries, promoting joint research in dance, music and theatrical forms and traditions, conserving, preserving and protecting old manuscripts, heritage sites and artifacts, providing scholarships and translating classics. The Vientiane Declaration in fact proclaimed the commitment of the member countries to develop transport in the region for strengthening inter and intra-regional linkages between people. The member states are also committed to deepening cooperation in the development of IT infrastructure and networks.

At the Second MGC Ministerial Meeting held in Hanoi on 28 July 2001, the member countries adopted the 'Hanoi Programme of Action' which provides specific actions to be taken in four sectors that had been earmarked by the Vientiane Declaration as priority areas of cooperation. The Hanoi

Programme of Action has a six-year time frame covering the period from July 2001 to July 2007 and the progress of its implementation was to be reviewed every two years in coincidence with the Mekong-Ganga Cooperation Annual Ministerial Meeting.[15] Amongst others, it highlighted the need for coordination and transparency and it underlined the need of using IT technologies and knowledge for education and training and also endorsed the use of websites to share information for efficient and effective planning. It also emphasized the essentiality of initiating and developing projects involving more than one MGC member countries but not necessarily all of them.

At the 3rd Mekong-Ganga Cooperation Ministerial Meeting held in Phnom Penh on 20 June 2003, the member countries adopted the 'Phnom Penh Road Map' as a plan to accelerate the implementation of all Mekong-Ganga Cooperation projects and activities. The member states reviewed the progress of the Hanoi Programme of Action and 'noted that the progress was slow and much remains to be done to translate idea to be reality'.[16] They reaffirmed their commitment to the implementation of the Hanoi Programme of Action for cultural cooperation and supported the trilateral road linkages among India, Myanmar and Thailand. Apart from the priority areas, member states acceded to develop affordable medicine for tropical diseases to help the MGC member countries, encouraged cooperation and joint ventures in pharmaceutical and harmonization of drug standards and revealed enthusiasm in exploring new vistas of cooperation. The Mekong-Ganga Cooperation emphasized on the connectivity of India based on cultural and civilizational similarities. In operational terms the project is an attempt to enhance cooperation in the fields of transport and infrastructure with special focus on overland connectivity.[17] The inclusion of Myanmar as member of the ASEAN in July 1997 brought the region to India's border and provided an impetus to extending the road and rail connectivity. In fact, the India-ASEAN Car Rally in November-December 2004 was an enterprising demonstration of the proximity of India and South-East Asia and an endeavour to promote regional connectivity. Under this cooperation, there is a proposal to set up a railway line from Delhi to Hanoi. India has proposed to extend the India-Myanmar-Thailand trilateral highway to Laos and Cambodia. After the completion of this project it has planned to enhance the possibility of setting up special economic zones at borders – India-Myanmar and Myanmar-Thailand.[18] Being land-linked, India's North-Eastern Region can serve as a 'hub' for trade between Mekong and India.[19] It has already been mentioned in this chapter that the MGC initiative primarily focuses on certain core areas of cooperation like tourism, culture, education, transport and communication among the six countries-India, Myanmar, Thailand, Laos PDR, Vietnam and Cambodia and the leading responsibilities of dealing with the focused areas rotate among the six countries.

TOURISM

In the area of tourism intense cooperation is required in sectors like tourism policy planning, human resource development, marketing and environmental preservation through the strengthening of existing linkages and the acceleration of the pace of collaborative dynamics in the field of tourism by the member countries. The onus is primarily on the development and expansion of the tourist destinations, which would share linkages with more than one member country. Transparency in exchange of tourist information is extensively encouraged.

The following measures seek to facilitate the prospect of tourism:

- Promoting awareness of the enormous cultural richness and diversity of the fascinating tourist destinations of the MGC region.
- Undertaking initiatives for organizing familiar trips with the participation of the member-countries' officials, tour-

ism agents and mass media circles to study and promote the tourism potential of the member countries.

- Encouraging cross-border tour packages with the aim to discover the rich cultural and civilizational affinities of the MGC region.
- Organizing MGC-wide cultural festivals so that the visitors can experience a full spectrum of exciting cultural and traditional events across the region.
- Developing Mekong-Ganga tourism through the establishment of Mekong-Ganga tourist booths in international tourism fairs, the publication of Mekong-Ganga tourism map, Mekong-Ganga travel guides and brochures, multi-media promotional materials to be distributed and circulated in different areas through international events on tourism and organizing workshops and seminars.
- Encouraging the development of an MGC Directory of Tourism Products and Services, in printed form as well as on-line information, among the tourism agencies of member countries and designing the logo for Mekong-Ganga Tourism Cooperation to be used by the member-countries in tourism promotional campaigns.
- Sharing information on the eco-tourism promotion programmes, air linkages and religious tourism circuits.
- Strengthening tourism investments
- Promoting distinctive MGC tourism products so as to attract investment in the tourism sector of the member countries.
- Establishing and developing an MGC tourism investment guide with a view to fostering transparency of the systems, procedures and regulations related to tourism investment in the member countries so as to highlight the region as an attractive area for tourism investments.
- Stimulating cooperation in tourism education and training.
- Earmarking and sharing the resources, skills and training facilities, the networking of tourism training centers, institutes, provision of technical assistance and experts, training of trainers.
- Exchanging missions among the member-countries to share

experience and knowledge in the development of the tourism industry.

- Sharing information on tourism statistical data and other related information; facilitating information access with regard to cultural and historical heritage in the MGC countries and exchanging information related to publication in each member country.
- Smoothening the travel of tourists among the member countries.
- Simplifying tourist visa procedures and removing the barriers impeding tourism growth in order to further develop tourist traffic. For instance, there is about 4.2 per cent increase since 2007 in direct air links between major cities and tourism areas of the MGC region.
- Promoting eco-tourism.
- Devising guidelines for assessing and monitoring tourism impact on the natural environment.
- Bolstering public information and awareness, especially at the local community level, so as to educate the public and gain its acceptance of environmentally sustainable tourism.

CULTURE

MGC focuses on preserving and developing the shared cultural and traditional values of the member countries for the purpose of enriching mutual understanding. Certain initiatives are being encouraged to promote cultural development among the member countries:

- Promoting joint research on the cultural heritage of the member counties especially dance, music, theatrical forms and traditions.
- Developing, disseminating, publishing and sharing information on culture, which the member countries can translate and replicate for teaching and learning of the MGC cultures.
- Exchanging missions and experts among the member coun-

tries for the purpose of joint research on the MGC's cultural heritage.

- Undertaking conservation, preservation, protection and promotion to revitalize and further develop the MGC's cultural heritage.
- Conducting surveys on heritage sites and artifacts to compile and publish a directory on heritage sites and artifacts for the MGC region.
- Holding special events at important cultural heritage sites in the MGC region with the participation of representatives from the member countries and from the international organizations with a view to promoting international awareness of the member countries' cultural heritage.
- Making joint efforts to expand the export market for cultural products of the member countries as well as promoting cultural exchange among the member countries.
- Establishing and strengthening networks for the exchange of information and for regular dialogue on cultural exchange among the member countries.
- Promoting the exchange and exhibition of all performing arts, visual arts and literature including traditional dance, music and theatre and boost people-to-people contact among the member countries.
- Encouraging the participation of the member countries in important traditional ceremonies and cultural festivals organized in the region.
- Facilitating roundtables for journalists, writers and experts in literature, arts, women's empowerment, health and nutrition.

EDUCATION

In the sphere of educational cooperation the MGC emphasizes on the promotion of closer interaction in areas of distance education, use of information technology for capacity building in key areas of e-development, education planning, research and language training.

- Encouraging the exchange of students and faculty among the MGC member countries.
- Organizing the awarding of scholarships to member countries' students to pursue studies in important areas.
- Strengthening collaboration between MGC universities and education research and management institutes.
- Establishing a directory of universities, education research and management institutes and information technology training centres in the MGC countries.
- Developing networking and twinning arrangements among the MGC universities and institutes.
- Creating a forum for the exchange of experience in teaching, learning and education policy-making.
- Promoting joint education and training projects for gaining language proficiency including English language training.
- Organizing symposiums and seminars on education-related issues of the member-countries.
- Promoting cooperation programmes in illiteracy eradication, continuing education and distance education for the poorer sections of people in remote areas.
- Developing education and vocational training programmes for community development including the benefit of women and children.
- Translating the classics of each MGC country into the languages of the other MGC countries with a view to contributing to the preservation of cultural identities and traditional values of each member country. Such programmes can be coordinated in cooperation with the existing ASEAN programmes.
- Organizing education exhibitions and book fairs in the member countries.
- Encouraging member-countries' publishing houses and concerned organizations to participate in MGC education exhibitions and book fairs.
- Cooperation in publishing and marketing books of common interests among the member-countries.
- Information Technology training and development.

- Promoting IT connectivity of educational institutions in the MGC region.
- Developing course content and impart educational programmes on the internet to expedite human resource development and upgradation of skills to reinvigorate the industrial revolution.
- Promoting connectivity of libraries for sharing publications.
- Encouragement of internet-based education.

TRANSPORT AND COMMUNICATION

MGC looks upon developing transport and communication facilities as being of immense significance. Smoothening the movement of people and goods among the MGC member countries is regarded as being conducive to socio-economic development, the promotion of trade and better communication facilities and networking. In this respect it is oriented to:

- develop transportation networks among the MGC countries.
- Assess the present status of the transportation networks in the region.
- Foster cooperation in cross-border facilitation, multi-modal transport, infrastructure development, maritime and inland water transport, civil aviation and human resource development.
- Enhance the implementation of transport facilitation within the East-West Corridor, Trans-Asian Railway and the Asian Highway projects.
- Promote cooperation in air services and linkages.
- Develop air services information networks among the MGC countries.
- Cooperate in air services and linkages among the MGC countries to enhance aviation competitiveness of the region.
- Communication and networking.
- Strengthening rural communication networks.
- Training of telecom professionals.
- Establishing a regional hub for meeting communication requirements of the MGC countries.

Crucial initiatives have been adopted for the funding arrangement. It has been decided that each country should consider the possibility of contributing seed money to the MGC fund for each sector. Efforts should be made to seek technical assistance and financial support from donor agencies and countries and international organizations as required.

Certain institutional arrangements were being decided after the formulation of the project:

- Ministerial meetings would be held every year in an MGC member country on an alphabetical rotation basis.
- For the purpose of facilitating the implementation of cooperation arrangements agreed by the ministers, MGC Senior Official Meetings was decided to be held annually, back to back with ASEAN – India Senior Officials' Meeting (SOM) if the latter is hosted by an MGC member country. In case ASEAN-India SOM is hosted by a non-MGC country, the MGC SOM shall be held separately in an MGC member country on an alphabetical rotational basis.
- It is on the part of the hosting country to do the secretarial work for Ministerial Meetings and SOMs.

The successful implementation of the Programme of Action demands intense dedication, commitment, coordination and cooperation of the member countries.[20]

Though India shares deep historical and cultural traditions with the countries of Indochina it was essentially India's economic reforms in 1991 and the robust enunciation of the Look East Policy, which steered it to reformulate its worldview on the economic and political issues as also about its strategic space in the Greater Mekong Subregion.[21] The successful pursuit of India's LEP with the original six of ASEAN, and the appreciation amongst those original six of ASEAN that Indochina requires special attention for economic and social development has greatly forwarded India's engagement with Greater Mekong Sub-region.[22] At the same time, the shared histories and the geographical contiguities of these Mekong

Basin countries with India and China complemented by the current politico-economic drive of the latter two into dynamic Asia has accorded a new strategic value to the Mekong region. For both India and China, Mekong countries provide strategic accessibility to reach the heartland of Asia-Pacific region. Development assistance and transport linkages are the two basic parameters that constructively engage India and China to the Mekong region, an immensely potential feasibility conceived by the then Secretary-General of ASEAN, Rodolfo C. Severino in the year 1999 he stated about the implicit credibility and prospects for the ASEAN to engage the two giants in constructive and balanced relationships. Economic ties could be deepened through the development of infrastructure and human linkage facilities across the common borders providing further fillip to the boosting of trade and people-to people contacts along with the modernization of transportation, communication and other connectivity linkages. The potential for tourism thus would be considerably high.[23] The end of the Cold War presented a new opportunity to revive the relationships among the neighbouring nations. India's economic liberalization initiated in 1991 by PM Narasimha Rao therefore has opened up new vistas for regional integration with the global economy.[24]

From New Delhi's point of view, India's politico-strategic partnership with the Indochina states and Myanmar is progressing at an impressive pace. The Mekong-Ganga Project in fact strengthened India's economic clout in the South-East and Asia Pacific regions and had somewhat balanced the Sino-Pak strategic and security linkages, which in Yashwant Sinha's view is known as 'India's "Look East" Phase 2'. Thus, from New Delhi's point of view, India's politico-strategic partnership with the CLMV countries seems to be immensely vital. The fact that successive governments in India since the 1990s have been endorsing this policy signifies a fundamental consensus regarding its implementation.

But, if we evaluate New Delhi's Look East diplomacy among developed and less developed countries of South-East Asia, the outcome is not that impressive. India, after a decade of economic, political and diplomatic investments in the countries of South-East Asia, has produced a somewhat mixed result. Its economic performance with the CLMV countries reveals a vulnerable economic performance compared to the developed countries of the region. From India's perspective, the weak economic infrastructure of the Indochina states and Myanmar, their late entry within the ASEAN and the financial crisis of 1997, were probably the fundamental causes behind New Delhi's weak economic ties with these countries. However, India's foreign policy makers' failure to cultivate economically strong Brunei for political, economic and strategic reasons remains a major flaw in the pragmatic vision of India's Look East diplomacy. India has no territorial problems with any country of South-East Asia. Therefore it must envisage more vigorous trade and commercial ties with the members within the region. India, through its emerging economic clout and strategic potential, needs to implement its LEP in a manner which might ultimately drive the countries of South-East Asia to look more deeply towards their west. The Vientiane Declaration, the First ASEAN-India Summit and India's wholehearted support for bridging the development gap between old and new ASEAN members through the Initiative for ASEAN Integration programme finally might remove the major stumble blocks of India's Look East policy by achieving the much needed integration and symmetry in its South-East Asian vision of an Asian economic community.[25]

MGC AND INDIA'S NER

The basic thrust of the MGC is to undertake economic development of the Mekong region by developing the infrastructure facilities. For India, MGC offers immense scope for creating linkages with the Mekong countries by connecting them to the subcontinent's economically backward North-Eastern Region. Indian policymakers believe that the development of the North-East is crucial to the promotion of trade and industrial cooperation with the ASEAN countries and the Mekong countries in particular. Road construction linking the North-East and MGC will facilitate quicker overland transportation of goods between the two regions. The Asian Highway on its completion will link Singapore with the Indian mainland via the Mekong cities and the North-East Region.[26] Tourism is a field where immense prospects are possible. The inauguration of the Moreh-Tamu-Kalewa Road on 13 February 2001 by the then Minister of External Affairs, Shri Jaswant Singh, had generated enthusiasm for the improvement of the infrastructure facilities and to devise considerable plannings for a multiple transport links between Tamu (Myanmar) and Thaton (Thailand) connecting India to the larger rail and road grid in the Greater Mekong subregion. The long-awaited Fourth MGC Initiative Ministerial Meeting was held in New Delhi on 12 October 2006. The then India's Minister of External Affairs, Shri Pranab Mukherjee reiterated India's commitment to strengthen India's cultural and commercial ties with the GMS countries. Of all the GMS countries Thailand has traditionally been the closest country to India and has also been one of the most influential players in the GMS. While being a host to over 1,00,000 members of the Indian Diaspora, it shares extensive socio-cultural and economic linkages with India. Compared to the Indian Diaspora in Myanmar the Indian Diaspora in Thailand has been far more active, prosperous and influential. However, for long, a robust economic engagement has not been considerably visible and it is only recently (coinciding with the MGC Initiative) that India-Thailand bilateral trade and investments have picked up momentum making India's corporate conglomerates like the Birla Group and Tatas be actively engaged in business sectors in Thailand. Thai interim Prime Minister, General (Retd.) Surayud Chulanont visited India during 25-8 June 2007, which ushered in the opening of newer avenues of cooperative cooperation. In a joint statement the two countreis decided to move their ties beyond traditional social and economic linkages and to expedite negotiations for stronger defence and security relationships. They also expressed confidence in boosting up India-Thailand bilateral trade which has related US $8.66 billion in 2014 and both the countries was enthunatic in signing an FTA on goods. India also announced a THB10 million grant for setting up the Sanskrit Studies Centre in Thailand. There was unanimity between India and Thailand to forge stronger ties especially for developing India's North-Eastern Region. On invitation of India's minister in charge of Department of North-Eastern Region, a Thai delegation led by its Commerce Minister, Krirk Krai Jirapaet, had visited Tripura, Assam, Meghalaya and held meetings in North-Eastern Council headquarters in Shillong in June 2007.[27] All those visits were indicators of the intent of the MGC Initiative towards the progressive development of the NER. The MGC was a Thai initiative which India supported readily and in fact suggested that the title entails the confluence of the ancient two civilizations on the rivers Mekong and Ganga based upon their rich shared heritage of Buddhism and culture.[28] While stressing on the historical and cultural links between the NER and Thailand the then Chief Minister of Tripura, Manik Sarkar mentioned, 'due to geographical location, Thai culture has always interacted and shared deep influences with the Indian as well as the neighbour-ing cultures of SEA'. The focus has been on identifying and highlighting the Thai-Ahom linkages with the primary objective of developing a level of comfort while interacting with the people of the region and ensuring smoother economic endeavours, which can face socio-cultural resistance from the local people of the region. The four ethnic groups in Assam – the Khamyangs, Turungs, Aitons and Khamitis essentially belong to Tai community.[29] Keeping in mind the close pro-ximities of the NER with South East Asia it can be asserted that India's NER is its umbilical link with East Asia and ignoring this can only result in stunted 'Asia' policies for the country. Therefore it can also be stated that the LEP of India has to take into its fold the NER in its eastern initiatives, myopia towards its North-Eastern region will end up not yielding any tangible outcomes.[30]

The NER of India has immense potential to contribute as it is a treasure trove of tourism potentials. It forms a part of the great tropical rain forest that stretches from the foothills of the Himalayas to the tip of the Malaysian peninsula and the mouth of Mekong river as it flows into the Gulf of Tonkin.[31] The countries to India's east constitute a region and a market of about US $2 billion. Thus understanding and integrating the NER with them and embedding ourselves in their consciousness are crucial. Taken into consideration the complexities the region has historically confronted, in contemporary times, it conjures up certain perturbed issues of violence, civil strife, ethnic identity crisis, ethno-nationalistic aspirations, marginality and the essence of modernization and development that have shaped the recent political landscape of the NER. The varied dynamics and the complex intricacies of the region are little known to the outside world. The limitations like physical isolation from the rest of India, inefficient political control and the reluctance to provide foreign visas to foreign scholars have restrained the scope and ambit of contemporary research on political relations with its neighbours along with issues of border-trade and transnationalism. The region represents a unique place, a meeting ground of many civilizations. The landscape also represents multiple ethnic identities and competing ethnic aspirations that are distinct from the mainland subcontinent.[32] Most of the ethnic groups of the NER are not Indo-Aryan by origin, but primarily consist of peoples of Mongoloid origin who have migrated here centuries ago from Mongolia, Tibet, China, Thailand, Burma and other SEA countries. Peter Kunstadter explained, while analysing the region as 'Assam has a large population of tribal and minority peoples whose languages are more closely related to the languages of SEA than to those of the Indian subcontinent. Their cultures too resemble the cultures of their neighbours in SEA.[33] There are other instances of the NER's enduring cultural forms and social practices and of the people maintaining inter-racial bonds and complex tribal relationships across international borders as the Tai-Ahoms or Ahoms, who are an off-shoot of the Tai people and are called Shan in Myanmar, Thai in Thailand, Lao in Laos, Dai and Zhuang in China and Tay-Thai in Vietnam. Similarly Kunstadter stated that the Khasis of Meghalaya had pioneered rice farming in Vietnam's Red River delta before losing out to the Vietnamese. Then they moved up the Red River across Myanmar into Yunnan before crossing into India.[34] India's many tribes and communities including the Nagas and Kukis are thus living across the international border between India and Myanmar. On the other side of the spectrum, despite the fact that the LEP has been in existence for more than two decades and even as it has substantially benefited other regions of India, specially Chennai, Hyderabad, Bangalore and Delhi, its spill-over effects to the NER have been minimal.[35]

India's former Minister of State for Commerce, Jairam Ramesh argues that the future of North-East India lies in the closer political integration with the rest of India and economic integration with SEA. India should capitalize on NER's historical and traditional cross-cultural linkages with the SEA as a soft power resource. This was completely ignored in the past which was a possibility for cross-cultural region-building much before. It never featured in India's foreign policy making. Therefore, India needs to explore more meaningful engagement in the cultural line and promote cross-border economic activities by fully exploiting NER's history and culture. In this regard, as far as the NER is concerned the first and foremost concern is to tackle insurgency and maintain law and order and rule of law. India's inability to contain prolonged insurgency and violence in the region has now become a major obstacle in cross-border region building. Hence, the government should give utmost priority with sincerity to solve the problem through political dialogue and constitutional arrangements and not resorting to military means. After all, it is the government's responsibility to address the resentments of its own people and eradicate the menace of insurgency. Otherwise, opportunities created by the LEP would never be materialized successfully in this part of the region. The continuance of insurgency will impede the prospect of foreign investment and possible transnational cooperation.[36] Human security and favourable human resources are necessary in the current context to keep up the pace of development in today's highly competitive environment. Moreover, the low degree of population mobility might be recounted as one of the main reasons for the backwardness and isolation of the region. In other words, most of the communities of the NER are less mobile and are hardly exposed and barely interact with the outside population. This makes the people of the NER inherently inward-looking. As a result, growth and development among local communities are not at an expected level. The realization of the LEP mandates the opening of the region, which will endow the NER with the competence to avail the benefits of international cooperation.

Political reasons like the old colonial policy and to a certain extent post-colonial order are also responsible for making this region isolated and not providing adequate opportunities to interact with other regions. For example, the old Inner Line Permit System introduced by the British is still in operation in North-Eastern states like Mizoram, Nagaland and Arunachal Pradesh and even Indian nationals cannot enter without the permission of concerned state authorities. The advocates of local community rights have also championed the cause to put in practice this law permanently in the name of preservation of tribal culture and identity. The pursuit of economic development does advocate the replacement of this policy as well as to enhance the competitive spirit and spontaneity of the local people for the sake of their own well-being. There can be other potent measures of preserving tribal culture, identity and community rights that are better than putting obstacles like the Inner Line Permit System. It is also necessary to ensure local community participation in the overall process of regional economic activities. For realizing such a goal it is necessary to encourage people-to-people contacts and community-to-community dialogue by emphasizing more people-friendly exchanges between the two regions.[37]

NER'S TOURISM POTENTIAL

The cultural relations of North-East ethnic groups with the SEA groups, which have remained completely untapped, also open a new dimension in the current context of the LEP. North- East India is the epitome of diverse and rich cultural heritage of India and the chain of festivals like Hornbill in Nagaland, Bihu in Assam, and Kharchi Puja in Tripura manifest the potentiality of the NER of being the harbinger of economic progress through a comprehensive manoeuvring of cultural exchanges with South-East Asian neighbours. In this chapter an attempt to highlight the prospect of tourism of North-East India through a case study of the Hornbill Festival of Kohima has been made. The credibility of the Hornbill Festival, appreciated through my fascinating experience as a participant observer at the venue of the Festival in December 2012, substantiates the tourism prospect of the NER as a means to its economic development. The NER despite being the epitome of rich and diverse cultural heritage of India has often being defamed as a 'backward' region. But festivals like this signify the potentials of the region as the harbinger of economic progress through a comprehensive manoeuvring of tourism perspective with South-East Asian neighbours. The LEP can promote the tourism credibility of the region through the portrayal of the cultural performances of the festival not only at the domestic level but at the international domain too. To promote tourism intense cooperation is required in sectors like tourism policy planning, human resource development, marketing and environmental preservation. The intent is to develop and expand the tourist destinations, which in turn would accrue economic benefits to the region.

Nagaland, the land of the hospitable and warm Nagas, lies in the corner of North-East India bordering Myanmar. It has always evoked a sense of awe and wonder in the minds of people including visitors. Although most of the Nagas have now become Christians, they still preserve the remnants of their early animist culture and ancient traditions. Dimapur, the only airport in Nagaland, is connected by air to Delhi, Kolkata, Chennai and Bangalore is a splendid place to experience the panorama of nature, the warmth and hospitality of people, lavish blossoms and coy rivers making their way through the rugged terrains. Nagaland tourism can bring solace to the victims of hectic, monotonous and rigorous lifestyles. Moreover, Nagaland exhibits its adequacy not only in the cultural dimension but also in bravery, prowess and heroism. Khonoma Gate of Nagaland reflects the courageous nature of the local indigenous inhabitants of Khonoma village who had built the huge gate to protect themselves from the British intruders. Endowed with natural magnificence, the gate draws visitors from far and wide.

Exposure to Hornbill Dynamism

My visit to Nagaland during the Hornbill Festival in 2012 has enlightened me with the cultural assets of the region. Nagaland is nestled among the hills of the NER. Bounded on one side by Myanmar and the states of Assam, Arunachal Pradesh and Manipur on the others, it is a cornucopia of nature's abundance. Its beauty is evident through its unmanicured and coarse woods, its vicious wilderness not leading to gracefully enclosed gardens or parks but bumpy roads. While travelling through the uneven stretches of land one will have a glimpse of dazzling waterfalls escorting to a nearby village wherein one may experience enthusiastic hospitality. Every corner of Nagaland reflects divine beauty and its people really mesmerize the visitors with their warm and informal demeanour conveying their innate competence to make visitors feel like family. Rural life is markedly dynamic and variegated, encouraging a visitor for an all-embracing study of their lifestyle. Nagaland's engrossing scenic beauty, enthralling music and dances, exciting historical sites and above all spectacular hospitality largely overwhelm tourists.

The exposure has inculcated an intensive appreciation of the richness of the cultural diversities of the region. All the enticing panoramas of Kohima get a fillip during the Hornbill Festival, which motivates inquisitive minds to experience the specracte. The Hornbill Festival is a competent tool to corroborate the versatile talents of the region. Nagaland is a cultural mosaic of multi-ethnicity represented by myriad tribes inhabiting the state. Each community celebrates its respective festivals revolving round the agrarian calendar that makes Nagaland a land of festivals. It was in the year 2000 that the state government in its thrust to promote tourism initiated an innovative strategy to exploit as well as showcase the cultural assets of Nagaland through a weeklong festival to coincide with the celebration of Nagaland Statehood Day, which is on 1 December 1963. The Nagaland Hornbill Festival is named in collective reverence to the bird idolized in the cultural ethos of the Nagas to uphold the essence of unity in diversity. The festival, made up of collective celebration of various tribes, vividly illustrates the versatility, productivity and ethos of Naga life stimulating cultural sensitivities, which is undoubtedly unique to the region. The weeklong festival brings all the tribes and sub-tribes to the venue of the festival, which lies at the foothills of the towering Mount Jafu in the Kisama Heritage Village. The name Kisama is derived from two villages namely, Kigwema (KI) and Phesama (SA) and 'MA' means village, on whose land the Naga Heritage Village is established and commissioned by the State Government of Nagaland. It is situated about 10 km from Kohima and offers a panorama of nature, and cheerful hospitality of the people. The objective of the Heritage Village is to protect and preserve all ethnic cultural heritages by establishing a common management approach and comprehensive database for perpetuation and maintenance for promotion of tourism. It also aims to uphold and sustain the distinct identity of dialects, customs and traditions of all the ethnic tribes of Nagaland. The Heritage Complex also hosts the World War II Museum, Bamboo Heritage Hall, Bamboo Pavilion, Kids Carnival, Horti-Scape, food courts, a stadium for live concerts, Naga Idol, a beauty pageant and fashion shows. It also has the Naga chilli eating contest. The Naga chilli has a Scoville Heat Unit (SHU) of about 2 million, making it the world's hottest. It see participation from locals as well as tourists. The Department of Women Development provided a glimpse of 'Naga Traditional Designs and Prints' which was showcased through a fashion show. In support of the Spastic Society, Nagaland hosted the Hornbill Charity Ball to help the individuals with disabilities.[38]

The festival becomes the magnificent centrestage of a weeklong medley of cultural performances, indigenous games, craft bazars, music events, fashion, motor sporting events, kids' carnival, floral galleria and a series of competitions which sees both indigenous and global participation. At the festival one is introduced to the craft artisans displaying exemplary skills in bamboo, wood, textiles and other craft activities. What emerged from a local heritage has changed into a national and international festival that is now a must-visit and notable attraction in the travel itinerary of both domestic and international travellers. Alongwith the events mentioned earlier there is a series of art, photography and film screenings by Naga film makers placed in different venues around Kohima. The Hornbill Festival is to experience first-hand both sides of the coin – the rich cultural and vibrant heritage of the Nagas and their cultural pride in juxtaposition with modernity. It is the coming together of synergistic elements that make up Nagaland.[39] The Hornbill Festival imbues the spirit of involvement and enjoyment among the people irrespective of age and gender and fills the environment with the ardor of amusement like any other major festival any in other state of India. This festival can be a captivating source of tourist enchantment spearheading towards economic prosperity. The indigenous strengths and abilities enlarge the ambit of accrediting the assets of Nagaland and can be utilized for professional opportunities and gains. Tourism therefore can act as a competent tool to develop the region as a gateway to the thriving equations between India and its South-East Asian neighbours.

Possibilities for Tourism Promotion

For facilitating essence of greater economic integration the LEP has emphasized on boosting cultural cooperation among the neighbours. An economically robust NER can strengthen and deepen the economic linkages between the ASEAN economies, China and mainland India, a process set in motion by the rapidly growing structures of globalization and LEP. The LEP has to be a state-driven policy to accrue benefits to the eight North-Eastern states. And the NER on its part has to act collectively. There should be coordination in demands and actions and most importantly consensus among the eight North-Eastern states. Synchronization of policies between the Centre and all the state governments is imperative to make the NER an attractive and profitable tourist hub. Too much dependency on policy formulation prevent the North-East states from achieving mileage from the Look East Policy. Despite being located at an advantageous position in the South-East Asian economic corridor, the North-Eastern states have been found to be over-dependent on the Centre and when it comes for Centre's decision, in most of the cases the Union Government pays little interest.[40]

To earn revenue from the tourism potential of the NER certain recommendations can be put forward:

- Resource mapping is required. There is availability of resources but what is lacking is the proper or the adequate exploitation. The differential advantage that the NER can offer in its tourism prospect has to be identified.
- Strategic strength with this potential needs to be designed for which collective planning is needed.
- Proper marketing of the scenic possession and indigenous abilities is required. For example, Myanmar, Thailand, Vietnam and Cambodia have strong Buddhist leanings but of all these countries Thailand is reaping maximum benefits due to the portrayal and showcasing of its attributes.

My field trip to Singapore conducted from 8-16 September 2014 greatly rekindled my understanding about the prospect of tourism in the NER. Singapore is known to the outside world as the most enthralling tourist spot with multitudinous potentials. The factors behind the prospect of tourism in this South-East Asian country might be one of the primary causes inducing my field trip to Singapore. My research interest centres around the North-East Region of India, which is undoubtedly a treasure-trove possessing intense tourism potentials but is deprived of its due in international relations because of a number of constraints. The thrust of the academic visit to Singapore has been to explore the facets contributing to the perceptible growth and development of the commercial hub. The striking feature of this South-East Asian country, which is the conglomeration of Chinese, Malays, Indians and Eurasian population, is its paramount level of development. The predominant facets like developed infrastructure and communication facilities, advanced technological knowhow, modernized centres of excellence and health care as well as most importantly the efficient law and order system, prevailing civic sense, obedience and conformity to the rules on the part of its people, prevalent security and safety of the people and the essence of hygiene, cleanliness have acted as boon to Singapore's prosperity and development in all possible means. In Singapore I stayed in a place called Little India which bears little resemblance to the so-called swanky ambience of the rest of the country. There is a huge market complex called Mustafa Centre which remains open for 24 × 7 and the commendable aspect has been the attitude of the salespersons, who greet and attend to the customers with profound enthusiasm and composed demeanour. Despite higher cost of living in the country the above characteristics stimulate the prospect of tourism, which truly upholds the spirit of cultural affinity along with lucrative package facility. The development of the NER through the exploitation of its tourism potentials mandates the formulation and implementation of concrete measures different from rhetoric by the Indian government. Singapore, as a South-East Asian neighbour thus offers a lot to learn and acts as an exemplary in India's venture of 'Act East'. But it is mentionworthy that the onus should not only be on the government as in this endeavour the enthusiastic participation and engagement of the populace of the country is imperative in order to boost the prospects of development-starved North-East India. This will also mitigate the grievances and frustrations of the NER in terms of economic opportunities.

The new government's 'Act East' policy's renewed emphasis on a more vigorous trading regime with the countries of South-East Asia adds momentum for the eight North-Eastern states to renew their promise of tourism potential. Indeed connectivity between the NER and the South-East Asian countries can spur cultural and educational exchanges and also health, religious and sports initiatives between the neighbours. All these undoubtedly will lead to a boom in the tourism industry of the NER. But at the same time an analytical comprehension of the availability of opportunities and the existing constraints is required to shortlist and prioritize high-return investments in physical and institutional infrastructure, identify crucial institutional and structural reforms necessary for development and utilization of the NER's tourism resources. India's LEP has corroborated to economic development, increased educational possibilities, commercialization of livelihood and growing interactions between the people of NER, with the rest of the country and the nations of South-East Asia to change the region's socio-economic condition. But to its dismay belying its multifarious potential the region continues to lag behind the rest of the country in economic matters. Among the impediments we can cite the issue of low connectivity with the rest of the country as the greatest economic hurdle. With limited geographic outreach and relatively less access to markets the region is somewhat at a disadvantage to attract investment. Moreover civil strife, insurgencies, inter- and intra-state conflicts pose a significant constraint on the economic prosperity of the region. But paradoxically acute poverty, competition over rare resources and massive underdevelopment are the factors fuelling conflicts thereby disturbing the law and order situation of the region. The dilemma for resource-rich economies is that development and growth are the prerequisites for addressing grievances. But the pursuit of growth through resource-intensive development also creates underprivileged people and thus induces conflict. The remedy therefore lies in policies and institutional reforms that explicitly identify and address the negative impacts of development.[41] To facilitate the potential of tourism promoting economic development in the NER a supportive environment providing incentives and institutions capable of grasping opportunities, businesses advancing investments and educational systems enhancing human skill is essential. Here the government's initiative of launching online visa facility for 43 countries acts as a springboard for boosting tourism among the neighbours. A policy reorientation in terms of heightened people-to-people contacts in the form of tourism rejuvenates confidence-building measures thereby leading to the fruition of greater economic ties among the neighbours.

CONCLUSION

It is evident that reinventing India's relations with the countries of the ASEAN region has been a predominantly significant factor in this evolving global power balance. It forms the crux of India's Look East Policy. The LEP is in fact a revival of India's enduring engagement with its South-East Asian neighbours which unravels a series of opportunities and possibilities for our own times. Intra-regional trade in the ASEAN countries is growing faster than their trade with the rest of the world and India needs to reinvigorate its economy by linking itself to the ASEAN growth. However, unlike in the past, merchandise trade alone cannot drive India's deeper engagements with the ASEAN.[42] East Asian leaders have often traced India's LEP to the diplomatic realism of former Prime Minister P.V. Narasimha Rao at a time of national crisis in the 1990s. Against this background, the overriding view in East Asia was that India was setting the terms for India's long-term engagements with key regional powers. Inevitably such diplomacy would extend beyond the economic realm. India's strategic calculations were easily discernible too.[43]

The essence of physical connectivity is a matter of immense importance in the world today. The crux of integration makes the presence of borders largely irrelevant in this era of globalization. India too, in its quest to accelerate cooperative endeavours, is venturing into the connectivity drive. This bears a positive orientation as the freedom to travel and communicate ends the barriers of language, culture and tradition as well as opens up newer possibilities for trade, investment with exchange of innovative ideas and information. The signing of the FTA between India and ASEAN has undoubtedly facilitated the pace of connectivity initiatives undertaken by India under its Look East Policy. The Mekong-Ganga Cooperation Initiative can be viewed upon as an undertaking driven by the avowed intension to promote connectivity facilities through cooperation between India and its South-East Asian neighbours to a greater extent. The India-MGC project could also help balance China's Look West strategy of gaining access to the Indian Ocean through its south-western province of Yunnan, and Myanmar and Bangladesh. China's three largest defence importers are Pakistan, Myanmar and Bangladesh. A China-Bangladesh defence pact was signed in 202 and the Chinese involvement in the development of Myanmar's roads and ports and installation of defence surveillance facilities on Myanmar islands near the Andaman's is a very significant endeavour. In fact, Myanmar has emerged as the Sino-Indian strategic signpost on either side of the Malacca divide. Moreover India and Myanmar have extensively cultivated their bilateral cooperation and the expanding Chinese supremacy as well as Myanmar's ASEAN membership have boosted India-Myanmar cooperation. India had successfully completed the 135 km Kalemyo-Kalewa-Tamu road link which connects Manipur with Myanmar, a historic event which marked the 'the first official (Indian) delegation to cross the land border since independence,' as claimed by the then Indian Minister of External Affairs.[44]

India faces stiff competition while trading with the ASEAN countries as there is increasing keenness from the whole world to trade with the region given its immense potentials and prospects. Thus in this competitive atmosphere it is difficult for India to cultivate special relationship with the ASEAN. However, India's unique advantage is the historic legacy of its shared religious and cultural ties with the region. India's LEP should thus be oriented to leverage this asset in reinventing its engagement with South-East Asia. If a vastly expanded portfolio of relationship-building initiatives is to be financially sustainable, these initiatives must be designed as commercially viable activities financed and managed through public-private partnerships. A field, possibly the most important for relationship building, is specialized higher education, engineering, management, law and medicine. India has many excellent institutions in these fields that enjoy global recognition. Moreover, they offer courses in English, the international language that students in the ASEAN countries are aspiring to master. An offer to establish such institutions in the ASEAN region will be largely welcomed.[45]

For the successful implementation of the program of the action of the MGCI a sense of community needs to be evolved within which collective commitment, coordination and cooperation of the member countries are ardently required. Recent years are witnessing major powers and agencies getting increasingly interested in the GMS. India's MGC Initiative has been conceptualized as an integral part of India's economic diplomacy with strong cultural underpinnings. By encouraging business contacts between people on both sides, the MGC Initiative intends to build bridges and stabilize commercial relations with the least developed countries where India's presence was not so dominant. This also seeks to underline the social responsibility of the private sector and to emphasize on the prospect of reaping benefits in the long run. Some of them, like the economies of Thailand and Vietnam have been booming rapidly in recent years. In this backdrop the MGC presents an opportunity for Indian companies, which can provide world-standard products at competitive prices to the GMS countries, which will also enable Indian companies to enhance their competitiveness globally. India has the capability to assist the CLMV countries, especially in the agricultural sector, in terms of technology transfer and skills training. Moreover initiatives like the MGC are also expected to facilitate the economic development of India's North-East which has continued to present both a political and development challenge to New Delhi. Trade promotion and industrial development in India's NER are required for flourishing overland trade via Myanmar to many MGC countries. By strengthening relations with Myanmar, India could emphasize pan-Buddhist links with the ASEAN. MGC Initiative has the potential to deliver increased volume of trade if the highway linking the countries of the region would be extended to link Singapore with New Delhi through regional capitals such as Kuala Lumpur, Ho Chi Minh City, Phnom Penh, Bangkok and others. In its Vision 2020 and the Hanoi Action Plan, which provides a detailed roadmap for socio-economic development of the region, ASEAN remains focused on creating incentives to integrate CLMV countries in the region. India with its traditional and cultural linkages with this region has a unique advantage and can play a crucial role in realizing this ASEAN vision.

However, in the last few years inspite of the high-level visits, the MGC Initiative has not been competent enough to keep pace with all the initial diplomatic rhetoric. For instance, India's Ministry of External Affairs has played limited role on its initiatives with the GMS countries or for the MGC initiative. Its official website has very limited reach and little to offer in terms of any information or outline on India's policy or activities with regard to the MGC Initiative, which poses an impediment for the realistic pursuit of the MGC Initiative. Focus on open sources, following the Asian Development Bank's strategy, should be encouraged for developing cooperation with the GMS countries. In this endeavour India's IT capabilities and experiences could be actively utilized for cultivation of the GMS and for proactive involvement of the non-governmental agencies. Institutions like the Research and Information System (RIS) for Non-aligned and Other Developing Countries, Consumer Unity and Trust Society (CUTS), and the Confederation of Indian Industry (CII) have done some commendable work in holding awareness workshops and in imparting training to GMS compatriots, further strengthening the official MGCI. Secondly, India's IT and pharmaceutical sectors have witnessed great demand within the MGC Initiative but often the human capital constraint has acted as a deterrent in quality training in these countries. India's credibility in institutional arrangements for bringing about high-quality manpower can act as a catalyst in this aspect.

In the area of cultural relations, though there have been exchange of artists, scholars and educationists between India and the GMS, they should have wider access and must not remain confined to the capitals and big cities alone. And finally, beyond periodical meetings and exchanges of officials, academics and experts for training and exposure, greater emphasis needs to be put on people-to-people contacts for enhancing mutual awareness and on technology transfers for accommodating the huge gaps in our priority areas. Concrete measures need to be implemented in order to fully utilize these vast potentialities, which promise to generate considerable tangible and intangible benefits for both the sides. In principle, the MGCI remains an important symbol of India's trust and India's growing stakes in promoting multilateralism in international relations.

To sum up, the idea of the MGCI has been driven by the desire to explore alternatives to the realist paradigm and to emphasize on norms and values becoming the basis of inter-states relations. The MGC Initiative was conceptualized not only to strengthen military and economic cooperation on the basis of India's engagement with the GMS but to foster the links apart from the many other objectives for mutual benefit.

The main areas of cooperation within the MGCI remain culture, education, tourism, and transport and communications. In the words of India's former Minister of External Affairs, Shri Jaswant Singh, spoken at the inaugural MGC Initiative meeting in Vientiane on 10 November 2000, leaders had agreed to launch the MGC Initiative with a 'political willingness and aspirations aimed at strengthening our traditional bonds of friendship' and it is in this larger perspective that New Delhi continues to evolve its future initiatives cultural and civilizational linkages. The interactions have also since grown from being purely cultural to economic and military, as also from being purely multilateral towards deepening bilateral initiatives that both strengthen cultural and people-to-people cooperation, as also their infrastructure within the MGCI.[46]

To promote tourism the Governor of Nagaland P.B. Acharya inaugurated the 'Business Promotion and Tourism Summit' at the Hotel Vivor on 4 December 2014. The Nagaland Federation of Chamber of Commerce and Industries organized the summit to hold discussions with the Maharashtra Chamber of Commerce, Industries and Agriculture (MACCIA) on tourism potential of the region. The Governor stated that the movements of people in India had always been one-way traffic, that is, people from North-East Region moving to the rest of India, while the inverse incidence was quite limited. In his opinion, the North-East Regions contributions to the country and its economic potentials were only recognized during the Chinese aggression and has never been adequately endorsed by the people of its own country. The Governor stated that it is the responsibility of the better-offs of the society to uplift and promote the underprivileged sections of population for sustainable development of the region. The Chief Minister of Nagaland, T.R. Zeliang opined that the people of Nagaland need a change in their mind-set and in the work culture. Prolific encouragement was expected of Maharashtra towards formulating policies in commerce, industries and agriculture. The CM was of the view that the onus should be more on the production and marketing of products, especially organic agro-products. Lok Sabha MP and former Chief Minister of Nagaland, Neiphiu Rio divulged that the 'summit' was the manifestation of the enthusiasm of the people of Nagaland in making the region a tourist hub. Rio said that the state paradoxically was poor in many ways but rich in many aspects. He felt that the uncongenial environment, political sensitivities and incompetent governance often pose hurdles in the tourism potentials of a region. He said that therefore the Naga political issue was of great importance and needed to be seriously addressed as peace was essential for the development of tourism. Taking cognizance of the dependence of the people on the government for growth and development instead of private entrepreneurial endeavours he eulogized that the LEP of India should be 'Look East through North East India'. He asserted that the people of Nagaland have missed out on social revolutions and developments due to the state's political problem. However, he highlighted the relative strengths of the region in terms of IT and nature-based resources, for which Nagaland Assembly had passed resolutions for the creation of Special Economic Zones to facilitate growth of business. Rio expressed optimism that the country would not leave any of its corners behind in growth and stated that 'unless there is trust there is no business transaction'. Emphasis on small and medium industries was discussed upon and the necessity of skill development and vocational education was also been nurtured in the summit. It has also been highlighted that a congenial social eco-system is a pre-requisite for industrial development. The state needs to develop in industry related to natural resources of oil, coal and medicinal herbs.[47] India's Minister for Tourism and Culture and Civil Aviation, Dr. Mahesh Sharma toured India's remote NER in April 2015 and in a bid to boost tourism laid the foundation stone for the new Regional Convention Centre of North-East Zonal Cultural Centre (NEZCC) at Dimapur.

Cooperation is the key word of the MGC Initiative. It is the driving force behind the success of this dynamic endeavour, which promotes the formation of community feeling among its member states. The respective repositories of the members can be exchanged for the optimum utilization of the available resources, thereby enhancing the possibility of reaping benefits. Under the essence of cooperation the member countries acquire the opportunity of wider intermingling and of knowing each other deeply, which provides the ground for understanding among the member countries wherein each expand its perimeters of cooperation sidelining differences. For the successful pursuit of the sub-regional initiatives the member countries should be tolerant towards fellow-members' limitations and should function cooperatively to overcome the obstacles. They should nurture and encourage the quality of respecting mutual proficiencies and abilities. There is considerable scope of development of the MGC Initiative by tapping the opportunities and possibilities of the changing dynamics generated in the process of integration of the economies. There is no doubt that the competition for growth and development between the member countries will drive innovation and new avenues of change to Asia. Collaborative endeavours accelerating the essence of solidarity will spur the development and prosperity of the region's nation states.

NOTES

1. Dilip Gogoi, 'East through Northeast: India and Southeast Asia in the new Asia', in Dilip Gogoi (ed.), *Beyond Borders: Look East Policy and North East India*, Guwahati, DVS Publishers, 2010, p. 38.
2. Jayanta Brahma, 'Revisiting Indian Foreign Policy: Mapping the North-East on the Foreign Policy Agenda', in Gogoi (ed.), *Beyond Borders*, p. 6.
3. Ibid., p. 21.
4. Subir Bhaumik, 'Ways to Create a Better Neighbourhood', *The Telegraph*, 19 August 2014.
5. Speech by the Minister of External Affairs, Pranab Mukherjee at the Seminar 'Look East Policy', Shillong, 16 June 2007.
6. Sanjib Baruah, 'Between South and Southeast Asia: Northeast India and the Look East Policy', *CENISEAS*, no. 4, 2004, p. 3.

7. Tridib Chakraborti, 'India's Southeast Asia Policy in the 21st Century: Perambulating the Horizon', in Y. Yagama Reddy (ed.), *Emerging India in Asia-Pacific*, New Delhi, New Century Publications, 2007, p. 154.
8. Prime Minister's address to the Second Northeast Business Summit in New Delhi, 20 January 2003, accessed electronically at http://pib.nic.in/release.asp?relid+754 on 14 July 2014.
9. 'The Mekong 6 Axis', *Outlook India*, 3 April 1996.
10. Renaud Egreteau, *Wooing the Generals: India's New Burma Policy*, New Delhi, Authorspress, 2003, p. 110.
11. C.S. Kuppuswamy, 'India's Policy: Looking Eastward', *South Asia Analysis Group*, 27 December 2000.
12. 'Looking East', *Frontline*, vol. 17, no. 24, 8 December 2000, p. 50.
13. Egreteau, *Wooing the Generals*, p. 112.
14. 'Vientiane Declaration on Mekong-Ganga Cooperation', 10 November 2000, Vientiane, Lao PDR, accessed electronically at www.mfaic.gov.kh>Top Bulletin>2000 on 17 April 2013.
15. 'Hanoi Programme of Action for Mekong-Ganga Cooperation', 28 July 2001, Hanoi, Vietnam, accessed electronically at www.mfaic.gov.kh/Products/1529-ha-noi-programs-of-action-for-mekong-ganga-cooperation.aspx on 17 April 2013.
16. Report of the Third Ministerial Meeting on Mekong-Ganga Cooperation, 20 June 2003, Phnom Penh, Kingdom of Cambodia, accessed electronically at http://thecalibre.in/in-depth-current-affairs/6th-mekong-ganga-cooperation-meeting/092012/?p=1214/ on 18 April 2013.
17. 'Ganga-Mekong Swarnabhoomi Project', accessed electronically at http://meaindia.nic.in/onmouse///ganga.htm on 7 September 2011.
18. *Mekong Ganga Policy Brief No. 1*, Research and Information System for Developing Countries publication on India-Mekong Economic Cooperation, March 2007, p. 4.
19. Prabir De, 'Connecting Mekong Region with India through Infrastructure linkages', *Financial Express*, 5 February 2008.
20. Electronically accessed at file:///D:/Documents%20and%20Settings/user/My%20Documents/Mkng-Ganga%20Cooperation.htm on 7 June 2011.
21. Swaran Singh, 'Mekong-Ganga Cooperation Initiative: Analysis and Assessment of India's Engagement with Greater Mekong Sub-region', *IRASEC Occasional Paper*, No. 3, 2007, p. 19.

22. H.E. Rodolfo C. Severino, 'The Greater Mekong Sub-Regional and Regional Peace and Security', Address at the International Conference on the Greater Mekong Sub-region', 6 July 1999, accessed electronically at http://www.aseansec.org/3317.htm on 7 September 2011.
23. Rodolfo C. Severino, Jr., *ASEAN Rises to the Challenge*, Jakarta, The ASEAN Secretariat, 1999, p. 209.
24. Dilip Gogoi, 'East through Northeast: India and Southeast Asia in the New Asia', in Gogoi (ed.), *Beyond Borders*, p. 34.
25. Tridib Chakraborti, 'Explaining the Penumbra of India's Look East Policy', in K. Raja Reddy (ed.), *India and ASEAN Foreign Policy Dimensions for the Twenty-First Century*, New Delhi, New Century, 2005, pp. 68, 78.
26. P.V. Rao, 'Subregional Strategies of Cooperation in ASEAN: The Indian Approach', in K. Raja Reddy (ed.), *India and ASEAN Foreign Policy Dimensions for the Twenty-First Century*, New Delhi, New Century, 2005, p. 155.
27. Swaran Singh, 'Mekong-Ganga Cooperation Initiative: Analysis and Assessment of India's Engagement with Greater Mekong Sub-region', electronically accessed at (www.jnu.ac.in/Faculty/ssingh/Mekong-Ganga.pdf) on 13 October 2011.
28. Sudhir T. Devare, 'India's Look East Policy: As Seen from a Vantage Point', in A.N. Ram (ed.), *Two Decades of India's Look East Policy: Partnership for Peace, Progress and Prosperity*, New Delhi, Manohar, 2012, p. 92.
29. Vibhanshu Shekhar, 'Thailand's Look West Policy: Opportunities and Challenges for India's Northeast', in Gogoi (ed.), *Beyond Borders*, p. 174.
30. Prabhakar Menon, 'India and the World East of It – Past and Present: An Impressionistic Account', in A.N. Ram (ed.), *Two Decades of India's Look East Policy: Partnership for Peace, Progress and Prosperity*, New Delhi, Manohar, 2012, p. 119.
31. Sanjay Hazarika, *Strangers of the Mist: Tales of War and Peace from India's Northeast*, New Delhi, Penguin, 1995, p. xv.
32. Dilip Gogoi, 'Intoduction', in Gogoi (ed.), *Beyond Borders*.
33. Peter Kunstadter (ed.), *Southeast Asian Tribes, Minorities and Nations*, vol. 1, Princeton, Princeton University Press, 1967, p. 205.
34. Sanjib Baruah, 'Between South and Southeast Asia: Northeast India and the Look East Policy', *CENISEAS*, no. 4, 2004, p. 34.

35. Ibid., p. 5.
36. Dilip Gogoi, 'East through Northeast: India and Southeast Asia in the New Asia', in Gogoi (ed.), *Beyond Borders*, p. 51.
37. Ibid., p. 54.
38. *Hornbill Festival Guide*, Kohima, The Directorate of Tourism, 2012, p. 2.
39. Ibid., pp. 3, 4.
40. 'Former Indian Ambassador Suggests NE to Form separate Economic Zone', *South Asia Monitor*, July 2014, accessed at news.webindia 123.com/news/Articles/India/20140709/2421610.html on 5 September 2014.
41. Hiranmoy Roy, 'Regional Development Paradigm', *The Statesman*, 7 July 2014.
42. Sudipto Mundle, 'Fulfilling Eastern Promises', *The Statesman*, 26 January 2011.
43. P.S. Suryanarayana, 'New Economic Idiom in Look East Policy', *The Hindu*, 26 October 2011.
44. P.V. Rao, 'India and Regional Cooperation: Multiple Strategies in an Elusive Region', in P.V. Rao (ed.), *India and Indian Ocean: In the Twilight of the Millennium*, New Delhi, South Asian Publishers, 2003, p. 144.
45. Mundle, op. cit., 26 January 2011.
46. Swaran Singh, 'Mekong-Ganga Cooperation Initiative: Analysis and Assessment of India's Engagement with Greater Mekong Sub-region', electronically accessed at www.jnu.ac.in/Faculty/ssingh/Mekong-Ganga.pdf on 13 October 2011.
47. 'Business Promotion and Tourism Summit Held', *The Morung Express*, Nagaland, 5 December 2014.

CHAPTER 4

North-East India and Myanmar: Venturing New Opportunities

Pre-2010 Myanmar's lack of exposition towards the outside world and its isolationist position had not been in accord with the rich endowment of valuable natural resources of the country. Its advantageous geo-strategic location and prospective possession have in no way aided to its perceptible growth and development. Myanmar thus has been deprived of its due in the annals of international politics. But the post-2010 changing dynamics in Myanmar have imparted it a defined identity from a pariah state to a flourishing destination. In the last couple of years, the country has gained both strategic and political importance in international relations. My first exposure to Myanmar after landing at the small but new and modern Yangon International Airport left me puzzled. The perception gained from theoretical understanding of the country was quite contrary to the exposed reality. The first question that came to my mind soon after the landing at the airport, where tall green grass instead of concrete stretch touches the runway – whether Myanmar has advanced from its 'isolationist past' to a modernized liberal state. More than a week's stay in Myanmar gave me with the understanding that the country is still struggling to accommodate its past with its present, trying hard to synthesize its enduring historical and cultural dynamics with the contemporary economic and geo-political realities.

Myanmar is changing, and changing very fast. Located between the two rising Asian giants, India and China, Myanmar today wants to exploit its strategic and economic leverage for its own benefit without tagging to any one country. From pawn, it now wants to be a player unto itself. Especially, following its entry into the ASEAN and the recent process of reformation, it has emerged as a new opportunity as well as a new challenge both for India and China. This has imparted Myanmar its eminence in the South and South-East Asian geo-politics. In India's Look East Policy Myanmar acts as a gateway to the ASEAN which in turn, is conceived as a springboard by India to reach out to the wider Pacific Region. At the same time, China's pioneering and growing imprint in Myanmar is in fact a reawakening call for India to foster closer ties with this South-East Asian neighbour. It is against this backdrop that India and China's relative proximities to Myanmar to become the focal-point of an insightful academic research for experts. In Myanmar's transition to democracy – more specifically from 'isolationist past' towards a modernized liberal state – the study of the influences wielded by its two giant neighbours, India and China, therefore assumes special significance for both academic as also policy studies.

India's LEP has given considerable momentum to Myanmar, the gateway to ASEAN. India is conscious of the fact that Myanmar, straddling both South and South-East Asia, serves as the link between the two regions. Therefore, a cooperative relationship with Myanmar is the crux of its LEP to establish close physical and economic links with its eastern neighbours.[1] The People's Republic of China is also an important determinant in the realistic pursuit of India's LEP as Myanmar is strategically located and has tremendous political and economic influences in the South-East Asian region. Therefore, both China and India's approach toward South-East Asia including Myanmar should not be of detriment to each other. But it is an undeniable fact that India is bit sceptical about China's dominance in the political and economic domains of Myanmar.

MYANMAR: MELTING POT OF NEIGHBOURHOOD INFLUENCES

From the geo-strategic significance of the location of Myanmar it is pertinent to mention that it is the melting pot of the cultural influences of both the emerging giants, India and China. Myanmar's crucial geo-strategic location and its commonality of borders with two emerging giants is both a boon and a curse: to be either a booming economic centre or a strategic pawn. Myanmar's strategic importance has made it a witness to the race between two giant neighbours vying for supremacy.[2] Myanmar has had experiences of varried administrations – domestic policies have ranged from civilian rule to a socialist military junta, a military-dominated socialist single-party mobilization system along an East European model to an authoritarian military regime and in 2011 a 'discipline-flourishing democracy'. These varied administrations have largely influenced its foreign policy, especially Sino-Burmese relations. All have had profound implications on the strategic concerns between China and Myanmar.

China is cynical about India's LEP and its stance on the policy often exhibits its scepticism about Indian presence and influence in South-East Asia. Certain factors justify China's reservations about India's major role in the Asia-Pacific region. India's close cultural and spiritual liaison with South-East Asia poses threat to China's overriding dominance in the region. On the contrary, the close proximities in area of soft-power resources make the South East Asian neighbours more integrally related to India. Even though some Chinese scholars portray India as not being part of Asia and that the Chinese culture has a much greater influence than India's, they cannot undermine the fact that Indian culture has had an abiding influence on the region and India's attempt to rediscover Asia through the LEP substantiates that. China knows that India is the only country in Asia that could possibly challenge its domineering supremacy and political hegemony and therefore it exerts a vigorous attempt to restrain India's outreach in the region. Traditionally China had been dismissive of India, which it treated as a mere South Asian player. However, over the last decade the impressive rate of India's economic growth and its political stability drawing international attention has somewhat bewildered as well as perturbed the Chinese.

Therefore China is apprehensive about India's increasing involvement in South-East Asia. Beijing is anxious of India's rising political and military clout in Asia as it would constrain its ambition of controlling the power dynamics of the region.[3]

The bilateral relations between China and Myanmar had been on a consistent rise since the independence of Burma in 1948 and the founding of the People's Republic of China in 1949. This was of strategic relevance for both the countries as well as for the South-East Asian region, though the equations for the first forty years were under the penumbra of Cold War power politics and were also tuned in accordance with the formulation and reformulation of Chinese domestic and foreign policies. The post-Cold War power politics witnessed the emergence of a different set of traditional and non-traditional concerns involving the interplay of both strategic and economic interests. Myanmar as a core in Sino-Indian relations assumed a pioneering role. Myanmar's utmost dependence on China was an offshoot of certain geo-political considerations. But there prevail certain misinterpretations and over-simplified notions about the intricacies of the bilateral equations:

- Myanmar is a client state of China and that Chinese influence is monolithic.
- China is so dominant that the current and any future Burmese administration will be entirely dependent on its northern neighbour.
- Every move by the Chinese is part of a calculated plan to advance their power and interests in Myanmar.
- Burmese democratization is entirely dependent on Chinese attitudes.
- Chinese perception that the US policy changes towards Myanmar under the Obama administration were attempts to encircle China.
- The previous US policy of 'regime change' in Myanmar did not succeed because of Chinese support to the military junta.[4]

Though Sino-Myanmar relations are longstanding and their cultural heritage is enduring there are certain hiccups in the relations too. There have been apparent disagreements and differences on issues related to Myanmar between Kunming and Beijing and even between Kunming and Yunnan provinces. Myanmar and assorted military interests have been deviated especially in the Sino-Burmese border areas. And as Myanmar enters a democratic era, new and potentially ambiguous relationships might emerge affecting Chinese holdings in those regions.[5]

Another irritant for China in this aspect is the shift in the ASEAN stance, particularly after the recent assertiveness of China over the South China Sea. Beijing now realizes that the ASEAN nations are keen to balance their ties with a 'rising' China with support for the US presence in Asia as well as with the growing involvement of India. It is being asserted by China that the US is now on a course of containment of China with the help of allies and partners like India and Japan. Such perception has an impact on the precept of India's LEP. What has rattled the Chinese is India's close proximity with Vietnam. India's growing involvement in the Asia-Pacific region, more particularly the LEP, poses threat to China's growing aspiration as it contributes to a more balanced Asia where each country can pursue its legitimate interests without disturbing other's security thereby creating a stable regional order. China will fret about LEP but eventually it will have to accept it as a legitimate pursuit of India's interests as it has done in the case of India's participation in the Regional Comprehensive Economic Partnership that the ASEAN has floated and will soon begin negotiations for. It has come to see that the Parternship does not threaten China's security or legitimate interests, it only opposes Beijing's irredentist claims.[6]

Energy is the key resource for any country to grow and prosper. Myanmar is the repository of this asset and it uses its strategic leverage to gain economic growth to sustain its political system. Myanmar encourages the competition between China and India. The 2006-7 bidding war between India and

China for the Shwe project demonstrates Myanmar's importance in the growth of both countries. Myanmar appears to be rebalancing its ties with China and this rebalancing was vividly demonstrated in the suspension of the China-funded Myitsone Dam project. The dam, at the confluence of the Mayhka and Malikha rivers that form the Irrawaddy River – Myanmar's boon – was a vital one. With a reservoir the size of Singapore it would have flooded a sizeable Kachin population in an area that is regarded as a site of cultural importance. Protests been slaged and some bombings have taken place in the vicinity of the construction as it is causing environmental degradation. The Kachins have mobilized against this construction undertaken by the China Power Investment Corporation. China was to construct the dam at an initial cost of US $3.6 billion operate it for fifty years under a BOT transfer agreement and most of the electricity would go to China while Myanmar would collect substantial revenues from it – about US $54 billion over fifty years. On 30 September Myanmar's President Thein Sein announced the decison to suspend the Myitsone Dam because the project was 'against the will of the people'.[7] This is an unprecedented concession to popular opinion – unknown in half a century of military rule. In so doing, Naypyidaw seems to be stepping out of China's shadow, while carefully maintaining the strategic relationship with Beijing. It is significant to mention that Myanmar's chairmanship over the ASEAN in 2014 had profound relevance for the ASEAN as it has for China. While it accommodates China's regional strategic interests, it resists Chinese influence and interference in Myanmar's internal affairs when necessary. Certain impediments like border instability, growing resentment against Chinese dominance in Myanmar, unstable and weak Myanmar governance and growing international pressure on China might constrain the Chinese goal of exerting supremacy in Myanmar.[8] Myanmar's lack of expertise and knowledge on economic planning makes China's investments insecure. In 2007, China tried to establish Special Economic Zones (SEZ), but Myanmar's incompetence in comprehending the SEZ concept resulted in its failure to pass a law that would have ensured economic growth. Recent media reports communicate the intense interest of many countries including the US in exploring potential areas of collaboration with Myanmar. At this critical juncture India's cooperation is vital to Myanmar's reform projects in a wide range of areas such as telecommunications, education, trade and commerce, agriculture and IT. From an Indian perspective, Myanmar is an open door to South Asia and South-East Asia. From a Chinese perspective, Myanmar presents an untapped market, alternative routes for natural resources, and stronger influence in the region.[9] Against this backdrop the geographical advantage between India and Myanmar can dynamize the essence of cooperation, especially in the highly competitive geo-political atmosphere wherein countries like Japan, Korea, the United States of America, Norway, China, Thailand and Malaysia are all rushing to Myanmar driven by self-interest be it geo-strategic, commercial, political or military.

INDIA'S MYANMAR ENGAGEMENT

India's cooperative ventures with SEA encompass its renewed thrust in strengthening and deepening cooperation with Myanmar. 'As in the past, so in the future, the people of India will stand shoulder to shoulder with the people of Burma, and whether we have to share good fortune or ill fortune, we shall share it together', stated Prime Minister Jawaharlal Nehru on Myanmar's independence in 1948.[10] But with a coastline of 1,930 km, wide open on the Andaman Sea and the Bay of Bengal, facing the Indian territories of the Andaman and Nicobar Islands, Myanmar poses a strong strategic challenge to New Delhi. Thus, the control of cross-border insurgency and trans-border drug trafficking constitute an important dimension in the bilateral relations between New Delhi and Yangon and both these countries signed a treaty of friendship in 1951, a boundary agreement in 1967 and a maritime boundary delimitation agreement in 1986 in order to reduce cross-border insurgency and drug-trafficking.[11] The entry of Myanmar into the ASEAN has provided India a land boundary to go its long maritime boundary with the South-East Asian region. Myanmar, located between South and South-East Asia, is a natural bridge linking the two regions and by forming new communication links India can be connected to locations in the South-East Asian heartland and beyond. India's plan to draw on its historic links and develop its common land border with Myanmar to reduce the poverty and underdevelopment in the NER is a strategic initiative to enrich its cooperation with Yangon. Development of better ties with Myanmar may largely reduce cross-border drug trafficking and separatist insurgencies in the NER. So in early 2000, India-Myanmar relations received a new momentum.[12]

India's policy of reinforcing engagements with Myanmar is governed by crucial factors as boosting bilateral economic ties, seeking Myanmar government's critical cooperation in addressing the plaguing problem of insurgency in the NER, and checkmating China's overwhelming dominance in Myanmar. It is noteworthy to mention here that Myanmar's abundant resources, particularly natural gas can boost up the pace of mutual cooperation with India, the country starving for energy.[13] Moreover, there is an imperative of the synchronization of India's Myanmar policy for the substantial contribution by Manipur of the NER to the LEP.[14] Thus stabilizing the North-East Region of India, its clandestine flows and foreign connections taking advantage of the proximity of South-East Asian nations, especially Myanmar, to advance into the Asian diplomatic and economic scene and finally, measuring the impact of China's influence on the Myanmar regime and its consequences for the country's interests have been the primary determinants of India's Myanmar engagements.[15]

Myanmar is the only land bridge between SEA and India and is the largest country of SEA covering about 6,78,000 sq km. On 30 March 2011, the formation of the new government resulted in the formulation of procedures and reforms in economic policies, which were largely the off-shoots of past experiences. There is considerable scope for India to assume a vital role in the changing political, economic and strategic future of Myanmar. Myanmar's strategically important geographic location is crucial to its economic relations with India. The Indian policy towards Myanmar was throughout these important years a bit perplexing as Myanmar's disinclination towards democracy and democratic ideals made it difficult to cultivate bilateral relations with an important neighbour, India when India promised to look East.[16] But now the political transition in Myanmar is a positive yardstick of healthier and more cooperative ties between India and Myanmar.

The increasing Chinese influence in Myanmar and Myanmar's increasing relevance in the context of India's Look East Policy largely inspired India to flourish its relations with Myanmar.[17] As Myanmar is opening up again, the question that crops up is whether India or China would be Myanmar's primary link to the wider world.[18] The inclusion of Myanmar as one of the member countries of the ASEAN in the year 1997 accords extra momentum to India's NER. India has undertaken encouraging initiatives such as the development of infrastructure facilities in the NER as well as in Myanmar and military assistance rendered to the Myanmar government to make the border between the two countries an area of peace and tranquility. The imbroglio of ethnic insurrections, tribal rebellions and uncontrolled trafficking is a source of major instability in the NER and the internationalization of these secessionist movements has contributed to the worsening of security problems in India and Myanmar. Cooperation between the two countries was a prerequisite for securing the region. India needs Myanmar's cooperation to stabilize the insurgency situation in the NER. India has urged the Myanmar government to put an end to the sheltering, and providing financial and military aid to the India rebels. Myanmar has also communicated its enthusiasm to lend support to India in order to suppress the Burmese Kachin, Naga and Chin insurrections that have nexus with the Indian insurgents. The first joint counter-insurgency led by the Indian Army notably the

Assam Rifles, and the Burmese army took place in April 1995. The Golden Bird Operation, executed by the Chiefs of Staff of the two countries, was intended to dismantle the ULFA, PLA and NSCN-IM forces on the Indian side and the Chin National Front on the Myanmar side. The offensive dealt a mortal blow to senior members of the two terrorist factions, both of which had accumulated a considerable stockpile of arms on the Arakan coast and were in the attempt to transport them to their bases via the Kaladan River.[19]

Myanmar's reciprocity to these geographical and natural advantages is highly acknowledged and the potentials of the country required to be utilized to avail the competitive advantages brought about by regional and global market chain have also been recognized. India needs a set of strong and proactive neighbourhood policies in which Myanmar must play an immensely significant part. To promote bilateral cooperation India needs to prioritize the bilateral approach to an instrumental orientation, encourage competition instrumental in enhancing engagement and must be oriented towards consistent bilateralism and successful multilateralism. As a neighbour Myanmar is important not only for the Look East Policy but due to other priorities as well. There is competition with China but it should not only be the guiding spirit of a healthy engagement with an important neighbour. Myanmar's advantageous geo-strategic location provides an impetus to evolving India-ASEAN relations as the country is India's gateway to further development of collaboration with South-East Asia. There should be a strong mutual urge to build upon this cooperation in order to ensure strong neighbourly relations with India.

The 'Malacca Dilemma' plays an immensely vital role in China's relation with Myanmar. China is heavily dependent on foreign oil and approximately 80 per cent of these oil imports currently pass through the Straits of Malacca, near Singapore, one of the busiest shipping lanes in the world and just 1.7 mile across at the narrowest point. For the Chinese strategists, the straits are a natural chokepoint through which future enemies could cut off foreign energy supplies. Thus an alternative route needs to be found and Myanmar is the key.[20] The work on an oil and gas pipeline, which is supposed to pet implemented in 2017, would start to transport Myanmar's newly found offshore gas to China's Yunnan province, as well as oil from the Middle East and Africa. It is a strategic barrier against the Straits of Malacca that might bring Chinese political influence right upto the Indian Ocean for the first time in history.[21] Increasing Chinese forays into Myanmarese territory were worrisome for India and the Chinese supremacy and authority in Myanmar were unacceptable to New Delhi. So India began to compete with Beijing for securing access to and influence in Myanmar. The Indian government had embarked upon improving connectivity and infrastructure and boosting up of the investments with Myanmar. There perhaps exists a natural or historical communication or pull towards India which is missing towards China. Since 1993 India has been pursuing a realistic policy by redefining its stone towards Myanmar, setting aside its criticism of the Myanmar generals and its support to the Myanmar's democratic movements.[22]

Indian interests in Myanmar can be summarized by the following considerations:

- Containment of Chinese economic and strategic influences in South-East Asia in general and Myanmar in particular.
- Guiding Myanmar in exploring her rich gas fields and thereby exploiting the energy resources.
- Getting the Myanmar government to come down heavily on the North-East's insurgents and rebel groups that have taken shelter and been pursuing violent activities there.
- To obtain inter-modal transit facility for the goods and services being traded between India and South-East Asian countries.

These considerations led India to enter into a number of significant economic arrangements with Myanmar. Though the expansion of trade between the two neighbours has taken place at a considerable rate the share of the NER is negligible.[23]

Both these countries opened up border trade on 12 April 1995. According to this arrangement, trade is conducted through two points – one is the Moreh (Manipur) – Tamu (Myanmar) point and another is Champai (Mizoram) and Rhi (Myanmar) points. It was expected that the volume of trade would be around INR 3-10 billion annually.[24] Four NER states – Arunachal Pradesh, Mizoram, Nagaland and Manipur – share India's international border with Myanmar spanning 1,643 km. The Look East Policy is focused on the economic advancement of the states of the NER and the gradual economic integration of the latter with Myanmar and the suppression of any anti-India activities on Myanmar soil. In fact, one of the major factors that caused a shift in India's policy towards Myanmar was security concern. During World War II, K.M. Pannikar, a historian and a strategist par excellence explained Myanmar's strategic significance to India thus:

> The defence of Burma in fact is the defence of India's primary concern no less than Burma's to see that its frontiers remain inviolate. In fact, no responsibility can be considered too heavy for India when it comes to the question of defending Burma.[25]

SINO-MYANMAR COOPERATION

Untoward incidents like the military coup and the killing of students in 1988 in Rangoon, as well as the killings of Chinese students during the Tiananmen crisis in June 1989, evoked severe international criticism and elicited Western economic sanctions. The West's diplomatic isolation of Myanmar opened up new arenas of opportunities for Beijing to fill the strategic vacuum in Myanmar and forward collaboration with it. The geographic location does bear strategically important connotations for China as Burma is the land bridge for the People's Liberation Army Navy (PLAN) in the long term to reach the Indian Ocean via the Myanmar-controlled Coco Islands, which are about 30 km north of the Indian-controlled Andaman Islands. By the year 2050, China is expected to achieve world-class blue water navy status.[26] Myanmar's importance lies in providing China achieve direct access to the Pacific and the Indian oceans. In 1994, Japanese sources reported that China had completed the construction of radar and electronic surveillance facilities on the Coco Islands, which were on lease to China.[27] There was also a report that China and Myanmar were interested in joint development of a deep-water port at Kyaukpyu on Ramree Islands in the Bay of Bengal.[28] Furthermore, the alleged military installation at the Zadetkyi Island on Myanmar's southern tip close to Indonesia's Sabang Island, (off northern Aceh in Sumatra) raised considerable skepticism about China's future maritime ambitions in the Indian Ocean.[29] Thus China's bilateral equation with Myanmar is an imperative factor in the long-term strategic interests of India. Myanmar's overt inclination towards China since its entente with the neighbour from 1989 onwards (particularly after the installation of the military regime in Myanmar in 1988) was in a way reciprocation of China's foreign policy objectives towards Myanmar.[30] China's foreign policy pursuits with Myanmar emphasize certain significant paradigms as ensuring a stable external environment with this resourceful neighbour which would foster China's domestic modernization and development policy. China's cooperation with Myanmar can be evaluated as a strategy of keeping up the momentum of Bandung's policy of peaceful coexistence with its neighbours. Moreover, China considers Myanmar as a gateway to restore its southwest Silk Road from Yunnan province to Myanmar and westward to Bangladesh, India and the West. The development of this connectivity would accelerate bilateral trade by promoting the backward economies in the south-western part of inland China. Myanmar can incentivize China's Western Development Strategy as the realization of ASEAN Free Trade Area (AFTA) might provide Kunming with the probability of benefiting economically by getting connected to Myanmar for commercial purposes. The motive behind the link is to diminish the magnitude of economic disparities between China's affluent coastal and its own poverty-stricken inland provinces in the sout-west.

The growing importance of Yunnan in Sino-Myanmar economic cooperation became all the more discernible in November 1989, a year after the military coup, when the SLORC signed a multiple trade and economic agreement with the Yunnan authorities, including geological surveys, coal and tin mining and a television station.[31] A month later, in December 1989, the two countries signed an economic and technical cooperation agreement in which China agreed to offer an interest-free loan of Rmb 50 million (US $15 million) for the Rangoon-Thanhy in rail and road bridge construction project.[32]

China and Myanmar have made noteworthy headway in connectivity and infrastructure development. The roads of Kunming-Ruili-Yangon and Kunming-Tengchong-Myanmar-India are actually the updated versions of the Burma Road and the Stilwell Road. In recent years, Beijing and Yunnan have built and upgraded some roads in Yunnan extending to Myanmar and some leading to Yunnan in Myanmar territory. The built roads of China-Myanmar Transport Corridor are Kunming-An Ning Highway, An Ning-Chu Xiong Highway, Chuxiong-Dali Highway, Dali-Baoshan Highway, Baoshan-Longling Highway, Longling-Ruili Highway, Baoshan-Tengchong Highway, Tengchong-Myitkyina, Jinghong-Damenglong, Zhangfeng-Bhamo, Yingjiang-Nabang, Tengchong-Banwa highways. Besides the trunk highway stretching to Myanmar, China has built and developed many roads to Sino-Myanmar border ports, such as Jinghong-Da Menglong, Zhangfeng-Bhamo, Tengchong-Banwa, and Yingjing-Banwa, especially since 2005 when Yunnan began to implement the project of 'Prosper the Borders to Enrich Local People' (PBELP). In May 2008, a new three-year project of PBELP in Yunnan was conceptualized. The driving force of the project was the construction of a defence highway and the 'Yunnan International Passage', as well as expediting the construction of the highway net, developing the roads and striving for the completion of the 750-km trunk highway and 2,100 km of county roads in border region, gradually solving the transport bottleneck thwarting frontier development. In response,

Yunnan has pooled of 10.71847 billion Yuan for the new initiative.[33]

Premier Wen Jiabao visited Myanmar on 2 and 3 June 2010, which ceremoniously marked the 60th anniversary of the commencement of diplomatic relations between the two countries. During the two-day visit, the two premiers formally launched the construction of the Sino-Myanmar oil and gas pipeline project. China's official *People's Daily* on 5 June reported that 'there are 793 km of gas pipeline in Myanmar, and also a 771 km long crude oil pipeline. An oil port in Kyaukpyu as a facility is to be built for the planned China-Myanmar oil pipeline project'. The pipeline project will promote infrastructure facilities, particularly roads along the pipelines in Myanmar. The two countries, for example, signed an MoU on the development of cooperation in the Sino-Myanmar Corridor Project to link Ruli and Kyaukpyu, on 18 May 2010. According to the Corridor Project, China will help Myanmar construct railway and motorway from Kyaukphyu Township of Rakhine State to Ruili in China. The implementation of One Belt One Road (OBOR) will perhaps give a lease of life to the China initiated projected. It helps China to secure the supply of semi-finished materials for its growing economy.[34] The Kyaukphyu project is set in the troubled south-western province Rakhine in Myanmar. The Kyaukphyu SEZ project was awarded to a six-member international consortium headed by one of China's biggest conglomerates, Citic Group in December 2015. Four other Chinese industrial and investment groups and one of Thailand's biggest conglomerates, Charoen Phokphand, are among other members of the consortium. The project is expected to contribute about $10 billion to Myanmar's annual GDP by 2025, while 90 per cent of the project managers would be Myanmar citizens. The Kyaukphyu project is expected to provide China an effective connectivity with the Indian Ocean than any of the so-called 'string of pearls', including the Gwadar port in Pakistan. The current military government of Myanmar has set aside 1,708 hectares (4289.32 acres) for the SEZ, which would comprise two deep-sea ports of 148 hectares and 95 hectares, a 978-hectare industrial zone, and a high-end housing project covering 494 hectares. The project is close to the landing point of the dual pipeline that transports gas and crude oil to China. During President Thein Sein's visit to Beijing in May 2011, a Memorandum of Understanding (MoU) was signed between Myanmar's rail transport ministry and China's state-owned Railway Engineering Corporation to build a rail line linking Kyaukphyu with Kunming, capital of the Yunnan province of China. Later, in July 2014, it was announced by the construction ministry of Myanmar that the No. 2 Union Highway and the Kyaukphyu-Magway route would be promoted for better connectivity with the SEZ. Since Kyaukphyu SEZ is an economic-cum-strategic asset for China, it is cautious about local sentiment as it has faced local resistance in Myanmar earlier. Efforts have been undertaken to ensure that the Chinese-led consortium collaborates with the Myanmar government and upholds the interests of the local community.[35] China is careful of the regime change in Myanmar. It has had good equations with the military regime and conducted a number of trade and commercial activities with Myanmar. It had faced trouble in the form of local protests against the Letpadaung copper mine project in the northwest of Myanmar. Before, in 2010, Myanmar government had to suspend a $3.6 billion Chinese-led Myitsone dam project because of local opposition, as almost 90 per cent of the power was expected to have gone to China. Given its intense strategic value Beijing is very proactive in implementing its Kyaukphyu project and is mindful of the imminent hurdles.[36]

Sino-Myanmar railway will become one part of the 'Third Asia Europe Continental Bridge' conceived by China, connecting the east coast of the Atlantic Ocean with China's east coast via Yunnan. In South-East Asia and South Asia, both China and Myanmar have joined in China-ASEAN Free Trade Area, Great Mekong Subregion Cooperation (GMS), Bangladesh-China-India-Myanmar regional cooperation (BCIM). The two sub-regional development schemes are meant to boost economic development in the Yunna province and across the border. The construction of the Sino-Myanmar Transport Corridor accredits Yunnan the merit of promoting its transportation facilities and booming its political and economic status in China by acting as an access to the Indian Ocean. China's influence in Myanmar thus is often being connoted as a ploy to exert its dominance in both the Pacific and Indian oceans.[37] On 3 October 1988, Yangon legitimized and formalized the border trade with China and set up border trade offices in Lashio, Muse, Namkham and Kunlong. Myanmar started the implementation of the border trade system in 1991 with China and India. Upto 2009 Myanmar had opened four border trading posts with China points with China namely, Muse (opened on 21 January 1998), Lwejel (23 August 1998), Chinahwehaw (19 October 2003) and Kambaiti (reopened on 1 August 2009). Kambaiti and Laiza trading points were temporarily closed in June 2006. Myanmar has been working to transform border trade with China into a normal one to enhance the bilateral commercial interest between two countries. Myanmar will from 2016-21 add one more border trade point in the Kokang region built in Yan Loe Chai Township to facilitate trading between that region and Yunnan.

China's policies on border trading have also experienced adjustment and reorientation. In 1988 the Yunnan government formulated the policy of making full use of its geographical and resource advantages to develop South-East Asian markets.[38] Individual countries and autonomous prefectures in Yunnan have their own interests as well. The potential economic problem of refugees flooding into border areas was amply illustrated in the August 2009 Kokang affair when 37,000 fled into Yunnan. 'However some country authorities in Yunnan province and some Chinese companies have signed natural resource exploitation agreements with ceasefire groups in the northern part of Myanmar. This phenomenon persists even though China's central government forbids it.'[39]

Yunnan's energy requirement is a prime consideration in its economic needs, which in turn, is a driving force behind its strategic moves towards Myanmar. Not only has increasing access to Myanmar's energy profited Yunnan directly in terms of business, investment, energy supply and employment it also enables the province to benefit economically by supplying other provinces in the region – Guangxi, Guiztou, etc. – with energy they lack but need. Yunnan is thus a critical factor in advocating the Myanmar oil pipeline and was the first its propose it, thus strongly influencing Beijing's decision to proceed. Yunnanese trade banks on Myanmar for commercial purposes. Yunnan's progress to rise from one of the poorer provinces of China is thus largely being influenced by Myanmar's relations. In terms of transportation, Myanmar is an important avenue for Yunnan to have access to South Asia and to the Indian Ocean too. In terms of resources, Myanmar is rich in oil, gas, timber and gemstones. In terms of border security, initiatives like countering narcotic trafficking, money laundering and smuggling of arms are yardsticks of cooperation for both the countries. Myanmar is therefore considerably relevant in China's strategic design to develop its western region.

INDIA'S NORTH-EAST AND MYANMAR

The geographic location of India's NER is of crucial importance in the context of India's LEP (which is the main thrust of this chapter). The North-East of India is a diverse area with disparate characteristics and is the point where South Asia geographically integrates with SEA or vice-versa.[40] The North-Eastern states are situated between 22° 19' and 28° 16' N longitude and 89° 42' and 97° 12' E latitude. They are is surrounded in the north by Tibet, China and Bhutan and in the south by Bangladesh and Myanmar and on the east by China and Myanmar and on the west by West Bengal and Bangladesh, having an area of 2,55,089 sq km which is about 7.8 per cent of the all-India area of 32,87,089 sq km.[41] North-East India, consisting of contiguous seven sister states – Arunachal Pradesh, Assam, Manipur, Meghalaya, Mizoram, Nagaland, Tripura – and the state of Sikkim, constitutes a distinctive corridor connecting the Indian subcontinent to East and South-East Asia, thereby forming an exclusive possibility for human migration between these areas. Thus being cradled by the Himalayas in the north and the Bay of Bengal in the south the NER is being cited as a gateway to SEA. Except for Sikkim, the other states are geographically contiguous and have enjoyed economic and political relationships with each other over centuries.[42]

The current policy literature on the North-East is focused on the much-trumpeted LEP of the Indian government. Opening up the natural outlet for the North-East has been one of the foremost concerns for the Government of India. Indeed, even some of the most controversial debates regarding the artificiality of the colonial boundaries have found their way into the argument that the government should actually allow this natural economic region to prosper without the constraints of national boundaries.[43] With the motive of developing the NER by initiating certain developmental strategies like encouraging investment possibilities, alleviating poverty and boosting up the connectivity facilities Indian Prime Minister, Manmohan Singh, in July 2008 released the document 'North-Eastern Region Vision 2020'. It was a serious effort undertaken for the socio-economic development of this region to match with the objectives of the LEP.[44] Economic development experts opine that the proper balancing of the pro-market policies would eventually lead the underdeveloped countries to prosper. But the main problem lies in the geographic location, not in the policy formulation. Tropical landlocked regions never enjoy access to the markets and modern technologies which are the basic requisites to flourish in the global economy.[45] India's NER is where South and South-East Asia converge to form new identities based on respective traditions and possessing their own distinctiveness.[46] The NER, according to PM Manmohan Singh's 'Vision 2020' is perceived to be developed in such a way that the commodities by catering to the prospering foreign markets in the ASEAN countries can yield substantive commercial gains.[47]

INITIATIVES AND PROJECTS

India has pioneered a number of infrastructure projects in order to provide impetus to the political, economic and strategic aspects of the LEP. Among the notable joint initiatives undertaken, the ASEAN-India Car Rally of 2004 deserves to be mentioned. It was a decisive endeavour undertaken by the Indian government to focus on the geographic proximity between North-East India and SEA. The rally, flagged off from Guwahati travelled through Myanmar, Thailand, Laos, Vietnam, Cambodia, Malaysia and Singapore over a period of 20 days, before concluding at Batam, Indonesia, on 11 December 2004.[48] Indian Prime Minister Dr. Singh referred to India's North-East as the gateway to the 'Asian Century' while inaugurating the Asian Car Rally, which is deemed to be a successful Look East Policy pursuit. This rally uphold the credibility of the NER to be the commercial corridor of India linking the ASEAN nations and by enabling its people to harvest economic well-being through trade, transit and tourism. The success of the car rally event of 2004 inspired the flagging of another car rally initiative in December 2012 from Guwahati.

In addition to the car rally, India has undertaken considerable bilateral and multilateral projects for promoting connectivity between the NER and SEA. The orientation has successfully advanced from 'Look' to 'Link' East. The important ongoing and potential infrastructure projects in this regard are the Moreh-Tamu-Kalewa Road, India-Myanmar-Thailand Trilateral Highway, Trans-Asian Highway, India-Myanmar rail linkages, Kaladan Multimodal Project, the Stilwell road, Myanmar-India-Bangladesh gas or oil pipeline, Tamanthi Hydroelectricity Project and optical fiber network between North-East India and South-East Asia.[49] India and Myanmar have jointly ventured into building the Sittwe port, which is situated on the western coast of Myanmar, and it can constitute a significant milestone in the LEP. To implement the project India has decided to spend about US $10 million rebuilding this port and making the Kaladan river navigable. This would provide a new access not only for the NER but also for the rest of India to the rest of SEA.[50] The project was planned to be launched in 2007 and the tentative period for the completion of the project is 2019. There would be a modern port at Sittwe, the Kaladan river at Mizoram would be navigable providing the NER with an alternative route for engagement with Myanmar and the rest of Asia. So the NER will then be integrated via Sittwe into India and it will also have integration with the rest of SEA.[51] It would provide further fillip to highway projects like the Asian Trilateral Highway, which encompasses Thailand, Myanmar and North-East India. This would result not only in road integration but integration of the transportation network of Asia and India, which would ultimately lead to rail link from Kolkata to Hanoi via India's North-East. Efforts are being made to initiate a rail link from Jiribam in Manipur to Hanoi in Vietnam passing through Myanmar. In 2006, a proposal for a bus service between Imphal and Mandalay was considered and accepted by the Indian government. The proposal was reiterated with renewed emphasis during the PM's visit to Naypyidaw in 2012. The trial-run of the bus since was flagged off on 9 December 2015.

There lies an extensive possibility for the NER to be a potential beneficiary of India's LEP in two significant ways. The region enjoys ample scope to gain if the trade is conducted over land across the region. The region has the propensity to benefit directly from it through the enhancing of its proportion in the commodity composition in the thriving markets of SEA besides enjoying its direct spill-over effects. Secondly, the LEP can also promote the region, if it is oriented to invoke and emphasize geographical and cultural continuities between South and SEA by encouraging human movements across the international borders.[52] That would be an incentive for the Indian business sector too. The businesses which are ambitious and enthusiastic to acquire global access will find profitable share in these markets. Export will boom due to favourable factors such as low tariffs, collaborative pacts and agreements and Free Trade Agreements. It is glaringly evident that the accomplishment of the policy leading to the overall development of the region largely depends on the proper implementation of the projects proposed or undertaken jointly by India and ASEAN. Some of the important India-ASEAN projects can be evaluated in terms of their effectiveness in furthering India's LEP.

INDIA-MYANMAR-THAILAND TRILATERAL HIGHWAY

The Trilateral Highway project is a somewhat ambitious endeavour, which was initially undertaken under the initiatives of the Mekong-Ganga Cooperation (MGC) and later shifted to the transport sector of the Bay of Bengal Initiative for Multi-Sectoral Technical and Economic Cooperation (BIMSTEC) but till date it has not yielded any positive outcomes. With the motive to commence the project in early 2004, the construction of the 1,360 km highway at the cost of US $700 million was divided into three phases so as to connect Moreh (India), Mae Sot (Thailand) through Bagan in Myanmar. The motto behind the construction of the road was to serve the cardinal purpose of establishing a connection between North-East India and SEA. The project unfortunately has faced multiple problems along with acute financial constraints. India and Thailand have upgraded some of the link roads but due to lack of adequate funds in Myanmar, much work remains incomplete. Tensions have also flared due to Myanmar's demand for India and Thailand taking up the responsibility of bearing the costs of road construction in its territory. Moreover, there are certain crippling security issues in the region. Most crucial are the problems in India-Myanmar border regions, which are often severely afflicted by hazards like illegal trade, drug trafficking and insurgencies. Another tension crops up with China's overarching control over Kachin state, bordering the Indian state of Arunachal Pradesh, which China claims as its territory and it is apprehended that the commencement of the

Trilateral Highway could flood the state with Chinese goods and illegal weapons thereby hampering the security interests of India. Those have always been concerning factors for India, but the prospects of accruing long-term benefits from the highways are significant especially for India to secure its foothold in Myanmar. For India, however, the realization of the Trilateral Highway will be a bag of mixed opportunities. The project raises concern on its final destination as well, that is the Myanmar-Thailand border where ethnic insurgent camps are still in existence. Myanmar in the past had been sceptical of Thailand for safeguarding groups like the Karen National Union and the Chin National Liberation Front. The cross-border infrastructure has also been hindered due to Thailand's apprehension about the negative impact of the steady inflow of illegal immigrants and the rampant narcotic business. Apart from all these practical impediments in the pursuit of the Trilateral Highway the presence of profound tenets of regionalism could also be cited as a considerable reason for the delay. The quicker integration of the Greater Mekong Subregion (GMS) has overshadowed the performance of other regional organizations like the BIMSTEC and the MGC. While cross-border connectivity has been boosted between the GMS countries, it has considerably eroded the scope of projects like the Trilateral Highway as the Mekong region countries are increasingly getting entrapped into the economic clutches of China. Presently the GMS countries' concentration is on the upgradation and the construction of new highways under the Asian Highway Project and already approximately US $2.7 billion has been invested in this initiative.[53] The East-West Corridor, the North-South Economic Corridor and the Southern Economic Corridor are the three major projects being administered. The development of these highways and ratification of Cross-Border Transport Agreement (CBTA) have since quadrupled the intra-GMS trade. It is appalling to notice the inadequacy of the Trilateral Highway initiative due to severe political and financial incongruities. It is highly expected that the completion of the Trilateral Highway will promote greater connectivity between India and South-East Asia and the positives will inevitably outweigh the negatives in every sense. Connectivity will certainly open up vistas of cooperation with the neighbouring states and provide effective mechanisms for dealing with cross-border problems which hitherto have remained unresolved. Additionally, since the Trilateral Highway will connect India to the Asian Highway Network the prospect of booming trade between India and ASEAN is quite high and it will thereby accelerate the trade potentialities of India, Myanmar and Thailand which is mostly maritime in nature. Moreover, India's NER will function as a competent hub of trade and commerce. It is evidently reasonable to state that the development of the Trilateral Highway is an imperative greatly required for the success of the LEP and its failure might shake the edifice of the enterprising venture which India has embarked upon.[54] Therefore India needs to be more proactive in implementing this project since considerable progress from its counterparts, Thailand and Myanmar, has been made and India needs to catch up. Recent media reports communicate that Myanmar and Thailand have made considerable headway in their parts to promote this highway but there are lacunae in the case of India due to certain political issues claiming immediate attention.

MOREH–TAMU–KALEWA ROAD

There are two or more semi-official border crossings between India and Myanmar which can be used by the locals only. One of them is from Tamu on the Myanmar side to Moreh (Morei) in Manipur on the India side. The road NH 39 stretches from Moreh to Imphal and on to Delhi. On the Myanmar side there are roads connecting Tamu to Mandalay and ultimately Tachileik on the Thai border. India in its quest to stimulate its LEP and Thailand for the purpose of boosting trade aims to upgrade this route and enhance commerce between the two countries. India has even upgraded the road from Tamu to Kalewa, about 150 km inside Myanmar. But due to major shortcomings like the spiraling problem of insurgency, poor infrastructure, preference of sea route over land routes, the influence of various pressure groups, frequent bandhs and blockades, overarching uncertainties among the trading communities, the absence of proper electricity supply, telephone, internet and banking system in the Moreh-Tamu area, the route from India to Thailand through Myanmar is far from a realistic realization. The border area is the fulcrum of illegal transactions too. Thus the practical scenario is that there is no concrete land route between India and Thailand and no viable land – or water – route between India and its strategically significant neighbour, Myanmar.[55]

At the diplomatic level, the arrival of the Minister of External Affairs, Shri Jaswant Singh in Myanmar on 13-15 February 2001, marked an imprint in India's Myanmar policy. The momentous angle of this visit was the fact that the Indian delegation went to Myanmar by road for the first time.[56] On 13 February 2001, Jaswant Singh, along with Burmese military officials, inaugurated the only legal border custom post, opened along the 1,643 km long common borders. The city of Moreh got connected to the Myanmar city of Tamu (Sagaing Division).[57] India financed the construction of 160 km of the road leaving Tamu towards Mandalay, which ends in Kalewa, and Myanmar was entrusted with the responsibility of the planning and undertaking the rest of the construction by itself.[58] The ₹90-crore road built by India's Border Road Organisation was India's gift to Myanmar. In his speech, inaugurating the road, the honourable minister said that 'the natural movement of goods, people and services for the North East is not through Calcutta;' and he described the importance of 'opening up the natural outlet of the North-East'.[59] The project received a breakthrough in April 2002, when Jaswant Singh again visited Myanmar to meet both the Myanmar military representatives and Thai officials who were intensely interested in the construction of a commercial route linking India with Indochina via Mandalay and Myanmar. The highway project linking the countries was signed on 6 April

2002 in Yangon. Myanmar was deeply satisfied with this triangular economic partnership. It was agreed upon by Thailand to finance the work from its border to Mandalay and India decided to be in charge of the other side of the stretch. It was scheduled to open in 2016 but set delayed by few months.[60] Strong political will and determination of all the three countries are the basic prerequisites for the steady implementation of the project.

It is through the Chin state that the India-Myanmar Friendship Road (financed by India) passes, from the border crossing point of Moreh (Manipur, India) and Tamu (Sagaing Division, Myanmar) down to the Chin cities of Kalewa and Kalemyo in the Chindwin valley.[61] It is often alleged that Myanmar is one of the main drug trafficking centres in the world.[62] Most of the ethnic and political insurrections in the NER and Myanmar are widely involved in the drug-trafficking network. There is dearth of reliable data on the drug routes from western Myanmar to NER and Bangladesh, whereas the drug framework in northern Myanmar is quite popular. India is also a producer of caffeine and ephedrine as well as of codeine, products that are exported to Myanmar. The processed drugs are routed to Kolkata and Cox's Bazar (the Bangladesh port). Since the late 1990s this Indian route for drugs from Myanmar has expanded further thereby flooding the NER. A significant number of youth residing in the Indian states bordering Myanmar – Mizoram, Manipur and Nagaland – fall prey to the addiction of drugs, heroin as well as opium. The Indian and Myanmarese authorities lack the competence to control this menace and are often accused of being ignorant about the outcomes of these heinous activities involving drug-trafficking and money-laundering transactions.[63] The India-Myanmar Road has become a priority of India's diplomacy.[64] With the addition of the Thai projects, which also intend at establishing a link with this road by connecting Mandalay to the Thai border, Myanmar and especially the city of Mandalay could well become a major hub of terrestrial trade flows between South Asia, China and SEA.[65]

TAMANTHI HYDROELECTRIC PROJECT

Gauging the inherent significance of the project India undertook the initiative to rejuvenate the stalled 1,200 MW Tamanthi Hydroelectric power plant and 642 MW Shwezaye project on the Chindwin River, the largest tributary of the Irrawaddy, Myanmar's key commercial waterway. Though this momentous undertaking is undoubtedly indicative of India's quest to cultivate diplomatic and economic ties with its resource-rich neighbours like Myanmar. Still the project is not being pursued due to the social implications associated with the resettlement of people. Myanmar is endrued with resources particularly hydrocarbon reserves, which can be of great importance for India's energy security. India ranks among the top 10 oil-consuming countries. Myanmar has the world's 10th largest natural gas reserves, estimated at over 90 trillion cubic feet in 19 onshore and the 3 major offshore fields. Myanmar has natural gas reserves of 89.722 trillion cu. ft (tcf), of which 18.012 tcf are proven recoverable reserves, or gas that can be easily extracted and tapped.[66] Tamanthi is in north Myanmar. Once completed, the project is expected to control floods and provide water for irrigation in the region. India would be the recipient of the bulk of the power generated. Myanmar has a hydroelectric power potential of 39,720 MW and an installed capacity of 747 MW. A power transmission link with Myanmar would also help towards a power inter-link of countries of the SAARC which groups India, Pakistan, Nepal, Bhutan, Myan-mar, Bangladesh, Sri Lanka, Afghanistan and the Maldives. Appraising the utility of the project the SAARC grid has envisaged on meeting electricity demands and reinvigorating economic and political ties in the region. The projects are integral to India for its engagement with Myanmar.[67]

THE STILWELL ROAD

Arunachal Pradesh is an isolated state in North-East India awaiting an opening and a historic route like Stilwell can provide it with this opportunity. Debates and dialogues are on the pros and cons of reopening of the Stilwell Road and several efforts have been undertaken with respect to economic and security concerns. This historic road fascinatingly connects three backward regions – the NER, northern Myanmar and south-west China. It extends from Assam and links Kunming in Yunnan Province of south-West China through Pangspu Pass on the India-Myanmar border. This land route which was rebuilt in World War II was used for cross-regional movement between contiguous regions of India, Myanmar and China for various purposes. It was known by various names like Ledo Road, Burma Road, Bhamo Road, and was extensively used for various transregional movements. It was laid founded by King Sukama, the founder of the Ahom kingdom of Assam in early thirteenth century, the road was used for migration of people, culture and trade and maintenance of political and diplomatic relations between Assam and Myanmar till the early nineteenth century with the decline of Ahom kingdom and the advent of British rule the route lost its importance. It was rebuilt in 1942 as the western allies had to supply to the Chinese via an alternative route as the Burmese road had been cut by the Japanese forces. This road carries the history of World War II and conveys the story of General Joseph Stilwell, the man behind the construction of the road with at least 30,000 Indian, Burmanse and Chinese workforces at an approximate cost of US $173 million. The road was in full use for more than one and a half years for emergency purposes and military transport, but after the independence of both India and Myanmar the road was closed for security reasons though unofficial movements still exist. This meandering path which connects three close neighbours of this region with 61 km lying in Indian territory, 1,033 km in Myanmar and the rest 633 km in China, got truncated and lost momentum due to changed geopolitical realities and became a proud moment of the past. A fresh thought is now being given to this road as potential passage for socio-economic development of the future generation of this contiguous region. The border region of Patkai range is still inhabited by a dozen ethnic communities and the opening of this road will help to connect and restore lost links ethnically and culturally across borders. To these communities the reopening of the Stilwell Road will be a dream come true. All the chief ministers of the NER have come to a consensus and requested the prime minister to reopen the Road. Tarun Gogoi, the then Chief Minister of Assam, a Tai-Ahom himself, is undertook lots of initiatives to reopen the road. He said that the Gateway of India is Mumbai faces the West and it is time to build another gateway at the Ledo facing East, symbolizing the reunion of the past, yet heralding the begining of a great new future. There is no second opinion among the regional heads of the NER on the reopening of the legendary road. The Central Government should open the road to translate dream into actuality and to boost trade and commerce. Among the three nations through which the Road runs, China has already pursued the idea of reopening and has rejected the idea of the constructive stretch of the road with 6 Link Express Highway. On the contrary Myanmar was extremely indecisive as the road passes through its jungle-covered mountainous and the swampy valley of Kachin State – the most insurgency-prone area. India was also in an uncomfortable position and there was a ray of hope as Myanmar agreed to honour the long-standing need of the region by reopening Stilwell Road to facilitate trade with India and China. In the Indian Chamber of Commerce's 5th NE Business Summit at Kolkata in January 2010, Myanmar Foreign Minister, Nyan Win gave the assurance of reopening the Stilwell Road. He said that China has already constructed the road up to Ta Nai of Kachin district and the balance stretch from Ta Nai to Ledo on the Indian border via the Pangsu Pass – a stretch of 230 km could now be completed with support from the Government of India. With this assurance it was expected that the last obstacle was removed and there would be restoration of trans-border linkages. But over six years have passed without any concrete result. It seems that the MEA is still not very keen on reopening it for the same age-old security reasons though the Home Ministry has stated there should be trade across the borders. People-to-people contacts along with exchange of commodities and ideas has been the justification behind the reopening of the Road. But the presence of active groups dates the restoration of the same. It is expected that the re-opening of the road would be a win-win relation in terms of both trade and economy. The road will make it possible for the NER to use Myanmar for channelizing its goods to ASEAN countries. The Stilwell road is expected to cut transport cost between India and China by 30 per cent, thereby boosting Sino-India overland trade. Cargo could reach Yunnan in about two days in place of two weeks. Most importantly the other-wise isolated state of Arunachal Pradesh would be connected to Myanmar. Arunachal Pradesh therefore has submitted a proposal to the Centre beginning border trade with China and Myanmar from various locations. Apart from trade it would also be used to tap avenues like horticulture and flori-culture and tourism. It is meant for reviving closed cultural, spiritual and ethnic ties. However, the NER should not be used as a dumping ground for Chinese products. There should be very good intra-regional understanding for reopening of the road through intra-regional connectivity with appropri-ate laws, rules, customs regulations and security forces. State, market and civil society are the three pillars of development and are expected to feel less threatened by the vulnerability of insurgencies. Congenial negotiations and understanding are required for making the road workable.

China had already completed constructing their stretch of the Stilwell Road, but Myanmar apprehends that the Stilwell Road, which passes through its Kachin region, is primarily hassled with militant camps belonging to outfits from India's NER and hence reopening the road might provide easier access to the rebels.[68] That apprehension might be one of the vital causes behind Myanmar's reluctance in opening the road or delaying the implementation of the project.

The success and fruits of the project are not being experienced since the time of its initiation. The vital problem lies in the maintenance of the road. Since the stretch of the Stilwell Road cuts through three different countries, the problem over the responsibility of proper maintenance of the road is significant between three neighbours. In India the 61 km of the stretch is being shared by Assam and Arunachal Pradesh – 30 km lies in Assam and the other 31 km in Arunachal Pradesh. The border between Assam and Arunachal Pradesh – which has about 14 km of road was in a miserable condition but initiatives has been undetaken to rebuilt and renovate and to construct the international trade route to connect Myanmar at Pangsau Pass. The road is being repaired and renovated up to Nampong under the project and the expansion of the renovation work is extended up to Pangsau Pass. The portion of the road lying within Arunachal Pradesh has been maintained by the Government of Arunachal Pradesh and the section falling within Assam is being maintaned by the Government of Assam. The Government of India was enthusiastic about reopening the road as an international highway as trade link to Myanmar, China and other South-East Asian countries. The motive behind the reopening of this road lies in the fact that it will facilitate smooth interaction between the people of the neighbouring countries and will thereby nurture friendly and cooperative relationship among the member countries. It will also boost trade and attract inland and foreign tourists as the road itself is historically famous and significant due to World War II, which in turn will accelerate the socio-economic development of one of the most backward border areas, ultimately benefiting the local people. The NER, though rich in natural resources, is lagging behind other regions in terms of economic development. The trade routes to Myanmar from Nagaland and Manipur and to Bangladesh from Assam and Tripura are functional and contribute to an increased regional cooperation. Thus the reopening of the Stilwell Road is being conceived with great expectation as it bears the prospect of making the region a major international trade centre.[69]

The idea of this historic Burma Road actually cuts across

two projects based on two different communication routes, which would complement each other both geographically and economically. In fact, the first Burma Road follows the old route of the southern portion of the Silk Road that connected China with the Indian Ocean. The first Burma Road, from Chengdu (Sichuan) and Kunming (Yunnan) to Rangoon, passes through the cities of Ruili and Muse (both Chinese and Myanmarese border cities, facing each other on the Shweli river), then Lashio or Bhamo and Mandalay, where the Irrawaddy flows. Mandalay could be reached from Bhamo if one avoided the forest road passing by Lashio. Myanmar has long sold cotton to China in return for Chinese gold, silver and above all silk. With the advent of the British, Chinese products sold in Mandalay were sent to Rangoon and then exported through the sea.[70]

The second road dates back to British colonization when the British tried to reach China from their colony of Bengal and later Assam. The Ledo Road they began to build in the 1930s was supposed to connect the city of Ledo in Assamese territory to Yunnan, where British merchants and colonists hoped to hold back the commercial advance of the French.[71] Exchanges between China, Myanmar and Assam had to go through the Kumon mountains following an old but forgotten trade line from Yunnan to Myitkyina on the Irrawaddy, then to the Kachin and Naga territories and finally to Ledo which was connected to Calcutta by railways. The British never took interest in constructing proper railway infrastructure on this route from Ledo through Myanmar whereas they did develop an efficient railway system everywhere else in the region. It would seem that they were immensely sceptic about the development of uncontrollable flows from China and thus the Road was never fully developed.[72] For a long time the Kachin Independence Army (KIA) dominated the famous Stilwell Road, now densely covered by jungle, but conducive to clandestine flows that have kept the Christian Kachin and Naga guerrillas well supplied, making them financially and militarily autonomous. The KIA used the old allied facilities built along the Stilwell Road and abandoned the old forts built by the British during colonization.[73]

Thus the discussion of such geo-strategic roads like Stilwell Road must be carried on from the following three aspects:

(a) past or historical aspect
(b) present scenario and
(c) future prospect

Unfortunately unlike the Silk Route there is no major quantitative work on the Stilwell Road to emphasize on the quantitative development or economic prosperity. It should not just be a cultural and emotional route, it needs to be backed by economic pursuit. How the NER is going to be benefited economically from the Stilwell Road needs to be assessed thoroughly. The security implication for the NER in case terrorism is transported (if the road is developed) needs to be dealt with utter seriousness. Individual, cultural or emotional linkages will not serve the purpose there should be an economic implication of development. India, Myanmar and China should collaboratively arrive at productive conclusions.

The questions regarding the prospects of reopening the road often think beyond the security aspects and take into consideration the economic gains of the NER through such an open route policy. The NER has been a troubled spot for India due to historical reasons and due to the occurrence of insurgencies and violent activities. Only recently it is regarded as an important region and a ray of hope and optimism can be visible for the people. In the states of Tripura and Assam political leadership has been successful in transforming from pains of the past into hopes for the future, ushering in an era of competence and expectation. Mizoram can also be included in the list where militancy is a story of the past. But ages of disconnect and lack of infrastructure development have kept the region far from the limelight. Connectivity thus occupies the core area of concern. Disconnect has kept it in isolation from mainland India and with the close neighbours which share almost 98 per cent of boundaries with the NER. The end of the Cold War ushered in subsequent modulations and transformations of the contours of world politics. The LEP conceived of (a) rebuilding the lost relations with the fast growing SEA nations; (b) revival of land-locked and conflict-prone borderland of NER's with South-East Asian nations with Myanmar as a gateway so that it can be conceptualized as a trans-regional economic and cultural space to counter the long-standing issue of insurgency, poverty and economic backwardness.

Twenty years after the formulation of LEP it is high time to assess the fruits of the policy as well as the relevance of the region as an economic hub through connectivity and commerce. India's two most important neighbours Bangladesh and Myanmar are experiencing political transition and can be opportune facilitators of rejuvenating cooperative relations. Tripura had undertaken commendable initiatives to restore the links and opening trade routes with Bangladesh and more efforts are underway for opening of the Chittagong port. The visit of Prime Minister Sheikh Hasina to the state in January 2012, might be recounted as a friendship gesture. Important mentions of connectivity are Sikkim through Nathula, Manipur through Moreh-Tamu Road and Assam securing border problems with Bangladesh. Mizoram was waiting keenly for the Kaladan Multimodal Project to begin. The project which was concived in 2008 is ready to be commissioned. These are the innovative attempts of restoring linkages with neighbours. Moreover, in 2015 Bangladesh Prime Minister Sheikh Hassina visit to India strengthened India's integration with its North-East as well as SEA, particularly in the backdrop when India-Bangladesh relations are in need of transformation and modification for the strategic advantages of both the neigbours. This is a decisive drive of India's Act East Policy.

KALADAN MULTIMODAL PROJECT

India on 2 April 2008 signed the decade-long Kaladan Multi modal Transit Transport Project with Myanmar that opened India's access through alternative route to the North-East states. India is vividly exploring the possibility of harnessing Myanmar's Chindwin river (development of hydroelectric capacities that would be eventually redirected toward India's North-East) and especially the Kaladan river. Flowing from Mizoram to the Rakhine state (Arakan) of Myanmar, this river could be of strategic importance for India as it could enable it to develop a suitable communication route via the east, bypassing Bangladesh. In that perspective, India offered to upgrade the commercial port of Sittwe (formerly Akyab), where the Kaladan river falls into the Bay of Bengal. The commercial use of such a harbour could be valuable for India's traders, especially those interested in commercial transactions from Kolkata or the eastern coast of India to the North-East of India but through Myanmar and the Kaladan river instead of accessing through the Siliguri Neck and Assam. Moreover, collaboration between the Myanmar and Mizoram authorities was necessary for developing Mizoram's system.[74]

The project bears the potentiality of developing Burma's Sittwe port on Kaladan river from where goods will be transported. The US $120 million agreement was signed by the then Indian Minister of External Affairs, Shri Pranab Mukherjee and his Myanmar counterpart U Nyan Win. The completion of the Kaladan Project is expected to facilitate India an access route from any corner of the country to the NER. Moreover, the implementation of the project will provide India an alternative trading route thereby diminishing the need of transition through Bangladesh. Besides developing the ports the project is oriented to construct and develop a road linking Kalewa in Myanmar to Moreh, the border town in the NER of India at an estimated cost of ₹5.3 billion.[75] Highlighting the significance of the project, the Essar Group spokesperson, Manish Kedia reiterated that the project was to construct a port at Sittwe and a jetty at Paletwa aimed at developing infrastructure in Myanmar, which would be beneficial to the country itself as well as would promote employment opportunities. It was estimated that the contract was worth about ₹3.42 billion (US $75 million) to the Essar Group.[76]

India needs to have a developed and modernized Myanmar

as its neighbour, equipped with effective infrastructure, especially if it wishes to see its NER opened up and developed. The economic expansion of the region should not end at its border, but should include other regions: the Indian NER, Bangladesh and western Myanmar too.[77] India is keen in developing Myanmar's energy resources. An offshore natural gas deposit facing the Arakan coast is being developed by two Indian companies in cooperation with two Korean companies (Daewoo International with a share of 60 per cent, Korea Gas Corporation 10 per cent, Gas Authority of India 10 per cent and ONGC Videsh 20 per cent).[78] The pipeline project linking the Arakan deposit to Bangladesh and Kolkata has not been implemented yet because of the Bangladeshi reluctance to go ahead. The visit of Myanmar leader General Than Shwe, to India on July 2010 sparked a new excitement for India's LEP. It signalled decisive progress in the context of physical connectivity between India's North-East and Myanmar, an advanced step in LEP. After the Kaladan Multimodal Transport System, India has announced the building of yet another new road, the Rhi-Tiddin and Rhi-Falam road connecting Mizoram to Myanmar. The next stage of feasibility on the Tamanthi Hydel Project was also being discussed. India is proceeding carefully on this 1,200 MW project on river Chindwin in north-western Myanmar. Moreover, India has decided to grant of US $10 million for agricultural implements for Myanmar's farmers and boost telecommunication links by strengthening the optic fibre link with microwave. India will assist with an extra US $60 million for railway upgradation.[79]

LEP underscores the importance of new opportunities and openings for the development of the NER besides fostering trade relations with SEA. The development of the entire gamut of infrastructure covering roads, trading centres, land custom stations and power is ardently required for stimulating economic activities and promoting trade integration. The NER is endowed with immense potentialities but what is needed is the proper harnessing of the production capacities and surpluses. One of the prime motives of the LEP is to generate revenue from the East. For meeting this end India has to steer the strategy of positioning the surpluses and the capacities in the international markets and imbibing them with the required market power thereby strengthening its market presence. The qualities of the NER need to be showcased. For instance, in Meghalaya major investments can be done in cultivating organic ginger and turmeric. Similarly in Manipur the government has invested in mulberry silk, in rubber in Tripura while in Assam it is tea. Sikkim has developed international popularity for orchids. Each state is blessed with typical characteristics and it should capitalize on that unique feature to market itself internationally. This will eventually accelerate economic growth and the NER will reap economic benefits from trade. In order to accomplish this there should synergy and coordinated efforts between the Central and the state governments. The Central government has opted for granting huge amounts of funds for the progress of the region but the region suffers from a basic structural inefficiency. Every year the Central Government allots about ₹15,000 crore to the eight North-Eastern states with a combined population of about 30 million. There is no dearth of money in the region but there is inefficiency in the spending ability of the people for the development purpose of the region. The allotment of huge amounts of money does not guarantee the implementation of the projects undertaken. There is no accountability on public expenditure and lack of responsiveness of the people impedes the harnessing of abundant economic potentials ultimately shaking the prospect of a better future for the region.[80] Transparency, accountability along with proper and timely execution of projects should be the guiding spirit of the LEP. Prime Minister Modi's 2015 Bangladesh visit will stimulate the connectivity between the two neighbours which will benefit the NER. As we know that the opening of India to SEA is mainly through two countries namely, Bangladesh and Myanmar. Therefore promoting connectivity is a key aspect on the agenda of bilateral cooperation. A milestone in this endeavour is the initiative for road linkages between Bangladesh,

Bhutan, India and Nepal (BBIN). Once implemented vehicles from all four countries will be to transit each other's territories via transport corridors. This launch will add momentum to trade and commerce as well as business opportunities thereby rejuvenating people-to-people contacts. Moreover, India will gain easy access to its NER as transit through Bangladesh will decrease the travel time. The proposed Kolkata-Dhaka-Agartala and Guwahati-Shillong-Dhaka bus service bears much credence.

BBIN can boost regional integration but infrastructure development is required. India needs to comprehend that the relevance of its geo-strategic location and potential can be as decisive as China's Silk Road Economic Belt, substantiating the creation of conducive ecosystem, liberalized visas, easy trade permits and smooth conduction of trade thereby revitalizing regional growth by opening overland access to Bangladesh, Myanmar, Thailand, Malaysia and beyond.

CONCLUSION

The primary facets of the leading projects are being mentioned with due importance. The aforementioned projects are crucial in engineering India's LEP and promoting connectivity, thereby developing the NER of India. The implementation of the projects is the major yardstick for the competent pursuit of the policy. It is unfortunate that the fruits of the projects are not being yielded till date and are lagging far behind the desired result. Likewise, other projects are in the pipeline but not yet implemented rigorously. Practically it is found that the passion and the over-zealousness with which the agreements and projects are proposed lose their track midway and the bureaucratic hurdles detain and often stall their pace at the implementation level. The LEP needs to be nurtured over a long period of time without losing its primary focus and objectives. But obstacles like lack of infrastructure development, absence of enthusiastic response from local people, frequent insurgencies, poor governance in the states, the easy availability of arms and weapons from across the international border to be utilized in armed movements and criminal activities impede increased relations between the NER and SEA. It is surprising to encounter that it is the same geographic location which acts as a catalyst for the NER to reap the benefits from India-ASEAN cooperation, and at times, makes it vulnerable to be the core of hostility with massive adverse effects.

The geographical location of the NER has always been the central theme in India's cooperative equations with the ASEAN. In 2007, India's then Minister of External Affairs, Shri Pranab Mukherjee visited the cities of Shillong and Guwahati and promoted the geography of the North-East as an opportunity in India's Look East Policy. In addition to that he explained to the local audiences the promises of LEP for the region.[81]

North-East is blessed with abundance of natural virtues which seriously need to be showcased, otherwise the region will remain on the backburner instead of being in the limelight. Mooting the idea of 'Geography as Opportunity', in his famous Shillong speech, on 16 June 2007, Shri Pranab Mukherjee said:

> I am convinced that by gradually integrating this region through cross-border market access, the North-eastern states can become the bridge between the Indian economy and what is beyond doubt the fastest growing and dynamic region in the world . . . geography is opportunity and the very geographical location of the North-East makes it the doorway to South-East and East Asia and vice-versa, a doorway for these economies into India.[82]

Despite all the developmental initiatives and strengthening of bilateral ties with Myanmar India still considers China's influence on Myanmar as a challenging proposition for India.[83] Whether Myanmar's historical trajectories would influence its future discourses would depend on the intersecting and interfering factors. If the political and economic transformations are being properly installed and institutionalized the parallel socio-cultural changes are likely to follow. Though there are influences of India and China as neighbours on Myanmar's socio-economic and political track, Myanmar's future will still be shaped by its own past, its historical patterns, its own human and material contexts, its own beliefs but would not be dictated by anyone else's terms and conditions. Indeed Myanmar's priorities will be agrarian and domestic, its government will be a centralized hybrid of primarily indigenous and foreign ideas and realities and for the foreseeable future Myanmar's past will continue to be an indelible part of its present.[84] But the LEP has rendered an added impetus to India-Myanmar relations which are reinvigorated by the exchange of visits from both the neighbours. It is noteworthy to mention that from 2011 since Myanmar's transition to democracy, the relations are getting warmer. Myanmar has witnessed marked changes in its domestic policies and actions as well as security and foreign policy issues. Reforming the electoral system, releasing the political prisoners, encouraging media freedom, expanding civil society groups, establishing a national human rights commission and a peace-building institute are some hallmarks of the new Myanmar, which to some extent, have bewildered the international community. There are certain predominant aspects like the reunification, restoration of identity, self-reliance and return to identity, that are still crucial to the development trajectory of Myanmar. The Rohingya issue is playing a major role in India-Myanmar bilateral chemistry and India perhaps can play a leading role in addressing this matter. India has often espoused its humanitarian credentials through repeated life-saving interventions on behalf of the Rohingyas and has on a number of occasions hosted a sizeable proportion of that community. India has been by them in their times of distress and might provide an exemplary to other countries to take up the initiative to help ease the plight of this immensely deplorable community. This could be a worthy cause for the Indian government to espouse and promote.[85]

In this complex context taking cognizance of Myanmar's

resource riches and international dynamics, the US, China and Japan have been enthusiastically outlining their strategic priorities and requirements in the country. Their extensive engagements should incite India to strengthen its age-old connections with Myanmar. India needs to reorient the grand design of developing the NER like China's Western Development Strategy of transforming Yunnan into a world-class destination. Development of border trade mandates differential advantage for the NER by producing quality goods at competitive costs using resources of the region. It has been argued earlier that the North-East people's knowledge and command over the English language can facilitate the pace of cooperation with Myanmar over China. But there should be consensus among all the eight North-Eastern states and a collective plan of action is the need of the hour. Proper synchronization of the policies of the Central Government and the state governments is imperative to make the NER the harbinger of thriving cooperation between the neighbours, India and Myanmar. India must deepen its ties with its neighbour by its soft-power diplomacy and Track 2 initiatives wherein education, culture and democracy can play an effective and enduring role by leveraging such comparative advantages to build interdependence and mutual benefits, contributing to peace and stability in SEA and East Asia.

NOTES

1. *Strategic Digest*, New Delhi, January 2001, p. 152.
2. Thant Myint-U, *Burma and the New Crossroads of Asia: Where China Meets India*, London, Faber and Faber, 2011.
3. Baladas Ghoshal, *China's Perception of India's 'Look East Policy' and its Implications*, New Delhi, IDSA, 2013, p. 153.
4. David I. Steinberg and Hongwei Fan, *Modern China-Myanmar Relations: Dilemmas of Mutual Dependence*, Copenhagen, Nias Press, 2012.
5. Ibid.
6. Ghoshal, *China's Perception of India's 'Look East Policy'*, p. 153.

7. Steinberg and Fan, *Modern China-Myanmar Relations*, p. 353.
8. Billy Tea, 'China and Myanmar Strategic Interests, Strategies and the Road Ahead', September 2010. IPCS Research Papers, accessed electronically at www.ipcs.org/.../china/china-and-myanmar-strategic-interests-strategic -, accessed on 26 November 2012.
9. Gideon Lundholm , 'China Trumps India in Myanmar Gas Stakes', *Asia Times*, 11 September 2007.
10. Mahesh Kumar Saharia, 'Myanmar Calling', *Assam Tribune*, 2 June 2012.
11. Tridib Chakraborti, 'Explaining the Penumbra of India's Look East Policy', in K. Raja Reddy (ed.), *India and ASEAN Foreign Policy Dimensions for the Twenty-First Century*, New Delhi, New Century Publication, 2005, p. 60.
12. Ibid., pp. 68-9.
13. Samir Kumar Das, *India Quarterly*, vol. 66, no. 4, New Delhi, 2010, pp. 358, 459.
14. Thingnam Kishan Singh, 'Introduction', in Thingnam Kishan Singh (ed.), *Look East Policy and India's North East: Polemics and Perspectives*, New Delhi, Concept, 2009.
15. Renaud Egreteau, *Wooing the Generals: India's New Burma Policy*, New Delhi, Authors Press, 2003, p. 117.
16. Samir Kumar Das, 'BIMSTEC or the Big Leap Forward for India's Northeast', *World Focus*, New Delhi, January 2008, p. 19.
17. Accessed electronically at www.questia.com/PM.qst?a=o&se=gglsc&d=5007070379 on 14 June 2010.
18. Thant, *Burma and the New Crosswords of Asia*, p. 38.
19. 'India Seeks Burma Border Help', *BBC South Asia News*, 7 January 2000.
20. Thant, *Burma and the New Crosswords of Asia*, p. 29.
21. Ibid., pp. 30, 31.
22. 'Realism in India-Myanmar Relations', *The Financial Express*, Kolkata, 15 September 2003.
23. Thant , *Burma and the New Crosswords of Asia*, p. 29.
24. Das, 'BIMSTEC or the Big Leap Forward for India's Northeast', p. 19.
25. Laxman B. Bahroo, 'Myanmar: Intersecting Destinies of a New Asia', *Bharat Rakshak Monitor*, May-June 2003, p. 9, accessed at www.bharat-rakshak.com/MONITOR/ISSUE5-6/bahroo.html on 10 October 2011.

26. Shee Poon Kim, 'The South China Sea in China's Strategic Thinking', *Contemporary Southeast Asia*, Singapore, vol. 19, no. 4, March 1998, pp. 369, 387.
27. Peter W. Rodman, 'China Woos Burma', *International Herald Tribune*, New York, 30 May 1997.
28. *International Herald Tribune*, New York, 7 April 1995.
29. Donald M. Seekins, 'Burma-China Relations: Playing with Fire', *Asian Survey*, vol. 37, no. 6, University of California Press, June 1997, p. 535.
30. J. Mohan Malik, 'Myanmar's Role in Regional Security: Pawn or Pivot?' *Contemporary Southeast Asia*, vol. 19, no. 1, June 1997, pp. 52, 73.
31. Liang Chi-shad,'Burma's Relations with the People's Republic of China: From Delicate Friendship to Genuine Co-operation', in Peter Carey (ed.), *Burma, the Challenge of Change in a Divided Society*, London, MacMillan Press, 1997, p. 81.
32. Ibid., p. 81.
33. New Three-Year Plan for 'Prosper the Borders to Enrich Local People in Yunnan', *Yunnan Political Affairs*, no. 11, 2008, p. 23, quoted in Hongwei Fan, 'China's Look South: China-Myanmar Transport Corridor'. Available at r-cube. ritsumei. ac.jp/bitstream/ 10367/3399/1/asia10_fan.pdf (acccessed on 1 November 2012.)
34. Billy Tea, 'China and Myanmar: Strategic Interests, Strategies and the Road Ahead', Institute of Peace and Conflict Studies Research Paper, no. 26, New Delhi, September 2010, p. 8.
35. Joshy M. Paul, 'Myanmar in China's Push into the Indian Ocean', accessed at http://www.indiandefencereview.com/myanmar-in-chinas-push-into-the-indian-ocean/ on 16 March 2016.
36. Accessed electronically at http://www.indiandefencereview.com/ myanmar-in-chinas-push-into-the-indian-ocean/ on 16 March 2016.
37. J. Mohan Malik, 'Sino-Indian Rivalry in Myanmar: Implications for Regional Security', *Contemporary Southeast Asia*, vol. 16 no. 2, September 1994, p. 61.
38. David I. Steinberg and Hongwei Fan, *Modern China-Myanmar Relations: Dilemmas of Mutual Dependence*, Copenhagen, Nias Press, 2012.
39. Li Chenyang, ' The Policies of China and India Toward Myanmar', in Lex Rieffel (ed.), *Myanmar/Burma Inside Challenges, Outside Interests*, Washington DC, The Brookings Institution, 2010, p. 27.

40. Samir Das, 'Between South and Southeast Asia: Recasting India's Northeast in the Age of Globalisation', in Asok Kumar Ray and Satyabrata Chakraborty (eds.), *Society, Politics and Development in North East India*, New Delhi, Concept, 2008, p. 150.
41. R.P. Bhattacharjee, 'Demographic Profile of North-East (1991)', in Sanu Mukherjee, Fatima Imdad Hussain, Parjit Chakravorty and Gurudas Das (eds.), *Demographic Profile of North-East India*, New Delhi, OSMOS Publications, 1994, p. 8.
42. Alokesh Barua, *India's North-East: Developmental Issues in a Historical Perspective*, New Delhi, Manohar and CHS, 2005, p. 17.
43. Bodhisattva Kar, 'When was the Postcolonial? A History of Policing Impossible Lines', in Sanjib Baruah (ed.), *Beyond Counter-insurgency: Breaking the Impasse in Northeast India*, New Delhi, Oxford University Press, 2009, p. 72.
44. C.S. Kuppuswamy, 'India's Look East Policy – A Review', accessed electronically at www.southasiaanalysis.org/%5Cpapers37%5Cpaper3662.html on 14 March 2010.
45. Sanjib Baruah, *Durable Disorder Understanding the Politics of Northeast India*, New Delhi, Oxford University Press, 2005, p. 212.
46. Sanjoy Hazarika, *Rites of Passage: Border Crossings, Imagined Homelands, India's East and Bangladesh*, New Delhi, Penguin, 2000, p. 32.
47. Das, 'Between South and Southeast Asia', p. 152.
48. Accessed electronically at www.tatamotors.com/our_world/press_releases.php?ID on 26 October 2009.
49. Julien Levesque, 'North-East in India's Look East Policy', *Institute of Peace and Conflict Studies*, New Delhi, 6 May 2008, accessed electronically at (http://www.ipcs.org/articles_details.php?articleNo= 2558$cID=9) on 15 October 2009.
50. Jairam Ramesh, Keynote Address, quoted in Charles Reuben Lyngdoh Merostar Rani (ed.), *Look East Policy: Impact on North East India*, New Delhi, Akansha, 2008, p. 7.
51. *Hindu Business Line*, 13 July 2007.
52. Das, 'Between South and Southeast Asia, pp. 151-2'.
53. Accessed electronically at www.indoburmanews.net/.../india-myanmar-thailand-trilateral-highway/ on 9 July 2010.
54. Accessed electronically at www.indoburmanews.net/.../india-myanmar-thailand-trilateral-highway/ on 10 July 2010.
55. Accessed electronically at pad16.com/sea_broken/myanmar/burmaroad.htm on 15 June 2010.
56. 'A Rewarding Visit, Says Jaswant', *The Hindu*, 15 February 2001.

57. 'Myanmar Shows India the Road to Southeast Asia', *Asia Times*, 21 February 2001.
58. 'India's Road to Rangoon', *BBC South Asia News*, 14 February 2001.
59. *Assam Tribune*, 2001.
60. 'Green Light for Pan-Asia Road Scheme', *BBC South Asia News*, 6 April 2002.
61. 'Indian Insurgents Get Base in Myanmar', *Mizzima News Group*, 8 March 2002.
62. '1000 Acres of Poppy Fields Destroyed in Myanmar', *The Times of India*, 22 March 2002.
63. 'In a Vicious Circle', *Frontline*, vol. 19, no. 15, July-August 2002.
64. 'The Roads to Myanmar', *Frontline*, vol. 18, no. 5, March 2001.
65. *BBC South Asia News*, 6 April 2002.
66. 'Myanmar – Open for Business', accessed electronically at www. hfw. com/publications/client.../myanmar-open-for-business on 19 February 2013.
67. Accessed electronically at www.info.shine.com/Article/Power/ Indian... to... projects/... cid948.aspx on 9 July 2010.
68. Accessed electronically at www.thaindian.com/.../myanmar-says-no-to-reopening-stilwell-road-plan-shelved_100206308.html on 19 June 2010.
69. Accessed electronically at www. changlang.nic.in/stilwell.html on 19 June 2010.
70. Thant Myint-U, *The Making of Modern Burma*, Cambridge, Cambridge University Press, 2001, p. 142.
71. Renaud Egreteau, *Wooing the Generals: India's New Burma Policy*, New Delhi, Authorspress, 2003, p. 168.
72. P. Stobdan, 'China's Forays into Burma – Implications for India', *Strategic Analysis*, vol. 16, no. 1, April 1993, p. 31.
73. Richard Sola, *Birmanie, la Revolution Kidnappe, 1981-1995*, Paris, L'Harmattan, 1996, pp. 61-3, quoted in Renaud Egreteau, *Wooing the Generals: India's New Burma Policy*, New Delhi, Authorspress, 2003, p. 62.
74. Egreteau, *Wooing the Generals*, p. 161.
75. Accessed electronically at kaladan.com/kaladan-project/kaladan-mmtt-project/ on 29 June 2010.
76. Accessed electronically at www.indoburmanews.net/.../essar-signs-contract-for-2018kaladan-multi-modal-transit-transport-project2019 on 7 July 2010.
77. Subhash Kapila, 'India-Myanmar Strategic Partnership: Indian

Imperatives', Paper 197, South Asia Analysis Group, 6 February 2001.

78. 'ONGC plans to Invest ₹2,900 Crores in North East', *The Hindu*, 21 July 2002.
79. Indrani Bagchi, 'Gen Visit to Deepen Ties with Myanmar', *The Times of India*, 26 September 2012.
80. Ibid.
81. Sanjib Baruah, *Beyond Counter-Insurgency Breaking the Impasse in Northeast India*, New Delhi, Oxford University Press, 2009, p. 1.
82. Accessed electronically at www.kanglaonline.com/index.php?template=kshow... on 9 July 2010.
83. Malik, 'Myanmar's Role in Regional Security: Pawn or Pivot?' *Contemporary Southeast Asia*, vol. 19, no. 1, p. 56.
84. Michael Aung-Thwin and Maitrii Aung-Thwin (eds.), *A History of Myanmar Since Ancient Times: Traditions and Transformations*, London, Reakton Books, 2012.
85. Salman Haider, 'A Drift on Open Waters', *The Statesman*, Kolkata, 26 May 2015.

CHAPTER 5

North-East India: A Region of Promising Dynamics

The major findings of the study are being analysed in this chapter. The thrust of this research being the appraisal of the implications of India's Look East Policy on the development or the advancement of the North-East Region of India from 'backward' to a 'gateway' status has evoked certain arguments. It is undeniable that academic discourse on the development of the NER inevitably brings into focus the question of political integration of the NER with mainstream India. As has been discussed in the introductory chapter the historical inferences connote that the issue of political integration of NER with the India Union politically has been one of the prime concerns of the policy-makers of our country. The opening up of the Indian economy due to the onset of globalization and, regional integration since the nineties upholds the imperative of economic development of India's resource-rich NER due to its relative proximities with South-East Asian countries. The NER is extremely rich in biodiversity and is the possessor of a wide variety of spices, medicinal and aromatic herbs and a range of fruits and flowers that are yet to find their way to the malls of India and the world.[1] Herein the significance of political integration of the region with the mainland lies. Thus, the LEP is conceived with a precondition of developing the NER from its landlocked condition by ending its economic isolation, for which the opening of the region is must. This policy bears the prospect of reviving the ancient trade routes in North-East India, including the 'Southern Ancient Silk Road', and to potentially explore and utilize the rich resources through regional cooperation with its south-eastern neighbours. But it calls for an intense understanding of the pulse or the psyche of the people of the region too. The LEP aims to address to the political impasse confronted by the region as political unrest often leads to economic backwardness. It has often been experienced that the attempts of integration of the region and its people with the Indian mainstream have ignited discontentment and antagonisms amongst different ethnic communities of the region thereby defaming it as the hot bed of turbulence. The not-so-favourable situation of the region has on many occasions propelled the government to concede to the demands of autonomy and self-determination of many ethnic groups, ultimately leading to the creation of separate states. Therefore, the issue of political integration of the NER with the mainstream is a matter of grave concern and necessitates the adoption of substantive strategies by the state governments as well as the Central Government in addressing the issue. All the endeavours need to be conscious of the multifaceted traits, attributes and tenets of the eight North-Eastern states.

Strategic thinking involves perceptions of the policy-makers about the changing dynamics in international politics particularly in the backdrop of an evolving society and economy. During the post-Partition era, there was a great preoccupation with bilateral relationships the focus largely on Pakistan in relation to arms supplies and Kashmir issue. The growth of regionalism was being predominantly projected through the establishment of the South Asian Association for Regional Cooperation (SAARC) though even before the emphasis on regionalism and regional aspirations got portrayed through progressive inclination indicating how India used to perceive the areas around it. Gradually SAARC has emerged as an identity and has gained momentum as certain things occurred because of the existence of SAARC. It is often being debated that the essence of regionalism got restricted in SAARC as India-Pakistan animosity has not allowed a broader opening up of the initiative. But the worldview gradually expanded and the introduction of the BIMSTEC was an attempt to reach out across the Bay of Bengal to the littoral on the other side, particularly Myanmar and Thailand. India's maritime negotiations with its neighbours, its renewed cooperation particularly with the ASEAN and ARF in the nineties, then with the Gulf countries and then with Shanghai cooperation as Central Asia was of greater interest to India, underscored India's growing eminence as a global player. India was the founder of the East Asia Summit. Today India has interests in the development of the Trans-Pacific partnership and the security architecture. It is eagerly waiting to be a member of ASEAN and is towards the orientation of this regional organization. Five of the ten ASEAN members such as Myanmar, Thailand, Indonesia, Malaysia and Singapore have direct ocean frontier with the Indian Ocean and the Bay of Bengal, which itself projects the ocean interests that India has with many of the ASEAN countries.

Neighbourhood could itself go beyond boundaries because it is an area and it is a little amorphous. It is a kind of space that allows external players to enter, exit and operate. The inception of the LEP can be traced back to the changed geo-strategic dynamics in the post-Cold War international politics. There was a change in the government policies and foreign policy affairs under the prime ministership of the Narasimha Rao-led Congress government. India started to evolve out of the socialist framework to a more pragmatic phase in both its economy and its foreign policy strategies. She began to realize the benefits emanating out of the virtues of globalization and market-driven economy.[2] The LEP has been formulated to address certain constraints of contemporary dynamics predominantly emanating from the compulsions of economic stagnation and political unrest within the country. India's cooperation with South-East Asian neighbours is backed by certain pertinences aiming at preventing China from establishing its dominance that could be threatening to India's strategic moves and jeopardizing its interests and its freedom of action in the South or South-East Asian region. It was also a preventive measure to restrain China from coopling the regional states as allies or supporting policies with the ploy to exert sufficient regional influence undermining Indian security. It was also was intended to develop strategic relationships with key regional partners providing support and accessibility to India to operate in the region. Thus the major drive of the LEP initially has been the economic imperative which in due course of its development has been focusing on the strategic, security and development facets. In this study an analytical understanding of the factors inducing the evolution of the LEP has been pursued, of which the onset of globalization, liberalization, privatization and the emergence of regionalization played a vital role. It is often argued that the emerging trends toward regionalism and India's wariness of getting marginalized and isolated in the post-Cold War international system are the prime movers behind India's cooperation with the thriving economies of East and South-East Asia. The objective of the policy thus could well be accomplished through regional cooperation, which mandates the solution of the plaguing problems of the NER impeding the overall development of the region. The LEP strives for cooperation with the South-East Asian neighbouring countries in the tackling of menace of insurgency, undocumented migration and drug trafficking besides revitalizing economic cooperation. The available economic prospect of the sub-region can best be exploited with the expansion of trade and commerce at the borders in the region. The boosting of transport and communication systems diminishes the pace of illicit activities in the border areas.

The LEP is oriented to address the plaguing problems of the region keeping in mind the peculiarity and the multiplicity of the NER in order to ensure lasting peace and development in the region. The menace of underdevelopment and the incompetence in the utilization of available resources have thwarted many of the developmental or innovative moves of the eight North-Eastern states. In this regard the creation of Public Diplomacy Division of the Ministry of External Affairs and the opening of its branch office in Guwahati is an encouraging gesture which would assist in addressing the aspirations of the people of this region in having better liaison with the External Affairs Ministry on issues concerning foreign trade, foreign direct investment and cultural exchanges. Sanjib Baruah views that,

> If the Look East Policy is to live up to its potential of becoming North-East India's road to peace and prosperity we will have to face up to the risks that exist and actively assess and manage them. That would mean taking a long-term view and synchronizing our foreign policies towards China, Myanmar, ASEAN – as well as towards Bangladesh and Bhutan – and our domestic policies vis-à-vis North-East India.[3]

He endorsed the efficacy of transnational solutions for the economic and political problems of the North-East which is trapped in the geopolitics of the colonial and postcolonial order. It might seem a little incredible but enthusiastic and productive endeavours can make this possible and realistic in the future. Proactive government initiatives along with proper synchronization of the state governments' policies with those of the Central Government policies and dynamic regional and subregional cooperation as well as cooperation of the neighbouring countries are required. However, such a policy of strengthening of ties and deepening of cooperation with the Eastern and South-Eastern neighbours should be wide-ranging thereby encompassing a wide array of crucial issues including concrete measures in developing not only infrastructure but also political stability and good governance. India's LEP aims at improving governance, combating corruption, cultivating the spirit of intellectual and cultural openness which encourages public debate and participation as well as opening new vistas of cooperation in political matters and the economic arena.

India certainly needs to develop its economic capabilities and also needs to develop potentials as well as actualize potentials, develop standards and secure the ability to demonstrate itself as a productive, manufacturing country that can reach out to the wider neighbourhood. Cultural links can revitalize the process. Though there are political diversities in our neighbourhood, economic potentials need to be exploited. India should be enthusiastic in creating stakeholders for encouraging mutually beneficial relationships in our neighbourhood. FTAs are important and in this context conceptualization, negotiation and implementation of India-ASEAN FTAs, opening of trade, and trade negotiations should be taken into account in order to foster mutually supportive partnerships. Positive, proactive approach provides a niche to produce a win-win situation. India's LEP is an essential component of India's foreign policy strategies towards its South-East Asian neighbours.

South-East Asia's response to Sino-Indian strategic competition might be perceived in a number of ways. First and foremost the onus is on the economic dimension. As Indonesian President Yudhoyono commented in 2004, the economic challenge for the ASEAN can be described in two words: China and India.[4] While there are concerns about China and India in terms of potentially crowding out ASEAN's share of global trade and investment, ASEAN leaders generally see economic cooperation between India and China within South-East Asia in positive terms and in particular will continue to use it as an opportunity to encourage Indian economic integration into ASEAN and to open the Indian market to South-East Asian products and investment. The ASEAN states and India share the common interest of limiting the growth of China's political and military power in SEA for their mutual concerns. India is rarely perceived as a threat to its South-East Asian neighbours and is generally considered a benign player in comparison to China's domineering overtures for which it is often regarded by many as a potential security threat whose power needs to be balanced. In fact ASEAN has facilitated India's links with the region in order to reconcile with growing interests of China as well as the US and Japan. It should be viewed as an initiative to engage both China and India in a web of cooperative relationships thereby creating a balance in their power equations. The ASEAN states, should in no way encourage any overt confrontation between India and China in and around the region. While many ASEAN states are encouraging India to play a greater security role in SEA, without a major change in the security environment they will also want any Indian security presence to be discreet. For the same reasons, the ASEAN states, particularly Singapore, Indonesia and Malaysia have not denounced China's growing interests in the Indian Ocean and they are likely to encourage China to also be circumspect in developing such interests. Another pertinent facet is the potential for the ASEAN to use Sino-Indian rivalry for the sake of maintaining and enhancing its own strategic influence. ASEAN's performance in future regional security arrangements is quite ambiguous particularly in the spectre of perceived inadequacies in the competence of the ASEAN Regional Forum. It is often argued that India has an important stake in the continued relevance of ASEAN in countering domination of the region by the US or China. Arguably, the developing strategic concerns between India and China, may lead to the deepening of their respective institutional relationships with the ASEAN thus diminishing the scope of its marginalization. There might be a possibility for Sino-Indian rivalry to be a factor in intra-regional relations in SEA, something that receives relatively little attention. During the Cold War, rivalry between the Soviet Union, China and the US were significant factors in influencing intra-regional tensions. It is already possible to discern incipient Sino-Indian rivalry along potential faultlines within the ASEAN: in Indochina between Cambodia, traditionally sponsored by China, and Vietnam, a longstanding political partner of India; and in maritime SEA between Singapore, India's primary regional partner, and Indonesia. India and China could therefore be significant constituents in existing intra-regional affairs to the extent that ASEAN is not able to effectively manage tensions within a regional framework.[5]

The efficient exploration of the rich resources of the NER

under the purview of the LEP is a significant milestone for the economic development of the region as well as for eradicating the problems of insurgency, migration and poverty. The LEP does provide the NER with the opportunity to cooperate with the South-East Asian countries under subregional groupings like the BIMSTEC and Mekong Ganga Cooperation so as to counter the imminent threats of drug-trafficking, illegal immigration, poverty and insurgency impeding the economic development of the region. BIMSTEC's role as a subregional grouping to reinvigorate the essence of India-ASEAN cooperation is thus crucial. It elucidates that the BIMSTEC should be considered as a complement to SAARC, not to be viewed in opposition to SAARC. MGC as a subregional grouping in India-ASEAN cooperation is to emphasize that cooperation accelerating the essence of solidarity is the motivating spree of development and prosperity of the nationstates. The ASEAN membership of Myanmar in 1997 has accorded the NER with an enlightening impression. Myanmar's incorporation into the BIST-EC, transforming it into BIMSTEC reveals India's over zealousness to participate in the Asian 'constructive engagement policy' vis-à-vis the Myanmar government. Thus Myanmar's presence in the international domain became evidently palpable thereby shedding its image as a pariah state among its neighbours. In early 2002, the Burmese foreign affairs minister, U Win Aung, assured of Myanmar's willingness to offer its considerable resources for the success of regional cooperation. Both India and ASEAN were to gain immensely out of such an eventuality.[6] To bolster India-Myanmar cooperation it is ardent to boost up the magnitude of border trade. With India-ASEAN free trade (good and services) in place trade and economic engagements with ASEAN are getting further boost. Trade grown in 2010 to 55.4 billion, a growth of 41.8 per cent from 39.1 per cent in 2009 and had a target of US $100 billion in 2015-16. The annual trade between India and ASEAN touched approximately US $76.53 billion in 2014-15. But the volume came down to US $65.04 billion in 2015-16 privail due to the decrease in the princes of commodities because of the fall of global economy. (accepted electrically at http://www.mea.govn/assential 20 years.htm, on 13 July 2017). Myanmar is the second largest country of ASEAN in terms of land size and population. Total recorded bilateral India-Myanmar trade for 2010-11 was $1.06 billion out of which less than 6 per cent is traded through the land routes whereas 82 per cent of China-Myanmar trade and over 70 per cent of Thailand-Myanmar trade are via land route. The issues now are only logistics and administrative as notifications have been issued permitting normal trade through these routes.

Myanmar is experiencing significant changes in its political spectre, which might provide a fillip to reinvigorate India-Myanmar bilateral ties. Since 2011 it has been embarking on a series of widely praised reforms, including opening a dialogue with Aung San Sui Kyi and allowing her to run for a place in Parliament which she won with a huge margin. Myanmar has suddenly come to the centrestage and is drawing the attention of world leaders. Hillary Clinton, the then Secretary of State visited Myanmar. British Prime Minister made a visit in early April 2014. All these activities highlight that Myanmar in its political and economic reforms will not only receive unprecedented support from the ASEAN countries but also globally. There have also been carefully calibrated exchanges of high-level visits between India and Myanmar. Dr. Manmohan Singh concluded a historic visit to Myanmar in 2012, the first ever by an Indian prime minister in the last quarter of the century. This made a spectacular imprint on bilateral dynamics. In a significant move and ushering a new relation with Myanmar, Dr. Singh met Nobel laureate and democratic icon, the opposition leader Aung San Sui Kyi in Yangon, an indicative to foster the universal quest for democracy and freedom. The two countries have signed 12 agreements on various subjects including trade and energy. India has also agreed to extend a credit of $500 million through Exim Bank to assist primarily in infrastructure projects. A very significant project for the NER is the announcement of annual assistance of $25 million for next five years (2012-17) for meeting the development needs of Myanmar's border areas with India which is likely to go a long way to address some of the security issues. The prime minister was also accompanied by a business delegation of 25 senior industrialists and businessmen. There has been significant understanding in various other areas in agriculture, education, health care, connectivity, culture and direct flights. Myanmar's officials believe that future India-Myanmar's relations would be determined and redefined by how much India is able to contribute to the country's modernization. India and Myanmar encouraged intense collaboration in higher education. During Prime Minister's visit to Naypyidaw it was agreed Upon that Calcutta University and Yangon-based Dagon University will have academic cooperation facilitating exchange of students, academic materials and research endeavours. This is an opportunity for revitalizing the close relationship between University of Calcutta and Dangon University. Moreover, the IT sector holds maximum promise for cooperation. Myanmar wants to emulate India's spectacular IT success. Kolkata-based Indian conglomerates such as ITC have huge potentials to do business in Myanmar.[7] To provide further encouragement to the liberalization process the international sanctions that have been in place for over two decades over Myanmar are being progressively removed.[8]

One of my field trips to Moreh of Manipur has helped me assess the importance of the region as the gateway to Myanmar. The field trip gave me an all-encompassing impression about the economic opportunities implicit in the region, which need to be extensively exploited. In one of my chapters I have made a comprehensive discussion about my field trip to Manipur, which has enlightened me with the understanding of some core realities. Though officially there is one border post between India and Myanmar at Moreh (Manipur) there exist crossing points for smuggled products also. For instance, Longwa, a small border city in Nagaland is the route for illegal transactions. Indian traders import a number of Burmese medicinal plants, as well as precious stones while Burmese merchants come to stock up on Indian textiles and other finished products. Encouraged by the proportion of exchanges in the area, the Nagaland government requested the Central Government to make official this new border post for the purpose of opening up Nagaland.[9]

India-Myanmar border trade is expected to expand with the opening up of a land custom station in Mizoram. The Border Roads Organisation is being entrusted with the responsibility of constructing a land custom station estimated to cost about ₹5 crore at Zakhawthar, another gateway to ASEAN in addition to Moreh of Manipur. Zakhawtar (Mizoram) and Rihkhawdar (Rhee, Chin) have been the secondary gates for the border trade between India and Myanmar. Zakhawtar is 225 km from Aizawl, the capital city of Mizoram state. The whole stretch from Aizawl to Zakhawtar is largely two lanes and a highly mountainous terrain, although the surface is paved and fairly maintained as compared to the section between Palel and Moreh in Manipur. Reflecting the better security condition, there is no security checkpoint (Assam Rifles) along the route from Aizawl to Zakhawtar. The regulations on border trade are the same as those in the Moreh-Tamu border. In Zakhawtar, physical border facilities such as land customs station (LCS), post office, and a bank (State Bank of India) are already developed, and ready to operate. However, the development of 'official' border trade is much slower than in the Moreh-Tamu border. If the route from Aizawl to Agartala is improved, and the transit trade through Bangladesh is realized, this route will become the shortest land route connecting Myanmar and Kolkata via North-East India and Bangladesh.[10]

Moreh (Manipur) and Tamu (Sagain) have been the main gates for the border trade between India and Myanmar. The road from Imphal to Palel (49 km) is largely two lanes, flat terrain, and the surface is fairly paved and maintained. In contrast, the road from Palel to Moreh (60 km) is single-lane and mostly mountainous. The surface is paved but not maintained, therefore a number of sections between Palel and Moreh need to be repaired. The border area between India and Myanmar is the fulcrum of the drug problem. It is to be noted that Myanmar is one of the main drug trafficking centers in the world.[11] Most of the ethnic and political insurrections in the NER and Myanmar are widely involved in the drug-trafficking network. There's no formal foreign exchange facility in the border area. Due to these restrictions, official border trade has not been growing. According to the statistics of Moreh Land Custom Station (LCS), in the financial year 2010-11, India's export to Myanmar was INR 2.6 million of cumin seeds, and India's import from Myanmar was INR 32 million of betel nuts and INR 4 million of dry ginger. Instead, informal border trade has been growing. Data reveal that the total trade in 2010-11, at Moreh including informal volume was estimated at INR 2,800 million, which is far more than the official trade statistics of INR 150 million, indicating a significant amount of informal trade across the border, backed by a strong demand in the market. From the viewpoint of India, there is fear of a possible influx of Chinese products into the domestic market.[12] Proper management of the trade transaction by the governments would be of crucial importance to keep the trade flows under control. The cross-border markets in Myanmar are nearer than the far away main markets in the country. The cross-border markets may act as an avenue for the surplus produced in the NER as well as a source of cheaper imports. The production structure of the border states needs to be reorganized in line with the demand structure of the neighbouring country. As the import basket of Myanmar mainly consists of manufactured goods, NER could benefit from trade with Myanmar only if the region could industrialize itself. It is thus important to have a market survey in Myanmar and identify the products which NER can produce at competitive costs, preferably using its own resources. India needs to envisage border trade as a strategy for the development of the frige areas.[13] Keeping pace with the paramount changes in Myanmar's political and economic landscapes India needs to foster India-Myanmar bilateral dynamics by restoring the traditional links. People-to-people contacts, particularly in health and education need to be emphasized on. Movement of goods and services due to the haloes of globalization and liberalization would boost up India-Myanmar bilateral co-operation to a great extent. The mandates for the prospect of economic cooperation and trade facilitation between India and Myanmar include certain crucial aspect like a thorough and extensive understanding of the nature of market, thereby consolidating the economic growth and the distributive performances.

Even to this day experts of the region often voice their frustration with the government. It is alleged that most of the armed struggles of the NER originate from a sense of deep frustration at being repeatedly caricatured as minions of the Centre.[14] Even with its huge human resource potential and natural beauty, the NER could never be successful in realizing its economic potential. That was why it has failed to gain from economic development since independence. It is an undeniable fact that the significance of the geo-strategic location of Myanmar provides India an opportunity to promote the North-East region from a security burden to a region of economic prosperity. Moreover, by improving the road route between India and Myanmar via the North-East, New Delhi will eventually connect a section of the Asian highway from Singapore to Istanbul. When completed, this entire Asian highway project will link up Singapore with New Delhi in South Asia via Kuala Lumpur, Ho Chi Minh City, Phnom Penh, Vientiane, Bangkok, Yangon, Chiang Mai, Mandalay, Tamu, Kalemyo, Dhaka and Kolkata. India's initiative to reactivate ties with Myanmar is greatly governed by decisive factors other than promotion of border trade, like containment of Chinese economic and strategic influences in South-East Asia in general and Myanmar in particular. India perceived that engagement with the ASEAN might help New Delhi to counter China's influence in the ASEAN region and cultivate cooperative ventures with the South Asian Region.[15]

Another field trip to Kohima, Nagaland, has helped gather an intensive understanding about the richness of the cultural diversities of the region. The performance of cultural typicality of respective tribes in the Hornbill Festival exhibited the versatility and productivity of the inhabitants of the NER which is undoubtedly unique to the region. This festival can be a captivating source of tourist enchantment, which in turn would widen the ambit of accrediting the potentialities and proficiencies of Nagaland, ultimately steering towards economic prosperity. In Kohima I visited the World War II Cemetery, an outstanding place of historical evidence. Kohima city went through dark days during the World War II when the Allied forces fought a bloody and victorious battle against the Japanese in 1944. This cemetery comprises around 1,420 graves with stone markers. Another important place to visit is the Catholic Cathedral, which is considered as one of the biggest churches in the NER. My visit to the State Museum provided me illuminating insights into the evolution of Naga culture. Thus my field trip to Nagaland has acquainted me with the treasures of the region, which can easily be capitalized for uplifting the NER from a region of security threat to a region possessing abundant potentialities.

It sometimes seems that Delhi is jittery in opening up the NER for border trade, people-to-people contacts and perhaps the security prism engulfs the entire intellectual deliberations on the NER. It is high time to exploit the economic assets of the region and the NER should no longer be viewed as a mere corridor to the ASEAN. Its developmental aspect needs to be reconsidered. There should be a proper method to address the LEP, and to gauge the impact of the LEP on the NER. A reality picture needs to be seriously taken into account in utilizing the advantages of the NER as the gateway to SEA. The NER should also share the responsibility of realizing the policy. The issue of insurgency cannot be overlooked in the ambitious endeavour of showcasing the scenic treasure of the region. Certain initiatives like the reconciliation among the factions as also between the groups and the Centre is important for the development of the region. The Act East Policy has delved into the issue of resolving the insurgency issues towards a logical conclusion in parleys with the various factions and the Centre thereby arriving at a solution through negotiations at the policy and the political levels.

My field trip to Myanmar from 9-16 September 2013 has helped me in assessing the influence of India on Myanmar vis-à-vis China's influence. As Myanmar is understood to be the melting-pot of the cultural influences of emerging giants. India and China, the field trip was conducted with an aim to critically gauge whether India and China are heading towards conflicting or competitive dynamism in Myanmar. I visited the University of Yangon to interact with professors of International Relations and the faculty of Yangon School of Economics, visited the Indian Embassy in Yangon, Institute of Economics in Meiktila, and Chindwin College, Department of International Relations at the University of Mandalay and the Indian Consulate in Mandalay. I also availed the opportunity of visiting Napyidaw, the new capital of Myanmar on my way back from Mandalay to Yangon. While interviewing and interacting with the academicians, media personnel, government officials and most importantly the students I gained an enriching insight on India-Myanmar and Sino-Myanmar relations. Since contemporary Myanmar is encountering a transition the understanding of a historical set of relationships is necessary to decipher present attitudes and the formulation of policies. It is noteworthy to mention that since 2011, conciding with Myanmar's transition to democracy, India-Myanmar bilateral relations are making considerable headway. If we compare China with India on the basis of execution of projects, it is true that China is pacing much ahead of India but certain core realities need to be considered. China is not a democracy, so scope of divergence of opinion is less compared to India, which is a democratic country and every act on part of the government is answerable to the Parliament. Though India is gaining slow access to Myanmar, it is a steady progress and most importantly India does not compromise on quality. There are a number of areas like education, health and IT in which Indian companies working in Myanmar. Chinese endeavours in Myanmar are sometimes meant for pursuing their self-interest, even at the expense of Myanmar's gains. The geographical advantage between India and Myanmar can dynamize the essence of cooperation, especially in the highly competitive geo-political atmosphere wherein countries like Japan, Korea, the United States of America, Norway, China, Thailand, Malaysia are all rushing to Myanmar driven by self-interest, be it geo-strategic, commercial, political or military. Thus it can be asserted that in its endeavour to promote cooperation with Myanmar the positive aspects of the NER of play the role of a catalyst. But much homework needs to be done in respect of developing the NER. All the innovative undertakings spearheaded towards deepening the integrity of neighbourliness between India and Myanmar should be critically aware of China's proactive engagements with Yangon. Strategically located between two major regional powers Myanmar is composed of a multitude but disputed number of ethnic groups in a heterogeneous multicultural society that has been at odds or at war for generations. Its borders are ethnically amorphous often with polarized internal and external relations. While its extensive natural resources are in demand a worldwide its decision-making process has been opaque. The very complex nature of Myanmar internal regional and international relations is subject of intense research.[16]

My visit to Gangtok has added another significant dimension to my understanding of the diversities of the NER. Being one of the states of the so-called troubled NER, Sikkim portrays an altogether different picture. It is a highly cosmopolitan region where people are not very distressed about security and the bazaars reflect a very different picture from that of Manipur or Nagaland. It is a clean and tidy region and careless throwing of waste which is very much in practice in cities like Kolkata, is evidently absent in Sikkim. Moreover smoking in public places is banned in Gangtok and people are immensely enthusiastic and energetic in their professional and personal spheres. Apart from being a splendid tourist spot it has been the hub of progressive economic activities as there is huge propensity of booming border trade the through Nathula Pass. However, the existing ground realities portray the slow growth, rather the declining of border trade between the NER and the neighbouring countries in the east. Despite the enormous potentials of the LEP the Government of India has not been competent in fully harnessing the region's inherent strengths.

Thus it can be concluded that there is plenty of goodwill among India and the ASEAN which can be exploited if both partners candidly avoid the untoward attitude of mutual ignorance. This can be accomplished through enterprising undertakings like exchange of educational programmes, by promoting area studies in universities and colleges, cultural exchanges and two-way tourism with the countries of East Asia and South-East Asia. A profound understanding of these countries should be encouraged to bolster better understanding among the neighbours. India must reorient its LEP as well as AEP to break the artificial political barriers between the subcontinent and South-East Asia and try to gain entry into ASEAN+ three by cultivating relations with China. Apart from forging and strengthening relations with ASEAN three, India should also look for opportunities in the Asia-Pacific region as a whole. The Asia-Pacific region includes strong and vibrant economies like Japan, China, Taiwan, Korea, Australia and Hong Kong. It is not only the largest market and a rapidly growing region of the world but also a region strategically and economically important to India. India must also try to become a member of the Asia-Pacific Economic Community (APEC) which extends from the Pacific coast of the Americas to Australia and includes the whole of South-East Asia. In its attempt to attract FDI India should not only increase its trade with the South-East Asian neighbours but should form a broad agreement to complement one other and adopt joint strategies to increase their combined share of global trade. India's initiatives like trilateral India-Myanmar-Thailand highway project, the establishment of land and air links, innovative strategies facilitating trade may engender the problems of illegal immigration, drug-trafficking and population explosion. Thus it is a challenging task for India to maneuver its cooperation with the ASEAN efficiently as its Act East Policy needs to acknowledge not only the members of the ASEAN as also other powers that have an undeniable effect on the region.[17]

The surmounting efficacy of globalization during the last quarter of the twentieth century and the first decade of the twenty-first century raises a question on the pertinence of development of the NER. Globalization covers within its fold a number of issues which might at some point of time destabilize the democratization process of a country. It is often stated that economies have become global but politics remains national.[18] Globalization breeds consumerism and consumerism is unattainable for most common people and so creates frustration or alienation. The socio-political developments have created a much greater consciousness about rights among citizens that is conducive to greater sensitivity about social realities. Develop-ments associated with globalization often intensify the social and economic inequalities, and there is a possibility of deprivation. But the virtues of globalization which are manifest in the form of spread of information technologies, technological developments, communication technology, have crucial impact on the politics of a country. On the one hand, it can expand and strengthen political democracy and on the other it can widen the spectre of alienation among the people who are deprived of the fruits of globalization, particularly in a globalized world where citizens are conscious of the reality in other countries. The technologies associated with globalization that empower citizens through the spread of information and means of communication are conducive to political mobilizations on issues when the consequences of markets and globalization cross thresholds of tolerance in countries where democracy exists in some from. Efforts should be encouraged in terms of progress of human development through promotion of education ensuing creation of substantive capabilities for improving the well-being of the people.[19]

It can be emphasized in the context of the NER that land-lockedness can lead to little development. The region needs to be stabilized first and then development can be implemented through participation of the people. There is a clear cut sequential division between participation and development as the latter is expected to be preceded by some sort of participation. The LEP as well as the Vision 2020 envisage development as a trump by which we can actually address the issues of insurgency and violence. Development relates to the disappearance of the issues of violence and insurgency as eminent scholar Sanjib Baruah talks of making conflicts disappear by development. Therein lies the essence of the LEP as it signifies the relevance of paradigm shift. But much to the dismay of the NER most of the India-ASEAN trade is conducted through sea, through Vishakhpattanam port, which exhibits that the LEP happens independently of the NER. Moreover the natural and trade route reveal that the NER is relegated to the background and not at the centre of the LEP which it claims to be.[20] It has to be accepted that the LEP till date has failed to deliver much all the anticipated benefits to the NER. Then the question that crops up is why there is so much hype and enthusiasm regarding the positive fall-outs of the LEP on India's NER? This is pertinently because of the policy's inherent strengths and capacities to develop the region. But intent and determination will pay off through deliveries on the grounds. We are all aware of the economic and the strategic leverages that the NER has to offer, so it is an opportunity not to be missed and should be prudently utilized by the LEP not only to advance the region from the 'backburner' to the 'gateway' of India's foreign policy but also to elevate India's position as a global player.

The LEP's orientation towards the NER has directed attention to crucial neighbourhood issues too. It is to be ascertained whether the LEP, an offshoot of globalization, goes in tandem with the development of the NER, keeping in mind the political sensitivities of the region. Large-scale corruption, incompetent governance and the gradual decline of the local economy has aggravated the problem of insurgency and separatism and has facilitated the birth of new separatist movements thereby distorting the law and order system and posing threat to the security of the people and the region. Without solving these issues, economic integration of the NER with the neighbouring region is a distant reality. Structural dynamics within the neighbouring countries and the loopholes in our diplomacy to deal with neighbourhood policy are responsible for nurturing fluctuating impressions about India. We have proximities as well as power matrix. A coherent long-term policy serving long-term interests is very much lacking in India. Diverse and conflicting stakeholders in India's foreign policy make the job of evolving concrete policies somewhat complex. Therefore some of the faults in India's dealings with its neighbours need to be sincerely addressed. The development of the NER impinged more relevantly on the strategic and security questions imbued in India's long-term interests. The relative proximities of the NER with its South-East Asian neighbours have enabled it to assume a greater role in the security affairs of the region keeping in mind the fresh developments in the neighbourhood affecting the entire subcontinent. It has to be admitted that trade and commerce has grown exponentially due to which the security concerns have become more salient. There are a number of tricky issues wherein the state governments' interests might not be compatible with those of the Central Government. But that should not incite them towards confrontation; instead striking a satisfactory balance would be an important challenge for the future. What is desirable from the LEP is a solution to the problems that have for so long bedevilled India's NER, prevented it from being integrated with the mainstream and to accomplish its goal of developing to its capacity and potential. There should be far-reaching awareness of the need to advance in that direction.

The implementation of the projects engineered towards development of the NER should reflect the determination of the government to actualize India's LEP as with the aim to project NER as a gateway to SEA. The Look East Policy rightly seeks for the creation of an enabling environment so as to end the landlocked situation and isolation of the NER by opening up the borders and re-integrating the region's economy through improved trade and connectivity between North-East India and South-East Asian countries. New Delhi has increased its footprint in East Asia and solidified the cooperation. The eight states of the NER face the common problems of large population and dispersed geopolitical considerations, with different phases of development, diverse cultures, languages, dialects and multi-ethnic fissures. A competitive fervour among the eight North-East states for growth and development may be encouraged as it will drive innovation and new opportunities of development. This will open newer vistas to the region to learn from each other's strengths, experiences and also mistakes, which will inevitably add up to the benefit of all as this innovative drive will not only lead to harmony among the states but also strengthen the pace of integration with the mainstream. For that to materialize we need to emphasize on certain paradigms – we need to undo alienation with our neighbours, we need to bridge the delivery deficiency or the gap between word and action. India should harness its cultural and civilizational bonds and the relevance of soft power needs to be actively projected. The realization of India's Look East Policy is significant in extending its influence in the Asia-Pacific Region. The restructuring of power equations in the wake of China's supremacy resulting in unresolved territorial disputes have made the most flourishing Asia-Pacific region of the world merely unstable. The benefits of Look East Policy can enable India to influence the regional balance in the highly conflicting and competitive backdrop of the Asia-Pacific region.

NOTES

1. *The Statesman*, 16 July 2007.
2. Preet Malik, 'India's Look East Policy: Genesis', in A.N. Ram (ed.) *Two Decades of India's Look East Policy: Partnership for Peace, Progress and Prosperity*, Manohar, New Delhi, 2012, p. 33.
3. Sanjib Baruah, *Durable Disorder: Understanding the Politics of Northeast India*, New Delhi, Oxford University Press, 2005, p. 22.
4. Jane Perlez, 'Faster ASEAN Integration Urged', *International Herald Tribune*, 29 November 2004.
5. David Brewster, 'Sino-Indian Strategic Competition and the Asia-Pacific', in David Brewster (ed.), *India as an Asia-Pacific Power*, Abingdon, Oxon, Routledge, 2012.
6. Renaud Egreteau, *Wooing the Generals: India's New Burma Policy*, New Delhi, Authorspress, 2003, p. 106.
7. Manash Ghosh, 'Burmese Days', *The Statesman*, 13 June 2012.
8. Mahesh Kumar Saharia, 'Myanmar Calling', *Assam Tribune*, 2 June 2012.
9. 'Longwa Emerging as Major Trade Point between India and Myanmar', *The Assam Tribune*, Guwahati, 10 February 2003.
10. So Umezaki, 'ASEAN-India Connectivity: The Comprehensive Area Development Plan (CADP) Phase 2', *ICRIER Seminar*, New Delhi, 29 February 2012.
11. '1,000 Acres of Poppy Fields Destroyed in Myanmar', *The Times of India*, 22 March 2002.
12. Interviewing C.J. Thomas on 15 February 2012 at New Delhi.
13. Gurudas Das and C.J. Thomas, 'Economy of Myanmar: Trends, Structure and Implications for Border Trade with India's North-East', in Gurudas Das, N. Bijoy Singh and C.J. Thomas (eds.), *Indo-Myanmar Border Trade: Status, Problems and Potentials*, New Delhi, Akansha, 2005, pp. 1-32.
14. Patricia Mukhim, 'Voices from the Periphery', *The Statesman*, 30 July 2007.
15. Faizal Yahya, 'India and Southeast Asia: Revisited', *Contemporary Southeast Asia*, vol. 25, no. 1, April 2003, p. 93.
16. David I. Steinberg and Hongwei Fan, *Modern China-Myanmar Relations: Dilemmas of Mutual Dependence* , Copenhagen, Denmark, Nias Press, 2012, p. 347.
17. Sushila Narsimhan, 'India's "Look East" Policy: Past, Present, and Future', in K. Raja Reddy (ed.), *India and ASEAN Foreign Policy*

Dimensions for the 21st Century, New Delhi, New Century, 2005, pp. 38-40.

18. Deepak Nayyar, 'Globalisation and Democracy', in *Economic and Political Weekly*, vol. L, no. 19, 9 May 2015, p. 48.
19. Ibid., pp. 50-1.
20. Interaction with Prof. Samir Das, Dean of Arts, University of Calcutta, at University of Calcutta, Alipore Campus, on 4 March 2015.

Bibliography

PRIMARY SOURCES

Annual Report Ministry of External Affairs 2007-8, Ministry of External Affairs, Government of India.

Basic Statistics of North Eastern Region (2003), North Eastern Council, Shillong.

Draft Annual Plan (1990-91), Planning Department, Government of Manipur.

East India Human Development Report (2004), National Council of Applied Economic Research, New Delhi, Oxford University Press.

Interview with Amar Yumnam, Professor, Department of Economics, Manipur University, Imphal, 8 September 2011.

Interview with Ambassador Nyunt Maung Shein, Chairman, Myanmar-ISIS, Ministry of External Affairs, Yangon, 12 September 2013.

Interview with Chaw Chaw Sein, Professor, Department of International Relations, Yangon University, Yangon, 13 September 2013.

Interview with Chief Secretary, Government of Manipur, Office of the Chief Secretary, Imphal, 7 September 2011.

Interview with Dr. Bezbaruah, Professor, Department of Economics, Gauhati University, Guwahati, 5 December 2012.

Interview with Dr. Bhupen Sarmah, Director, Omeo Kumar Das Institute of Social Change and Development, Guwahati, 5 December 2012.

Interview with Dr. Nani G. Mahanta, Associate Professor, Peace & Conflict Studies, Gauhati University, Guwahati, 5 December 2012.

Interview with Dr. Neil Jain, First Secretary, Embassy of India, Yangon, 10 September 2013.

Interview with Dr. Sanjay Barbora, Associate Professor, TISS, Guwahati Campus, 5 December 2012.

Interview with Madan Mohan, Consul General of India, Indian Consulate, Mandalay, 11 September 2013.

Interview with Cho Cho Thein, Professor, Meiktila Institute of Economics, Meiktila, 11 September 2013.

Interview with N. Kulkarni Devi, Joint Director, Planning Department, Government of Manipur, Imphal, 6 September 2011.

Interview with Pradip Phanjoubam, Editor, *Imphal Free Press*, Imphal, 8 September 2011.

Interaction with Kanti Bajpai, Senior Professor at the Lee Kuan Yew School of Public Policy, National University of Singapore, at NUS, 11 September 2014.

Interaction with Dr. Tin Maung Maung Than, Senior Research Fellow of Institute of South East Asian Studies (ISEAS), at ISEAS, Singapore, 9 September 2014.

Interaction with Dr. Ian Storey, Senior Fellow of ISEAS, at ISEAS, Singapore, 10 Septmber 2014.

National Human Development Report (2001), Planning Commission, Government of India, available on <www.planningcommission.nic.in/reports/genrep/nhdrep/nhdch3.pdf>.

National Human Development Report (2011), Planning Commission, Government of India, available on <http://planningcommission.nic.in/reports/genrep/ar_eng1112.pdf>.

National Human Development Report (2013), Planning Commission, Government of India, available on <www. http://planningcommission.gov.in/reports/genrep/index.php? repts=b_repgen.htm>.

Ninth Five Year Plan and Annual Plan (1997-98), Planning Department, Government of Manipur.

Speech of Shri Zoramthanga, Chief Minister, Mizoram, 50th National Development Council Meeting on 21 December 2002 at New Delhi, available on <planningcommission.nic.in/plans/planrel/pl50ndc/mizoram.doc>.

Ved Marwah (2001), 49th N.D.C. Meeting, Vigyan Bhavan, New Delhi, available on <www.planningcommission.gov.in/plans/planre/pl49ndc/manipur.htm>.

SECONDARY SOURCES

Books

Abdi, B.L, *North-east Region: Problems and Prospects of Development*, Chandigarh, CRRID, 1984.

Agnihotri, S.K. and B. Datta Ray, *Perspective of Security and Development in North East India*, New Delhi, Concept, 2005.

Aung-Thwin, Michael and Maitrii Aung-Thwin, *A History of Myanmar Since Ancient Times: Traditions and Transformations*, London, Reaktion Books, 2012.

Bajpai, Kanti, 'Introduction: International Theory, International Society, Regional Politics, and Foreign Policy', in Kanti P. Bajpai and Harish C. Shukla (eds.), *Interpreting World Politics: Essays for A.P. Rana*, New Delhi, Sage, 1995.

Banerjee, Dipankar, *Myanmar and Northeast India*, New Delhi, Delhi Policy Group, 1997.

Bareh, H.M, *The Encyclopaedia of the North-East*, vol. 4, New Delhi, Mittal Publication, 2007.

Barua, Alokesh, *India's North-East: Developmental Issues in a Historical Perspective*, New Delhi, Manohar, 2005.

Baruah, Sanjib, *Beyond Counter-insurgency Breaking the Impasse in North-east India*, New Delhi, Oxford University Press, 2009.

——, *Durable Disorder: Understanding the Politics of Northeast India*, New Delhi, Oxford University Press, 2005.

Bhaumick, Subir, *Insurgent Crossfire: North-east India*, New Delhi, Lancer Publishers, 1996.

Brewster, David, *India as an Asia Pacific Power*, Abingdon, Oxon, Routledge, 2012.

Das, Gurudas, R.K. Purkayastha (eds.), *Border Trade: North-east India and Neighbouring Countries*, New Delhi, Akansha, 2000.

Das, Gurudas, N. Bijoy Singh and C.J. Thomas (eds.), *Indo-Myanmar Border Trade*, New Delhi, Akansha, 2005.

Das, Samir, *Blisters on their Feet: Tales of Internally Displaced Persons in India's North East*, New Delhi, Sage, 2008.

Datta, P.S, *Northeast and the Indian State: Paradoxes of a Periphery*, New Delhi, Vikas Publishing House, 1995.

Datta, Sreeradha, *Bangladesh: A Fragile Democracy*, New Delhi, Shipra, 2004.

——, *The Northeast Complexities and its Determinants*, New Delhi, Shipra, 2004.

De, Sibopada, *Illegal Migrations and the North-East*, New Delhi, Anamika, 2005.

Deb, Bimal J. *Development Priorities in North East India*, New Delhi, Concept, 2002.

Dutt, Sagarika and Alok Bansal (eds.), *South Asian Security: 21st Century Discourses*, London, Routledge, 2012.

Egrteau, Renaud, *Wooing the Generals: India's New Burma Policy*, New Delhi, Authorspress, 2003.

Ghoshal, Baladas, *ASEAN and South Asia: A Development Experience*, New Delhi, Sterling, 1998.

Ghosh, Subir, *Frontier Travails – Northeast: The Politics of a Mess*, New Delhi, Macmillan, 2001.

Gogoi, Dilip, *Beyond Borders-Look East Policy's North East India*, Guwahati, DVS Publishers, 2013.

Gordon, Sandy, *India's Rise to Power in the Twentieth Century and Beyond*, New York, St. Martin's Press, 1995.

Grare, Frederic and Amitabh Mattoo, *Beyond the Rhetoric: The Economics of India's Look East Policy*, New Delhi, CSH-Manohar, 2003.

Hazarika, Sanjoy, *Rites of Passage: Border Crossings, Imagined Homelands, India's East and Bangladesh*, New Delhi, Penguin Books, 2000.

Iralu, Kaka D, *Nagaland and India: The Blood and the Tears*, Kohima, Author, 2000.

Kothari, Rajni, *Politics in India*, New Delhi, Orient Longman, 1970.

Lintner, Bertil, *Land of Jade: A Journey from India through Northern Burma to China*, Bangkok, White Orchid Press, 1996.

Mishra, Om Prakash and Anindyo J. Majumdar (eds.), *The Elsewhere People: Cross-border Migration, Refugee Protection and State Response*, New Delhi, Lancer, 2003.

Misra, Udayon, *The Periphery Strikes Back: Challenges to the Nation-State in Assam and Nagaland*, Shimla, Indian Institute of Advanced Studies, 2000.

Mukherjee, Sanu et al. (eds.), *Demographic Profile of North-East India*, New Delhi, OSMOS Publications, 1994.

Myint-U, Thant, *Burma and the New Crossroads of Asia: Where China Meets India*, London, Faber and Faber, 2011.

——, *The Making of Modern Burma*, Cambridge, Cambridge University Press, 2001.

Nanda, Prakash, *Rediscovering Asia: Evolution of India's Look-East Policy*, New Delhi, Lancer, 2008.

Pakem, B., *Regionalism in India: With Special Reference to North-East India*, New Delhi, Har-Anand, 1985.

Pari, Peter A., 'Competitiveness and Leverage', in Michael G. Plummer and Chia Siow Yue (eds.), *Realising the ASEAN Economic Community: A Comprehensive Assessment*, Singapore, ISEAS, 2009.

Plummer, Michael G. and Chia Siow Yue (eds.), *Realising the ASEAN Economic Community: A Comprehensive Assessment*, Singapore, ISEAS, 2009.

Prakash, Shri, Vanita Ray and Sanjay Ambatkar, *India and ASEAN Economic Partnership in the 1990s and Future Prospects*, New Delhi, Gyan Book, 1996.

Pupphavesa, Wisarn, *BIMSTEC-Japan Comprehensive Economic Cooperation: A Step in the Future*, New Delhi, Bookwell, 2008.

Ram, Amar Nath, *Two Decades of India's Look East Policy: Partnership for Peace, Progress and Prosperity*, New Delhi, Manohar, 2012.

Rani, Charles Reuben Lyngdoh, *Look East Policy: Impact on North-East India*, New Delhi, Akansha, 2008.

Rao, P.V., *India and Indian Ocean: In the Twilight of the Millennium*, New Delhi, South Asian Publishers, 2003.

——, *Regional Cooperation in Indian Ocean: Trends and Perspectives*, New Delhi, South Asian Publishers, 2001.

Ray, Asok Kumar and Satyabrata Chakraborty (eds.), *Society Politics and Development in North East India*, New Delhi, Concept, 2008.

Ray, Asok Kumar and Sutapa Sengupta (eds.), *Population Dynamics in North East India*, New Delhi, Om Publications, 2008.

Ray, Jayant Kumar and Prabir De (eds.), *Promotion of Trade and Investment in Eastern South Asia Subregion*, New Delhi, Bookwell, 2004.

Ray, Jayanta and Rakhee Bhattacharya (eds.), *Development Dynamics in North East India*, New Delhi, Akansha Publishing House, 2008.

Ray, Sunanda K. Dutta, *Looking East to Look West Lee Kuan Yew's Mission India*, New Delhi, Penguin, 2009.

Reddy, K. Raja, *India and ASEAN Foreign Policy Dimensions for the Twenty-first Century*, New Delhi, New Century, 2005.

Riefel, Lex, *Myanmar/Burma: Inside Challenges, Outside Interests*, Washington, Brookings Institution, 2010.

Sachdeva, Gulshan, *Economy of the North-East: Policy, Present Conditions and Future Possibilities*, New Delhi, Konark, 2000.

Samaddar, Ranabir, *The Marginal Nation: Transborder Migration From Bangladesh to West Bengal*, New Delhi, Sage, 1999.

Sharma, R.R., *India and Emerging Asia*, New Delhi, Sage, 2005.

Singh, Thingnam Kishan, *Look East Policy & India's North East: Polemics and Perspectives*, New Delhi, Concept, 2009.

Sridharan, Kripa, *The ASEAN Region in India's Foreign Policy*, Aldershot, Dartmouth Publishing Company, 1996.

Stubbs, Richard, 'Regionalisation and Globalisation', in Richard Stubbs and Geoffrey R.D. Underhill (eds.), *Political Economy and the Changing Global Order*, Canada, Oxford University Press, 2000, 2nd edn.

Upadhya, Shashi, 'Challenges before SAARC', in Ramakant and P.L. Bhola (eds.), *Post Cold War Developments in South Asia*, Jaipur, RBSA Publishers, 1995.

Verghese, B.G, *India's Northeast Resurgent: Ethnicity, Insurgency, Governance, Development*, New Delhi, Konark, 2004, 2nd edn.

ARTICLES

Acharya, Amitav, 'Southeast Asia: Imagining the Region', *Himal South Asian*, vol. 16, no. 1, January 2003.

Bahroo, Laxman B, 'Myanmar: Intersecting Destinies of a New Asia', *Bharat Rakshak Monitor*, May-June 2003.

Barbora, Sanjay, 'Ethnic Politics and Land Use: Genesis of Conflicts in India's Northeast', *Economic and Political Weekly*, vol. 37, no. 13, 30 March 2002.

Baruah, Amit, 'Looking East', *Frontline*, vol. 17, no. 24, 8 December 2000.

Chakraborti, Tridib, 'BIMSTEC: Origin, Growth and Progress', *World Focus*, January 2008.

Chakraborti, Tridib, 'India's Look East Policy: Time for Stock-Taking', *World Focus*, Annual Number, November-December 2009.

Chatterjee, Shibashis, 'Conceptions of Space in India's Look East Policy: Order, Cooperation or Community?' *South Asian Survey*, vol. 14, no. 65, 2007.

Das, Samir Kumar, 'BIMSTEC or the Big Leap Forward for India's Northeast', *World Focus*, January 2008.

——, 'Gateway to the East: A Symposium on Northeast India and the Look East Policy: The Ethnic Dimension', *Seminar*, Special Issue, vol. 55, June 2005.

Das, Samir,'Imagining a New Geography of India's Northeast', *India Quarterly*, vol. 66, no. 4, 2010.

Dasgupta, Anindita, 'Small Arms Proliferation in India's North-East: A Case Study of Assam', *Economic and Political Weekly*, vol. 36, no. 1, 6 January 2001.

Ghoshal, Baladas, 'East Asian Miracle and India', *World Focus*, vol. 17, no. 1, January 1996.

Harshe, Rajen, 'South Asian Regional Cooperation: Problems and Prospects', *Economic and Political Weekly*, vol. 34, no. 19, 8-14 May 1999.

Huang, Yasheng and Tarun Khanna, 'Can India Overtake China?', *Foreign Policy*, vol. 137, July-August 2003.

Kapila, Subhash, 'India-Myanmar Strategic Partnership: Indian Imperatives', *South Asia Analysis Group*, Paper 197, 6 February 2001.

Lim, R., 'The ASEAN Regional Cooperation: Building on Sand', *Contemporary Southeast Asia*, vol. 20, no. 2, 1998.

Misra, Udayon, 'Naga Peace Talks: High Hopes and Hard Realities', *Economic and Political Weekly*, 15 February 2003.

Muni, S., 'India and Southeast Asia: Challenges and Opportunities', *Contemporary Southeast Asia*, vol. 19, no. 2, September 1997.

Murthy, Padmaja, 'BIMSTEC and SAARC: Understanding the Linkages', *World Focus*, January 2008.

Naidu, G.V.C., 'India and Southeast Asia', *World Focus*, vol. 17, no. 10, 1996.

——, 'BIMSTEC and its Geo-strategic Importance', *World Focus* 337, January 2008.

Oinam, Anand, 'Look East Policy and Manipur', *The Shanghai Express*, Imphal, Manipur, 27 December 2003.

Ojendal, J., 'Regionalism in Southeast Asia under Unilateral Pressure', *International Organization*, vol. 80, no. 3, May 2004.

Padelford, Norman J., 'Regional Organisation and the United Nations', *International Organisation*, May 1954.

Parthasarathy, G., 'Look Beyond "Look East"', *The Pioneer*, 21 December 2000.

Prabhakara, M.S, 'Is North-East India Landlocked?' *Economic and Political Weekly*, vol. 39, no. 42, 16 October 2004.

Sharma, Hanjabam Gyanendro, 'Look East Policy: The Gaze and its Dangers in the North East', *Alternative Frames*, Manipur, Centre for Alternative Discourse, 2006.

Sharma, Harvir, 'China's Interests in Indian Ocean Rim Countries and India's Maritime Security', *India Quarterly*, vol. 58, no. 4, October-December 2001.

Shimray, Ungshungm, 'Socio-political Unrest in the Region Called North-east India', *Economic and Political Weekly*, vol. 39, no. 42, 16 October 2004.

Stobdan, P., 'China's Forays into Burma-Implications for India', *Strategic Analysis*, vol. 16, no. 1, April 1993.

Suryanarayan, V., 'Prospects for a Bay of Bengal Community', *Seminar* 487, March 2000.

Suryanarayana, P.S., 'Emerging Asian Equations', *Frontline*, vol. 20, no. 22, 25 October-7 November 2003.

Yahya, Faizal, 'BIMSTEC and Emerging Patterns of Asian Regional and Inter-Regional Cooperation', *Australian Journal of Political Science*, University of Notre Dame, vol. 40, no. 3, September 2006.

Web Articles

'India's Look-East Policy: Prospects and Challenges for Northeast India-3', accessed electronically at <http://haokip.bandamp.com/blog/17831.html> on 26.10.2009.

'Myanmar-open for Business', accessed electronically at <www.hfw.com/publications/client.../myanmar-open-for-business> on 19 February 2013.

Kuppuswamy, C.S., 'India's Look East Policy: A Review', accessed electronically at <www.southasiaanalysis.org/%5Cpapers37%5Cpaper3662.html> on 14 March 2010.

Levesque, Julien, 'North-East in India's Look East Policy', Institute of Peace and Conflict Studies, New Delhi, 6 May 2008, accessed electronically at <http://www.ipcs.org/articles_details.php?articleNo=2558$cID=9> on 15 October 2009.

Mehrotra, Mansi, 'Management of India-Bangladesh Border', accessed electronically at <www.claws.in/index.php?action=master $task=316$u_id=51> on 1 November 2010.

Prime Minister Atal Behari Vajpayee's address to the Institute of Diplomacy and Foreign Relations on 'India and ASEAN: Shared Perspectives', at Kuala Lumpur, 16 May 2001, electronically accessed at <pib.nic.in/archieve/pm_vst_mal/pm_vst_mal.html> on 7 July 2012.

Khan, Rabb M. Shamsur, 'Towards Better India-Bangladesh Relations', accessed electronically at <www.idsa.in/Publications/IDSA Comment> on 27 July 2010.

Newspapers

Asia Times (Kolkata)
BBC South Asia News (London-based)
Dainik Janakontha (Assam, Silchar).
Gangtok Times (Sikkim, Darjeeling and Kalimpong)
Hindusthan Times (Kolkata)
Imphal Free Press (Imphal)
Nagaland Post (Nagaland)
New Light of Myanmar (Yangon, Myanmar)
Seven Sisters Post (Guwahati)
Sikkim Express (Sikkim)
Sikkim Mail (Sikkim)

Sikkim Reporter (Sikkim)
The Assam Tribune (Assam, Guwahati)
The Hindu (New Delhi)
The Shillong Times (Shillong, Meghalaya)
The Statesman (Kolkata)

Index